CATHEDRAL
ARCHITECTURE

*The architect . . . was a profound mathematician
as well as an artist: he calculated the quantity of weight,
and adapted his supports accordingly;
he designed his masses, filled up the enrichments,
and foresaw the effect.*

JOHN BRITTON, FSA, 1826

WHAT IS A CATHEDRAL?

If asked to define a cathedral, many people would reply that it is a large church presided over by a bishop. This would be incorrect in two respects. First of all, size is not strictly a criterion, for some parish churches and abbeys are larger than the smallest cathedrals; and secondly, a cathedral is in the care of its dean and chapter, who are responsible both for maintaining the fabric of the building and for conducting the services.

The Latin word *cathedra* comes straight from the Greek *kathedra,* which means simply 'a seat', and in the Church the word came to be used for the bishop's seat or throne. Hence, a cathedral is the church in a diocese that contains the bishop's throne, whatever the size of the building.

BELOW:
The font is used for Christian baptism, and usually stands near the west end of the building, sometimes in a special chapel called a baptistry. This late 12th-century font is in Winchester Cathedral.

BELOW:
St Augustine's Chair at Canterbury, where every Archbishop of Canterbury is enthroned. A cathedral is the church in a diocese that houses the bishop's seat (called the bishop's throne).

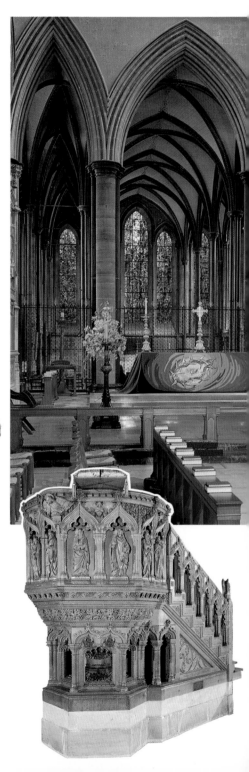

RIGHT, INSET:
Pulpits were seldom used in cathedrals and churches in England in medieval times (although the earliest known is dated 1330), but in 1603 their provision was made compulsory. This Victorian pulpit is in Norwich Cathedral.

Before the Dissolution of the Monasteries by King Henry VIII, many cathedrals – although not all – belonged to monastic foundations, and stood at the heart of other buildings, such as the monks' living quarters, some of which still survive. The covered walkways known as cloisters – from the Latin *claustrum*, an enclosed space – were usually situated on the sheltered south side, and provided a place for study or recreation on wet days. Many of these cloisters (such as those at Canterbury, Gloucester, Worcester and Lincoln) are beautifully vaulted in stone, with traceried windows overlooking the enclosed cloister garden. The cloisters also led to the chapter house, once used by the monks, and now by the dean and chapter, for meetings. Many English chapter houses are polygonal in plan, with a central pillar supporting a lofty vaulted roof of stone. A few are rectangular (for example, at Exeter, Canterbury, Chester and Gloucester), and that at Worcester is circular.

ABOVE:
The high altar at Salisbury Cathedral. The altar was placed at the east end of a cathedral and was usually several steps above the level of the nave, so that the ceremonial was more easily seen.

ABOVE:
The cloisters at Canterbury, built between 1396 and 1420. Monks used the sunlit north side of the cloister for study, while the south side housed the lavatorium *and linen cupboards.*

LEFT:
The circular chapter house at Worcester is one of the earliest and finest in England. The main structure is Norman, and the windows, in the Perpendicular style, were inserted later.

Most English cathedrals were built in cruciform plan, that is, in the shape of a cross. The long western arm or shaft of the cross is formed by the nave, the crossbar is the transept (usually called the north and south transepts), and the eastern arm is the choir (so-called because the choir is usually seated here). The eastern arm or choir is usually shorter than the western one, and is sometimes called the presbytery (from the Latin word *presbyter*, meaning priest), or the chancel (from the Latin word *cancellus*, for screen), because in the earliest Christian churches, as today, this part was divided from the nave by a low open screen.

The idea that a church was and is planned in the form of a cross to remind us of Christ's crucifixion is now rejected by many scholars, who consider that the transepts were included mainly to give a convenient increase of space. The provision of transepts is also attributed to a desire for more side-altars, or alternatively to bear the outward thrust of the great tower at the centre of the church. The high altar is placed at the east end, and the main entrance is at the west end.

The east end of most cathedrals is square, although some are polygonal or semicircular (known as an apse). A few have a ring of chapels around an apse and this arrangement, known by the French word *chevet,* may be seen at Canterbury, Gloucester and Norwich. More often, however, there is a large chapel extending eastwards from the main east end of the cathedral, and this is usually called the Lady Chapel because it is dedicated to the Blessed Virgin Mary.

The various small chapels situated around the *chevet*, or elsewhere, are often called chantry chapels because masses were sung in them for the soul of the person who originally built and endowed the chapel at his own expense. Each chapel contained a small altar.

This, then, is the general plan of an English cathedral, but the architectural style and features of the building changed over the centuries as alterations were made and rebuilding carried out. The dates of the various periods are given only as a rough guide to when they were flourishing, as each style overlapped the next.

The north wall (built 1118–40) of the presbytery at Peterborough shows the three stages or levels forming the basic construction of our medieval cathedrals. At ground level is the nave arcade, consisting of strong weight-supporting piers or columns. The second level forms the triforium or 'blind storey' (so-called because normally there was no opening or window behind it), and the third and uppermost level is known as the clerestory – literally, the clear storey. Windows placed here allowed more light into the nave.

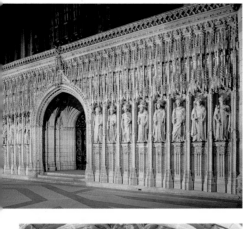

ABOVE LEFT:
The pulpitum, *or chancel screen, in York Minster dates from the late 15th century. These screens, of carved stone or wood, were built to separate the chancel and its adjoining chapels from the nave.*

RIGHT:
The great west door of Bath Abbey was given in 1617. Many items, such as lecterns, fonts and pulpits, have been donated by benefactors over the centuries.

NORMAN

(CIRCA 1066–1190)

Although the Christian Church in the British Isles was well established in the 4th century, it was almost destroyed, in what is now England, by the pagan Anglo-Saxons, and precious little remains of its ancient buildings. Indeed, hardly any actual part of an English cathedral exists today (with the important exception of some crypts) that is earlier than the Norman Conquest of 1066, though long before that time quite a number had been founded. These include Canterbury (597), Rochester and Old St Paul's in London (604), York (625), Lichfield (656), Winchester (662), Hereford (676) and Worcester (680), and

their foundation followed the gradual conversion of the English to Christianity. This began in 597 with the baptism of the Kentish king Ethelbert by Augustine, who led a missionary party from Rome and became the first Archbishop in 602.

Norman architecture is the term given to post-Conquest Romanesque in Britain, and it is usually considered to have run its course by the end of the 12th century. The style has been aptly described as powerful and masculine. It is marked by semicircular arches everywhere, deeply recessed doorways and windows with semicircular heads, occasional circular or 'bull's-eye' windows, thick walls, massive round pillars to carry the nave arcades (the lines of arches), bell towers decorated with rows of small arches and crowned with pyramidal roofs or spires, vigorous carved ornament such as zigzag moulding and animal forms, and very primitive 'stained' glass in a few of the round-headed windows.

Where vaulting was used (for example in some of the cathedrals whose timber roofs had been destroyed by fire), it was often very thick and heavy. In form it resembled a barrel, and is commonly called 'barrel' or 'tunnel' vaulting. It was carried by massive stone arched ribs between the supporting pillars and walls.

ABOVE:
This sturdy Norman doorway at Worcester shows the semicircular arch which is so typical of the period.

RIGHT:
The crypt of Worcester is a striking example of early Norman work. Note the simple bases to the plain piers, the cushion capitals and the groined roof with square-edged transverse arches.

LEFT:
The Norman arches of the crossing in St Albans are rounded, chunky, and just as their builder, Paul of Caen, left them.

LEFT:
The characteristics of Norman workmanship are clearly seen in the nave of Durham Cathedral: round arches, stout columns, cushion capitals and zigzag ornament. The enormous pillars are incised with different geometric patterns.

RIGHT:
England's finest Norman apse, at Norwich Cathedral, surmounted by a later clerestory and vault. Norwich retains its original ground plan almost unaltered.

EARLY ENGLISH

(CIRCA 1190—1300)

The next style in our cathedral architecture is variously referred to as Early English, Pointed or Lancet. Perhaps Early English is an inappropriate description because our Norman architecture, in spite of its name, is in many ways distinctive to England rather than to France, and was of course earlier than Early English! Nevertheless, this style is even *more* English, and, however we describe it, nothing quite like it exists anywhere else in Europe. The style developed through a Transitional phase and marks the beginning of the three Gothic periods of cathedral architecture, known as Early English, Decorated and Perpendicular. It was during the Early English period that the typical heavy, rounded Norman arches gave way to lighter, pointed arches in nave arcades, windows and doorways.

BELOW RIGHT:
A view of the entire length of Salisbury, looking from east to west. The length of the nave is about 230 feet (70m).

BELOW LEFT:
The magnificent west front of Peterborough. The cathedral was started in 1118 and completed by 1238. Building programmes worked from east to west, so although the east end of Peterborough is Norman, the west front is Early English.

Salisbury Cathedral is unusual in that it is Early English throughout. It is the most complete cathedral in a single style – a style that is easily recognisable from the tall lancet windows. Begun in 1220, Salisbury is thought to have been virtually finished by 1258, when it was consecrated. The cloisters and chapter house were added later and completed by 1280. The tower and spire were probably begun in the 1290s and were certainly finished just before the Black Death ravaged Salisbury in 1348.

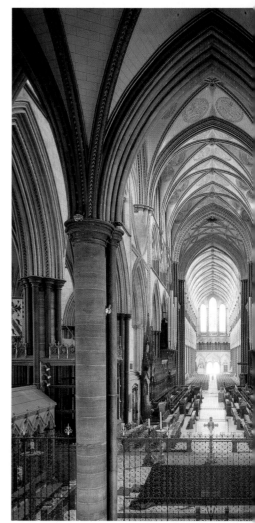

....

LEFT:
The Lady Chapel at Llandaff, with its elongated windows and lovely vaulted ceiling, is a fine example of the grace and proportion of the late 13th century.

Other important examples of Early English architecture are to be found at York Minster (transepts), Lincoln (nave, choir and chapter house), Rochester (choir and transepts), Wells (nave and west front), Ely (choir, transepts and Galilee porch), Worcester (choir), Bristol (Elder Lady Chapel), Durham (Chapel of the Nine Altars), Southwark (choir and retrochoir), Westminster Abbey and most of Lichfield.

ABOVE:
The Galilee porch at Ely is a beautiful example of Early English architecture, dating from about the time of the Magna Carta (1215).

LEFT:
The Lady Chapel at Hereford was built about 1220–30. The five stepped lancet windows are unusually elaborate, and quite unlike the heavier, rounded windows of the Norman style.

DECORATED GOTHIC

(CIRCA 1250–1380)

The second stage in English Gothic architecture is widely known as Decorated, from the type of window tracery that came into fashion at this time. The style is easily recognised because the windows are divided by moulded stone mullions (vertical stone bars) into narrow glazed 'lights' (openings), usually measuring one to two feet wide. Where the arch begins to curve upwards to a point, the mullions are twisted into graceful circles and other beautiful patterns to form tracery.

RIGHT:
The Percy Tomb at Beverley Minster is a glorious display of crisp, bold carving in the Decorated style, enriched by fruit, leaves, angel figures and symbolic beasts.

ABOVE AND RIGHT:
The east window at Ripon Cathedral (above) is in the Early Decorated style known as Geometrical, and is one of the finest examples of this type of stone tracery in England. As the style developed, the curves became more ornate and flowing, as seen in the Late Decorated (Curvilinear) west window at York Minster (right).

On doorways and elsewhere, the general character of the design became more free and more ornate, most surfaces being rich in carved texture. Beautiful and decorative stone details, such as ballflowers, foliated capitals, plants and animals, were freely and naturalistically carved – all in marked contrast to the conventional stiff foliage of the Early English period. Labour and expense were not a problem: England was extremely prosperous during this period,

with an increasing population, and the Church received a large income from the land it owned, which allowed many ambitious building projects to take place and much time to be spent in carving the many and elaborate details.

Nowadays, some scholars divide this period into Geometrical (Early Decorated) and Curvilinear or Flowing Decorated (Late Decorated), while others prefer the term Mid Gothic. Examples of Decorated architecture are to be found at Exeter (Lady Chapel, choir and nave), Ely (part of the choir and Lady Chapel), York (nave, west front and chapter house), Lichfield (nave and Lady Chapel) and St Albans (choir), and in the chapter houses of Salisbury, Southwell and Wells.

ABOVE:
The Lady Chapel at Lichfield was completed in 1330 and is Decorated architecture at its best. The nine enormous windows fill the whole of the space above the arcading of the lower wall.

LEFT:
The nave of Exeter Cathedral dating from 1353–69, a late example of the Decorated period. Four of the seven bays, the triforium blind arcading, the clerestory and the vault are seen.

11

PERPENDICULAR GOTHIC

(CIRCA 1350–1550)

The third and last of these three Gothic phases of English architecture is the Perpendicular period, sometimes called Rectilinear in order to distinguish it from the Curvilinear style mentioned in the previous section. It has been termed 'the architecture of vertical lines' and this can be seen from the illustrations shown here. It is interesting to note that after the Black Death swept across England in 1348, and the population was possibly as much as halved within a short time, the richly carved detail of the Decorated period became almost plain by comparison in the Perpendicular period (compare, for example, Bishop Fox's Chantry shown below right with the Percy Tomb illustrated on page 10.) However, in spite of the plague, English architects and craftsmen continued to become more skilful and daring.

It was also around this time that stained glass gradually became more fashionable. The intricate shapes created by the elaborate patterns of tracery in the upper part of windows were obviously unsuitable as frames for the pictures of saints and parables

RIGHT:
The Rectilinear style can be clearly seen in the Lady Chapel at Gloucester, completed c.1490. The more regular shapes made room for stained glass, and the simpler stone carving enabled much building to be carried out in spite of the loss of skilled masons from the Black Death.

BELOW LEFT:
Superb fan-vaulting in the 'New Building' at Peterborough, built between 1496 and 1508. The architect was almost certainly John Wastell, who went on to build the famous chapel at King's College, Cambridge.

that the people wished to see; so all these complicated patterns began to give way to more regular and rectilinear shapes which somewhat resemble a gridiron. The masons then started imitating this patterning in shallow panels carved on the solid masonry

LEFT:
Bishop Fox's Chantry at Winchester showing the Rectilinear design.

12

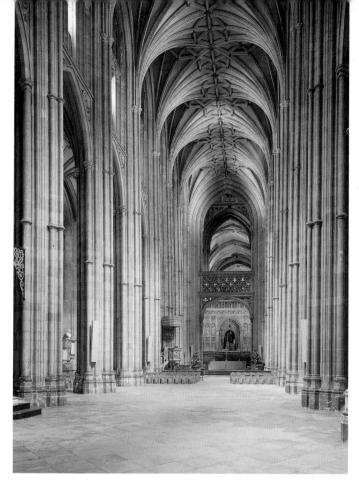

of the walls and parapets, purely for ornamental purposes. The piers became tall and thin and the vaulting above became ever more complex, resulting in the elaborate, marvellous, but structurally illogical fan-vaults that can be seen at their best at

ABOVE:
The nave of Canterbury, rebuilt between 1391 and 1405, has eight bays of pier arcading with three-light traceried clerestory windows.

ABOVE RIGHT:
Henry VII's Chapel at Westminster Abbey has been acclaimed as the magnum opus *of the Perpendicular style. The elaborate lace-like beauty of the fan-vault is one of Westminster's great treasures.*

LEFT:
The choir stalls at Chester were made in about 1380. Here is a wealth of carved canopies, elbow rests and misericords.

King's College Chapel, Cambridge, in Henry VII's Chapel at Westminster Abbey, the cloisters of Gloucester, the ambulatory of Peterborough, and in the choir at Christ Church in Oxford.

In Scotland also, Norman architecture had been succeeded by Early English; but, instead of the Perpendicular phase, a more florid development of the Decorated style replaced it under French influence, which was very strong there at the time. The results were such beautiful and fanciful forms as can be seen, for example, in the flamboyant tracery of St Giles in Edinburgh. The later phases of Perpendicular Gothic architecture in England are sometimes called Tudor, but the term is more usually applied to the style of domestic buildings of that period than to cathedrals or parish churches.

ENGLISH RENAISSANCE

(THE 17TH CENTURY)

The 17th century, too, saw little in the way of cathedral-building – but there was one glorious exception!

The huge Gothic cathedral of St Paul in London, the largest in England, lost its tall spire when struck by lightning in 1561, and was in a very poor state by the time the famous architect Inigo Jones undertook its restoration between 1633 and 1643. Luckily Sir Christopher Wren, his successor, had already prepared a scheme for rebuilding most of the cathedral when, during the Great Fire of London in 1666, the whole structure was virtually destroyed. Wren set about rebuilding it between 1675 and 1710. His cathedral differs in almost every respect from any English cathedral that preceded it and is one of the greatest buildings in the world. It is un-English in style, yet also unlike the Renaissance buildings in Italy and France that had inspired him. And the dome, even by today's standards, is a remarkable architectural and engineering achievement – perhaps the finest ever designed by any architect in England.

Very little in the way of church-building took place in England or Scotland during the 16th century. The Reformation of the Church had started, and the Renaissance movement reached England from Italy and France at about the same time. During this period, c.1550–1660, there was a good deal of hostility towards extreme 'Popish' practices such as the veneration of relics and effigies of saints. A violent campaign of iconoclasm swept over many parts of England, and vast numbers of images were destroyed.

ABOVE:
The building of the new St Paul's began in 1675, and by 1710 the last stone had been laid. Among the great cathedrals of the world, St Paul's is unique – conceived by one man, constructed under his supervision, and completed during his lifetime.

14

RIGHT:
The magnificent choir of St Paul's. In the foreground is one of the round Italianate arches beneath the dome, enriched with panelling, mosaic, fluted pilasters and massive piers.

BELOW:
Wren gathered round him a remarkable team of craftsmen. Among them was Jean Tijou, a Frenchman, who made these glorious wrought-iron sanctuary gates.

MODERN

(THE 20TH CENTURY)

After the completion of St Paul's in 1710, no more cathedral-building took place until 1839, when Augustus Pugin, who designed the Houses of Parliament, built St Chad's Roman Catholic Cathedral in Birmingham. In 1880, work began on a new cathedral at Truro, incorporating the old parish church of St Mary. J.L. Pearson's building, in the Gothic tradition, was completed in 1910.

The Roman Catholic cathedral at Westminster dates from 1895. J.F. Bentley's exotic Byzantine building was inspired by St Mark's at Venice, San Vitale at Ravenna and St Sophia at Constantinople.

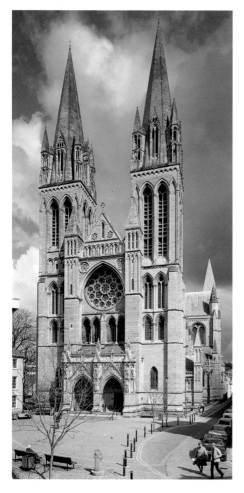

ABOVE:
The exterior of Westminster's new Roman Catholic cathedral is of red brick and stone. Parts of the interior have been completed with mosaic and coloured marble.

LEFT:
The new cathedral at Truro, built in the Gothic tradition, was completed in 1910. It has strong continental influences and the tops of the spires stand 204 feet (62m) high.

The three 20th-century Church of England cathedrals (Liverpool, Guildford and Coventry) are of great interest. The foundation stone of Liverpool Cathedral was laid in 1904, and it is almost certainly the last of the great Gothic cathedrals built in the old tradition. The cathedrals at Guildford and Coventry are in striking contrast. The familiar details, such as arcades, roof vaulting ribs, an east window and triforium, are still present at Liverpool, but have been much modified at Guildford, and are almost completely absent at Coventry. The vaulted roof still seen in Liverpool and Guildford, supported on massive piers, becomes in Coventry a webbed canopy supported on slender reinforced concrete legs, structurally independent of the roof above it.

All cathedrals, old and not so old, are living, working buildings, needing constant and expensive attention. Over the years many have suffered from the effects of general wear and tear, from frost damage, car exhaust or acid rain. With help, they can all be kept in good condition for future generations to enjoy.

LEFT:
Guildford, designed by Sir Edward Maufe RA, is traditional in its general layout, but the design has moved into the modern age. The exterior is of brick while the inside is faced with an almost white limestone, creating a light and spacious feel.

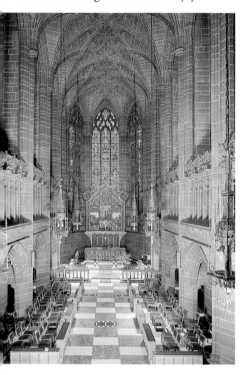

ABOVE:
The architect of Liverpool was Sir Giles Gilbert Scott OM, who was only 22 when he won a competition with his design for the new cathedral, built of the local red sandstone. This view shows the Lady Chapel.

RIGHT:
Coventry is unique in England and represents a complete departure from the traditional design of English cathedrals. Designed by Sir Basil Spence OM, it was consecrated in 1962.

GLOSSARY

ABACUS
The load-bearing flat slab or block, made of stone or wood, that forms the top of a capital.

ABUTMENT
The part of a stone or brick wall that sustains an arch.

APSE
A semicircular or polygonal projection.

ARCADE
A row of arches, e.g. between the nave and aisles, or between the choir and aisles, of a cathedral, supporting the main wall which is pierced by windows in a clerestory.

ARCADING
Rows of small arches used mainly for effect, either on the lower part of an internal aisle wall, or as a decorative feature on external walls, below the eaves or parapet.

ARCH
A self-supporting arrangement of bricks or stone blocks (voussoirs) carrying the weight of a wall over an opening. The width of the arch between its supports is the 'span', its height from base or 'springing line' to top ('crown') is called the 'rise'.

ARCUATED
A term describing a building in which arches are used to support the structure, as opposed to a 'trabeated' building, where columns and beams are used. All English Gothic cathedrals are arcuated.

BARREL VAULT
A continuous semicircular arch or tunnel, used in English Norman architecture.

BELFRY
A bell tower or campanile.

BLIND STOREY
An alternative name for the triforium.

BOSS
In medieval architecture, a keystone usually carved ornamentally and sometimes also painted and gilded, at the intersection of ribs in a vaulted roof.

BUTTRESS
A vertical mass of masonry or brickwork projecting from a wall to resist the outward thrust of a roof-truss or vault or simply to stiffen the wall.

CAMPANILE
A term usually applied only to a bell tower which is detached from a church. These are very rare in England. One was demolished at Salisbury Cathedral in 1789; but one example still survives, at Chichester Cathedral, erected c.1410.

CAPITAL
The moulded or carved block on the top of a column. It is often richly ornamented but it actually served a utilitarian purpose – to distribute weight from above on to the shaft of the column.

CHANCEL
The part of a cathedral or church east of the crossing.

CHAPTER HOUSE
An assembly place for the governing members of an ecclesiastic foundation.

CHEVET
A semicircular apse with radiating chapels.

CHEVRON or ZIGZAG
A Norman ornamental moulding, the actual ornament being shaped like a V.

CLERESTORY or CLEAR STOREY
In an aisled building such as a cathedral or church, the part of the main wall, below the eaves and above the top of the aisled roof, which is pierced with windows giving light to the main interior.

COPING
A protective covering of brick or stone on the top of a wall, usually projecting slightly in order to throw rainwater away from the face of the wall below.

CORBEL
A stone block, built into and projecting from a wall to carry the end of a roof-truss or a beam; these are often carved with grotesque human or animal figures.

CORBEL TABLE
A row of stone corbels or brackets carrying a parapet; often carved into grotesque heads.

CORNICE
A continuous horizontal member, usually moulded, crowning an external wall, or around the top of a room internally.

CROSSING
In any cathedral or large cruciform church, the square space formed by the intersection of nave and transepts.

CRYPT
An underground chamber or cellar, usually vaulted; found in most English cathedrals.

CUSHION CAPITAL
In Romanesque architecture, a plain cubic capital with its lower corners cut off and rounded, so that it resembles a cushion.

DOG-TOOTH MOULDING
An ornamental moulding in stone, much used in English cathedrals (for example at Salisbury) during the 13th century. It consists of a row of pyramidal projections, each carved into four leaves.

DOME
A convex roof, usually hemispherical, over a square, circular, or octagonal space.

FAN-VAULTING
The latest and most elaborate phase of English Gothic vaulting, very complicated and structurally somewhat illogical.

FLYING BUTTRESS
A stone buttress consisting of an arch serving as a prop, its upper end resting against the high main wall of a church, its lower end against a pier, in order to take any transmitted thrust. To increase the stability of the buttress, a pinnacle is usually built on the top of the pier.

GABLE
The triangular piece of wall at the end of a ridged roof.

GALILEE
A porch or chapel at the west end of a cathedral, for example at Durham and Ely.

KEYSTONE
The wedge-shaped central stone of an arch, on which the efficiency of the arch depends.

LANTERN
A turret or other small structure erected on the top of a tower, a roof, or a dome, to give light to the interior of a building, for example at St Paul's and Ely.

MISERICORD
In the choir stalls of a medieval church, a bracket (often grotesquely or humorously carved) beneath a hinged seat which, when the seat was tipped up, gave some support to a person standing during a lengthy service.

MULLION
A stone or wood vertical bar dividing a window-opening into 'lights'.

NAVE
The main body of a church, with or without flanking aisles, but excluding the chancel and transepts (if any).

OGEE ARCH
A pointed arch of double curvature – convex above concave.

PARAPET
A low wall built around a roof or platform to prevent people from falling over the edge.

PIER
In architecture, a solid vertical mass of stone, brick or concrete, supporting a vertical load.

PILASTER
A flat and often ornamental column, partially built into the wall of a structure, and projecting from it very slightly.

PLATE TRACERY
A primitive form of Gothic tracery, in which geometrical openings, such as circles, were pierced through a solid slab or plate of stone.

PRESBYTERY
The area near the high altar.

PULPITUM
A screen dividing the choir from the nave.

REREDOS
An ornamental screen standing above and behind the altar.

RETROCHOIR
In some cathedrals and large churches, the portion of the chancel behind the high altar, at the extreme east end.

ROSE WINDOW
A circular window containing tracery and often resembling a rose.

ROTUNDA
A term occasionally applied to a dome or to a circular domed building.

SANCTUARY
Either the holiest part of a church, that is, in the chancel, or any portion of a church in which a medieval fugitive from justice could claim sanctuary and escape arrest, under an ancient church law.

SANCTUARY KNOCKER
Ornamental knocker on the door of a church (notably Durham Cathedral) which a fugitive could touch when claiming sanctuary.

SEDILIA
A range of stone seats, generally three in number, on the south side of a chancel, for the use of the clergy.

SHAFT
The main part of a column, from its base to its capital.

SPAN
Of arch or beam, the distance between its points of support.

SPANDREL
The triangular space between the outer curve of an arch and an enclosing frame of mouldings, often richly carved with foliage.

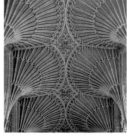

STAINED GLASS
Glass that is 'stained' or coloured by the addition of a metallic oxide during its burning, but usually painted afterwards with delicate foliage and other detail.

STELLAR VAULTING
Vaulting of a type in which the converging ribs form a star-like pattern.

TIERCERON
In vaulting, a minor rib springing from a main rib and leading to the ridge-rib.

TRACERY
In Gothic architecture, slender moulded stone bars, intersecting to form patterns at the tops of windows.

TRANSEPT
In any cruciform cathedral or large church, the transverse arm running north and south. The term is generally used in its plural form, as 'transepts', otherwise one speaks of 'the north transept' and 'the south transept'.

TRANSOM
In any large window with mullions, a horizontal bar across the whole window, of the same section as the mullions, to stiffen them transversely.

TREFOIL
Literally 'three-leaved'. Either a carved three-leaved ornament, or a three-lobed or three-leaved panel or opening in tracery.

TRIFORIUM or BLIND STOREY
In a medieval cathedral or large church, the portion of the internal wall above the arcade and below the clerestory, behind which is the dark or blind space over the aisle. The name blind storey is used as a contrast to the term clerestory because the latter is pierced with windows.

TUNNEL VAULT
Another name for a barrel vault.

TYMPANUM
The semicircular space over a round-headed doorway, above the lintel and beneath the enclosing arch, often decorated with sculpture; or space within a pediment.

UNDERCROFT
In a medieval monastery or a formerly monastic cathedral, a vaulted cellar or range of rooms used for storage, etc., often with a dormitory above.

VAULT, VAULTING
The covering of a building, or part of a building, with a roof formed of concrete ('monolithic'); or of stones in mortar, or bricks in mortar, and in any case forming a continuous semicircular or pointed arch.

Thinking about Inequality

What is inequality? In recent years there has been an explosion of interest in the subject that has yielded a substantial body of formal tools and results for income-distribution analysis. Nearly all of this is founded on a small set of core assumptions – such as the principle of transfers, scale independence and the population principle – that are used to give meaning to specific concepts of inequality measurement, inequality ranking and, indeed, to inequality itself. But does the standard axiomatic structure coincide with public perceptions of inequality? Or is the economist's concept of inequality a thing apart, perpetuated through serial brainwashing in the way the subject is studied and taught? Amiel and Cowell examine the evidence from a large international questionnaire experiment using student respondents. Along with basic 'cake-sharing' issues, related questions involving social welfare rankings, the relationship between inequality and overall income growth and the meaning of poverty comparisons are considered.

Y. AMIEL is head of Economics and Management at the Ruppin Institute. His previous work has been published in *Economica*, *Economics Letters*, the *Journal of Public Economics* and the *Scandinavian Journal of Economics*.

F. A. COWELL is Professor of Economics at the London School of Economics and Political Science. He is also Editor of *Economica* and Associate Editor of the *Journal of Public Economics*. His previous books include *Measuring Inequality*.

Thinking about Inequality

Personal Judgment and
Income Distributions

Y. AMIEL AND F. A. COWELL

CAMBRIDGE
UNIVERSITY PRESS

PUBLISHED BY THE PRESS SYNDICATE OF THE UNIVERSITY OF CAMBRIDGE
The Pitt Building, Trumpington Street, Cambridge CB2 1RP, United Kingdom

CAMBRIDGE UNIVERSITY PRESS
The Edinburgh Building, Cambridge CB2 2RU, UK   http://www.cup.cam.ac.uk
40 West 20th Street, New York, NY 10011-4211, USA   http://www.cup.org
10 Stamford Road, Oakleigh, Melbourne 3166, Australia

First published 1999

Printed in the United Kingdom at the University Press, Cambridge

Typeset in Monotype Times 10/13pt [SE]

A catalogue record for this book is available from the British Library

Library of Congress Cataloguing in Publication data
Amiel, Y. (Yoram)
Thinking about inequality / Y. Amiel and F. A. Cowell.
        p.   cm.
Includes bibliographical references (p.   ).
ISBN 0 521 46131 6 (hb) – ISBN 0 521 46696 2 (pb)
1. Income distribution.   2. Equality.   3. Poverty.   I. Amiel, Yoram.   II. Title.
HB523.C694   1999
339.2–dc21   99-13081   CIP

ISBN 0 521 46131 6 hardback
ISBN 0 521 46696 2 paperback

Contents

Figures

Tables

Preface

This book started life during a conversation at the LSE in the late 1980s. One author suggested to the other the shocking thought that the standard approach to the study of economic inequality and income distribution might be all wrong. Somehow this led to an even more shocking thought: that we might investigate whether this was so by asking other people, lots of them. This led to a full-scale research project which resulted in a number of papers (see Amiel and Cowell, 1992, 1994a, 1994b, 1995, 1996, 1997a, 1997b, 1998a, 1999) and finally to this volume which draws together the main results of the research project.

The number of people to whom we have become indebted in the course of preparing this book is enormous. First, our thanks go to Hayka Amiel who started the thought running that eventually led to the research for this book (see chapter 1 for this story). We would also like to acknowledge the input of Avraham Polovin, who has collaborated with us in our related work on risk, and of Eytan Sheshinski, who acted as joint supervisor (with Frank Cowell) of Yoram Amiel's Ph.D. thesis; some of the ideas which have been developed in this book had their origin in Yoram's thesis. Our thanks too for the patience of Mary Roye, Erik Schokkaert and colleagues at the Ruppin Institute who read the text and provided many useful comments. We are also grateful to Tony Atkinson, Gary Fields, Serge Kolm and Amartya Sen for helpful discussions, to Janet Stockdale for helping us with the questionnaire design, and to all those colleagues who patiently ran questionnaire sessions in classes or lecture groups: Gideon Amit, Gershon Ben-Shahar, Stuart Birks, Dieter Bös, Sorel Cahan, John Creedy, Rolf Cremer, Wolfgang Eichhorn, Gideon Fishelson, John Formby, Wulf Gaertner, Jim Gordon, Charles Greenbaum, Boyd Hunter, Jochen Jungeilges, Karl Jungenfeldt, Reuben Kahana, David Levhari, Avishai Margalit, Dalia Mor, Mårten Palme, Tomasz Panek, Wilhelm Pfähler, David Pines, Avraham Polovin, Eli Sagi, Abba Schwartz, Moshe Semionov, Ramii Shalom, Jacques Silber, Dan Slottje, Tehila Tamir, Harald Wiese, Yossi Yahav and Yitzhak Zilcha. After the running of all the questionnaire series some 4,000 questionnaires had to be processed and we are very glad to have benefited from the help of Trudy Ackersveen, Yafit Bar-David, Sue Coles, Anja Green, Hanana Giladi, Ann Harding, Chen Michaeli, Ceema Namazie, Elisabeth Steckmest and the data-processing staff of the Ruppin Institute. Tasneem Azad, Paolo Belli, Lupin Rahman, Christian Schluter and Silva Ule provided valuable help in the preparation of this text. We also wish to acknowledge the Hebrew University, the Ruppin Institute and STICERD all of which in many ways made our collaborative work easier. Finally, we want to thank all those students in many countries who completed the questionnaires; without them, none of this would have been possible.

Yoram Amiel   Frank Cowell
Ruppin Institute   STICERD
Israel   London School of Economics

1 Introduction

1.1 A look at inequality analysis

Thinking about inequality is not always a fashionable topic amongst economists. But thinking about inequality actually goes on all the time. Perceptions of inequality affect economic choices and political decisions. A sensitivity to inequality coupled with compassion for the poor motivates charitable giving by individuals and states. Notions about inequality appear to inform popular views about the appropriateness or otherwise of pay awards. And any parent with two or more children needs no formal analysis to be persuaded of the importance of distributive justice. Fashionable or not, thinking about inequality plays a part in the judgments and actions of politicians, planners and ordinary people.

Of course the study of economic inequality has not just been a matter of fashion. It has been an integral part of the general historical development of political economy and economics, and the approach to the topic has changed with the passage of time. While this is not the place for an extensive treatise on the history of economic thought about inequality, a brief sketch to introduce conventional wisdom on the subject may help to put into context what we want to tackle in this book.

This century has witnessed a shift in emphasis in thinking about inequality. It used to be commonplace to set the analysis of economic injustice within a particular social or institutional framework – such as Ricardo's or Marx's class-based theories of political economy. Alternatively, issues of inequality used to be cast in terms of specific models of income distribution – such as Vilfredo Pareto's famous laws of distribution. However, in more recent times, there has been a move away from these narrowly focused perceptions of the problem to an approach founded upon general principles. What principles?

A cursory review of recent literature suggests that the principles encompass a wide range of theoretical and applied economics. But all the same it is possible to simplify them down to a relatively few essentials. In practice we may usefully distinguish four major building blocks that are required in the analysis of income distributions:

- *The definition of income.* We need to specify carefully, or to be told clearly, what the thing called 'income' is.
- *The income recipient.* We also need to be clear about the nature of the entities – persons, families, households or whatever – that receive those incomes.
- *The reference group.* We should explicitly define the 'universe': the collection of persons or groups within which inequality comparisons are to be made.
- *The calibration system.* The 'inequality thermometer' – the inequality measurement tool – has to be precisely specified.

These four main components of inequality analysis get unequal treatment in the literature. As a sweeping generalisation we may state that items one, two and four in this list get a lot of attention; item three does not.

For example, theoretical economists focus principally on the fourth item in the list: the specification of a system of calibration. This forms a natural extension to a substantial literature on social choice and welfare economics. The way the analytical problems are formulated has close connections with other related issues such as the assessment of risk, the meaning of individual utility and the construction of index numbers of prices and income. In fact, inequality presents a classic theoretical measurement problem, and is typically treated in a classic fashion by setting out a system of axioms that appear to be reasonable and by formulating key propositions that follow from the axiomatic base.

On the other hand, applied economists and statisticians usually pay close attention to the first two issues: it is widely recognised that practical matters in defining income (or wealth, consumption expenditure, or whatever) or the family unit that is the income receiver are essential to understanding levels and trends of inequality within most economies.

But as far as the third point on the list is concerned – the appropriate reference group – one is immediately struck by the lack of references in the mainstream economics literature. Why this apparent neglect of one of the main components of income distribution analysis? Perhaps the answer is that to many researchers the issue seems obvious or self-defining. For example, in an empirical study, the sample is what it is. The population which the sample represents – so it might be argued – does not really need more than the most cursory discussion. Yet in principle the 'universe set' on which income distributions are to be defined and inequality to be assessed is a matter of theoretical as well as practical debate. For example, in the world of Plato or Aristotle the issue of distributional justice was applied only to free men since, in a social system that tolerated slavery, economic injustice for slaves was not a particularly relevant concept (and, of course, women did not get a look in). Similar difficulties have been raised in connection with modern theories of justice: who is to be counted within the ambit of such theories, or who is to be party to the social contract? The voting public? All adults? The whole population? If the jurisdiction of nation-states can abruptly change, even this last broad definition may be imprecise. Matters become yet more complicated if we try to take account of all the citizens of the world or persons yet unborn. The question has also been raised as to whether the principles that are applied to people should also be applied to cats, dogs and other animals.[1]

Even on the empirical level the issue of the reference group can have a dramatic impact on the picture that emerges about the pattern of world inequality. As a simple instance of this consider the study of international income comparisons by Summers and Heston (1988, 1991). Their hundred-plus countries are divided into six broad groups (Africa, North and Central America, South America, Asia, Europe and Oceania) so that it is possible to obtain a broad-brush picture of world income inequality in 1985 and 1988. But at first glance this broad-brush picture looks rather extraordinary: we find that in 1985 per capita income in Oceania was remarkably low – below Asia and South America so that it ranked fifth out of the six world regions (were the New Zealanders and Australians really so hard-pressed?); but in 1988 per capita income in Oceania had seemingly jumped so that it ranked third out of six (after Europe, but above South America). The answer to this conundrum is not hard to find: in the 1985 data compilation the relatively poor Indonesia – with its 160 million inhabitants – was classified as being part of Oceania; in 1988 it was lumped in with Asia. So, by respecifying the groups only very slightly – in effect just relabelling one country – a substantially different story emerges of income inequality among different regions of the world. Clearly too, whether one counts Indonesia as an Asian country or part of Oceania is going to have a dramatic impact on the perceived inequality within Oceania.

This brief mention of theoretical and practical difficulties is not intended to imply that clear comparisons of inequality are usually impossible or meaningless. But it serves to highlight the importance of what might appear to be mere background features of the problem in making sensible inequality comparisons.

1.2 A second look

In our view there are deeper problems associated with the issue of the reference group. In fact it is arguable that the issue lies at the root of some of the more intractable problems in the assessment of income distribution. One of these problems – which we shall be taking up later in the book – is the relationship between the analysis of economic inequality and the analysis of poverty. Over recent years each of these two related topics has been extensively developed in terms of a mathematical approach founded upon a set of formal assumptions or axioms. But they have been developed separately, each using a distinct set of axioms as an intellectual basis. The intellectual divorce between the two branches of the

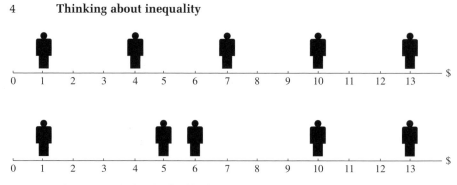

Figure 1.1. A simple distributional experiment.

subject can to some extent be explained in terms of different approaches to the idea of a reference group as we shall see further in chapter 7.

The way that reference groups are perceived also has a bearing upon some basic propositions in inequality analysis. In effect, what people mean by inequality can be crucially dependent on their perception of the relevant reference groups and in the ways that these groups are interlinked. The problem of the reference group and the way in which it relates to people's thinking about inequality is actually a convenient introduction to the case for a second look at the basics of inequality and income distribution analysis.

As an example of what is involved here, try a simple experiment. Figure 1.1 shows two possible income distributions in a very elementary economy. Each distribution contains five persons who have been arranged on an income scale in positions corresponding to their incomes, and the two distributions have the same total income ($35). The units of income are irrelevant in the experiment (the '$' sign has an unspecified value) but let us suppose that income tells us all that we might need to know about the 'well-offness', economic status or whatever of the persons; and we might as well assume that the five anonymous persons are as identical as the caricature suggests them to be. The experiment is simply this: write down which of the two distributions appears to you at first sight to be the more unequal and, if possible, give reasons for your answer.

Now, noting that the difference between the two distributions directly affects only two of the persons in the experiment, consider the slight modification of the diagram that is presented in figure 1.2. Here we have explicitly divided the population of five into two component groups, left and right, as indicated by the shading, but the distributions are in reality just the same as in figure 1.1. Notice that in each of the two subgroups taken separately it is arguable that the situation at the bottom of the diagram represents greater inequality than that at the top. The richest person in the left-hand group has a higher income ($5 rather than $4) and the poorest person in the right-hand group has a lower income ($6 rather than $7); so in both cases the income gaps within each reference group widen as we go from the top of the diagram to the bottom. However, that is not the end of the story.

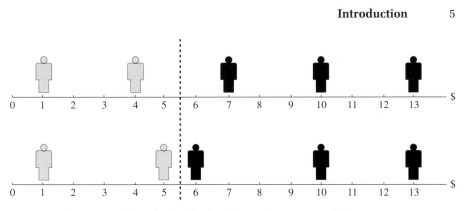

Figure 1.2. A simple distributional experiment: second view.

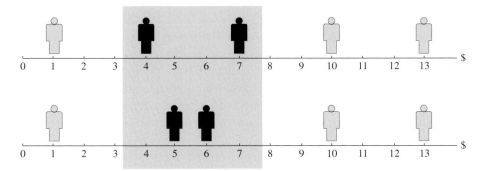

Figure 1.3. A simple distributional experiment: third view.

As a final step in the experiment have a look at figure 1.3, which again merely retouches the picture that was originally displayed in figure 1.1. In this case we have highlighted just the two persons whose incomes are directly affected in going from one distribution to the other. Put in this fashion there appears to be no argument whatsoever as to which distribution is the more unequal. Disregarding for the moment the persons whose income positions remain unchanged in going from one distribution to the other (the people with incomes $1, $10, $13) it is clear that there has been an unambiguous reduction in the gap between the two remaining persons: the gap closes from ($4, $7) to ($5, $6). Put another way, if we consider the top income distribution as the 'before' picture of inequality, and the bottom distribution as the 'after' picture, then there has been a redistribution of $1 from a richer to a poorer person: according to this view inequality *must* have fallen.

So we seem to have at least two stories about what is going on in this trivial problem of inequality comparison. How does one go about resolving the apparently contradictory pictures of inequality that emerge from even a very simple experiment such as the one we have been considering? Indeed, is there any point in trying to resolve such contradictions? Evidently the way that one tries to answer this sort of question will strongly influence one's entire conception of the meaning of inequality comparisons.

The conventional approach to the subject has been twofold. On the one hand there is the horny-handed practical approach to evaluating empirical income distributions: having argued about the right way to measure income, and whether we should view income receivers as individuals, families, households or other groups, you pick a measure of dispersion off the shelf and you estimate this along with mean income and other statistics (we shall be looking at some of these off-the-shelf measures later in the book). Alternatively there is a theoretical approach to the problem that appears to be full of the intellectual promise that accompanies analytical rigour: this method is to introduce a particular set of axioms which collectively define what is meant by inequality comparisons and hence what is meant by economic inequality itself. It is essentially the picture of inequality characterised by figure 1.3 that is taken to be the standard paradigm for the majority of theoretical and empirical work in the economics literature.

The ambiguity of answers from the simple experiment raises issues that are considerably wider than the particular principle or principles which may be brought to bear on the particular distributional problem highlighted in figure 1.1. It prompts the question as to whether the way in which inequality is conventionally presented in the literature on economics and in other related disciplines is in some sense 'appropriate'.

1.3　A guide to the book

Those who know the economics literature on inequality will say that we have presented the pictures in our little experiment the wrong way round. That is actually quite true. We deliberately put the unorthodox view of the inequality comparison experiment first, and followed up with the standard story. The reason for this has little to do with the grand sweep of the history of thought on the subject, and much to do with a small domestic incident.

A few years ago one of the authors, Yoram Amiel, was asked by his wife Hayka (who is a school-teacher and not an economist) to explain the topic of his research. To put the main ideas over concisely he gave her a little numerical example as an illustration – something close to the experiment that we have just been considering, in fact. Faced with the choice between the two distributions, Hayka gave the 'wrong' answer. Yoram concisely pointed this out: the answer should have been clear, unambiguous and the exact opposite to hers – according to the standard theory of inequality measurement. Hayka's reply was similarly concise: 'So change the theory.'

We make no claim to be changing the theory of inequality measurement in this book. But this issue did prompt an extensive research project which, amongst other things, resulted in the book. Along the way it also raised a number of provocative questions which we make no claim to have resolved. Is the standard theory 'right' and, furthermore, what does it mean for a theory to be 'right' in this context? These questions have in turn prompted the theoretical and empirical analysis which is reported in the following chapters.

Chapters 2 to 4 are principally about the problem of inequality in its purest form, the problem of dividing a cake of fixed size amongst a fixed number of people. Chapter 2 gives a summary guide to the standard approach in the literature on inequality measurement, chapter 3 explains the method we used to investigate the assumptions underlying the approach – a series of specially structured questionnaires – and chapter 4 reports the results of these investigations. These chapters also deal with elementary issues of how one can compare situations that have different sizes of cake or different numbers of people sharing the cake.

Chapters 5 to 7 extend the approach to three areas closely related to the pure inequality problem: social welfare (chapter 5), the relationship between income growth and perceptions of inequality (chapter 6), and poverty (chapter 7). Each of these additional topics requires additional assumptions on top of the structure used for the pure inequality problem, and we subject these to the same sort of investigative strategy; they also provide us with an opportunity to check our results on the pure inequality issue.

Chapter 8 makes a comparison of responses to our various questionnaire studies across countries and across academic disciplines, while chapter 9 sums up and suggests directions in which thinking about inequality may yet go. Finally, those readers who like to have assumptions and propositions tidied up in a concise mathematical format may want to use appendix A which sets out the main results in the conventional approach to inequality measurement; all this material has been parked in this unglamorous location because, although it has its uses, it is no substitute for thinking about inequality.

Notes

1 See, for example, Sen's discussion of Rawls's concept of the 'original position' (Sen 1970, p. 124).

2 What is inequality?
The economists' view

2.1 The axiomatic approach

As we mentioned in chapter 1 the standard approach to the problem of inequality comparisons is based upon a formal structure that is usually expressed in terms of precise assumptions – or axioms – and mathematical propositions. So, in order to grasp what is going on and what it is that we are investigating in the rest of this book, it may be helpful to have a brief introduction to the axiomatic methodology.

The axiomatic methodology is a grand name for an essentially simple approach to our subject. It consists of a rule-based system of thought which enables us to state precisely what we mean by inequality comparisons, and thereby what we mean by inequality. The axioms are formal assumptions which are taken as fundamental: they are not derived from even more basic assumptions; they do not have to be based on any real-world experience or observation; they require no appeal to any external value system. Whether the axioms are 'true' or not, and what is meant by the 'truth' of a set of axioms are moot points. What are the circumstances under which the axiomatic approach is valuable, and what is one trying to achieve by adopting this approach?

Perhaps a rough-and-ready description of the principal advantage of the axiomatic approach is that it acts as a systematic antidote to the trial-and-error approach of picking apparently suitable ready-made statistics. This description both overstates and understates the case. It is a slight overstatement because picking an axiom system can in fact amount to little more than the trial-and-error approach in a rather more sophisticated guise: if you happen to want to use a particular measurement tool anyway, it is not too difficult to write down a set of 'basic' assumptions which will imply that your pet measure is in fact the only one that is available for use. Our simple description also understates the rôle of the axiomatic approach: actually it is potentially quite powerful because, by adopting this method of analysis, it is possible to set out the exact relationship between

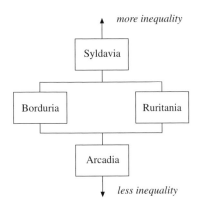

Figure 2.1. An inequality ranking.

particular principles or rules of comparison, and the types of specific mathematical formulae available for summarising income distributions. In fact it aids in formulating basic ideas about the meaning and structure of inequality comparisons.

2.2 Inequality rankings and orderings

Inequality comparisons are the basic idea with which we need to work. From several of these comparisons we may then build up an inequality ranking or, perhaps, an inequality ordering. An inequality comparison is simply a coherent rule for comparing distributions of income (or wealth, consumption, and so on) in two situations. Has the income distribution in our country become more equal over the last five years? Is Syldavia a more unequal society than Borduria? For an inequality comparison to be meaningful, then the answer 'yes, Syldavia is more unequal than Borduria' must also imply, in the other direction, 'Borduria is less unequal than Syldavia.' Of course this simple pairwise rule does not say anything about whether such pairwise comparisons can always be made, or whether connecting up different pairs of comparisons (where they can be made) is also possible. We can do more if the comparison rule is transitive, which means that inequality comparisons can be chained together: the statements 'Syldavia is more unequal than Borduria' and 'Borduria is more unequal than Arcadia' together imply the statement 'Syldavia is more unequal than Arcadia.' Given transitivity we can produce an inequality ranking such as that illustrated in figure 2.1.

A transitive ranking of distributions may nevertheless leave certain gaps in the set of possible pairwise comparisons. This is also illustrated in figure 2.1 where the inequality comparison rule implies that Syldavia is more unequal than Ruritania which in turn is more unequal than Arcadia, but that Borduria and Ruritania cannot be compared in terms of the rule. Notice that we are not saying

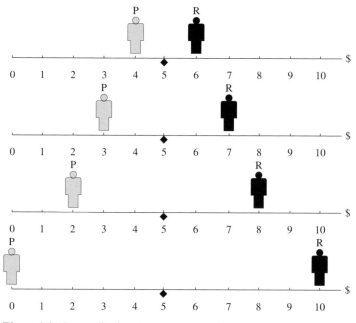

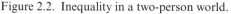

Figure 2.2. Inequality in a two-person world.

that the inequality rule indicates that Borduria and Ruritania have the same inequality, but rather that the rule is indecisive in this case. According to the rule that generated this ranking we just do not know which of the two is more unequal.

However, if the inequality comparison rule is always decisive (or 'complete' to use the standard jargon), then, combined with the property of transitivity we could obtain an inequality ordering. At one level this is just what we mean by 'measuring' inequality. As we shall see, the meaning of inequality comparisons depends critically upon the axiomatic basis that is specified for the inequality comparison rule.

In one very special case, virtually nothing is required in terms of axiomatisation. Given a two-person world with a fixed total income there is very little to say in terms of inequality comparisons. A brief look at the four distributions in figure 2.2 is sufficient to make the point. Because there is by assumption a fixed total income (in this case $10) the two persons (P and R) must be equally spaced around the position of mean income ($5); it is clear that as we move from the top of the diagram to the bottom, inequality steadily increases as the rich person R and the poor person P move farther apart. So what is inequality in this case? We could measure it as the income gap between the two figures ($2 in the first line, $4 in the second, and so on), or we could measure it as the proportionate gap between the two ($2/$10 = 0.20 in the first line, and so on); or, if we wanted to, we could use the square or the cube-root of the distance between persons P and R: it matters little except in terms of the scaling of the 'thermometer' by which we propose to measure inequality.

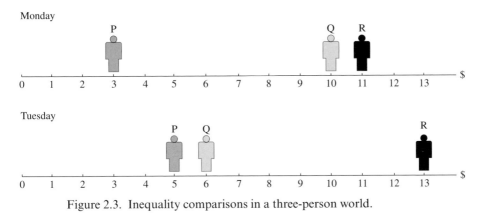

Figure 2.3. Inequality comparisons in a three-person world.

However, when there are three or more persons, matters are not so simple. Examine figure 2.3 which displays a pair of alternative distributions for three persons: Poor (P), Quite-well-off (Q) and Rich (R). To see the problem imagine that the top part of the picture represents the distribution on Monday, and the bottom part the distribution on Tuesday: then going from Monday to Tuesday we find that poor P gains at the expense of quite-well-off Q; but, along with the gains of P, the rich person R also gains: the Q–R gap widens. It is easy to imagine two different people looking at this situation and coming to diametrically opposite conclusions as to whether the net result constitutes a rise or fall in inequality from Monday to Tuesday, depending on whether they accorded priority to the P–Q change or the Q–R change.

As we shall see, further difficulties arise even if we stay with the two-person case, but attempt to compare distributions that have different totals of income. At this point the axiom system has a potentially important rôle to play.

If we want to go beyond the two-person, fixed-income situation, then putting the problem into a formal setting can assist in focusing the mind on the essential nature of these difficulties. In order to understand the way in which these issues are involved it will be useful to take a brief and informal overview of the main principles that are usually applied in the problem of making inequality comparisons.[1]

2.3 The transfer principle

Let us go a little deeper into the little experiment that we carried out in chapter 1. Recall that in comparing the two distributions illustrated in figure 1.1 the 'right' answer was that the top distribution was more unequal. The reason was that displayed in figure 1.3: the reduction in the income gap between the second and third persons in the distribution. The principle which we have highlighted here can be very simply stated: for any given income distribution if you take a small amount of income from one person and give it to a richer person then income inequality must increase.[2] This is the transfer principle, originally introduced by Pigou (1912) and developed by Dalton (1920). In fact we have stated this principle a little too casually because we have not specified the persons to whom it is to apply (Just to the poorest and the richest? Just to someone below and someone above average income? Or to any two persons in the population?). As we shall see in chapter 4 this point is quite important in terms of understanding the applicability of the transfer principle.

The transfer principle by itself is evidently not decisive in terms of inequality comparisons. This can be seen by looking again at figure 2.3. In passing from Monday's distribution to Tuesday's we find that there is an equalising change at the bottom of the distribution (the P–Q gap has shrunk), but that there is also a disequalising change at the top of the distribution (the Q–R gap has increased). A 'top-sensitive' observer of this situation (someone who attaches particular importance to what happens in the part of the distribution involving higher incomes) will conclude that inequality has increased from Monday to Tuesday: a 'bottom-sensitive' observer would come to the opposite conclusion. By appealing to the transfer principle alone we cannot resolve all possible inequality comparisons and build them up into a complete ordering of distributions by inequality.[3]

2.4 Income and population

One of the things that is left unclear by the simple example given in figure 2.2 is how one might systematically compare the two-person distributions illustrated there with two-person distributions of a larger cake (with higher mean income), or with apparently similar distributions having the same mean but with more individuals receiving each of the two incomes. Furthermore, the transfer principle is of no help on these issues: it applies only to the problem of slicing and reslicing a fixed-size cake amongst a fixed number of people.

We might guess that there ought to be some reasonable ways of extending the inequality orderings so that they apply not to this particular problem alone, but to more general situations involving cakes of arbitrary size, and arbitrary numbers of cake-eaters. There are indeed such 'reasonable' extensions. However, intuition can be an unreliable guide here, and we shall find more than one apparently reasonable way of extending the rules on inequality comparisons in the two-persons, fixed-cake situation to more interesting distributional problems.

Let us begin with the issue of the size of the cake. In other words we want to take into account the effect on inequality rankings of changes in aggregate income. Perhaps the idea that first springs to mind is that of *scale independence*: simply stated, for a given income distribution if you double, halve, treble everyone's income, then measured inequality should remain unchanged. This has become virtually the standard assumption in the literature, but let us take a moment or two to query it. Occasionally it is argued that the scale-independence

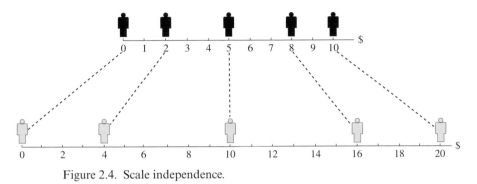

Figure 2.4. Scale independence.

principle is somehow the only reasonable assumption to make in view of the problem of arbitrary changes in the value of the monetary unit in which income is measured: if living standards are determined by real income and there is inflation so that the buying power of the dollar is halved, then of course the two distributions illustrated in figure 2.4 must be equivalent in terms of inequality. But this argument by itself is misleading: income can be measured in any way one wants – pounds, dollars, bars of chocolate – and so we can eliminate the problem of an arbitrary monetary scale by dividing all the incomes by an appropriate price index before carrying out any inequality comparisons. To get the sense of the scale-independence principle replace the '$' sign in figure 2.4 with 'chocolate bars' and suppose this chocolate to be an all-satisfying composite economic good (this trick eliminates the scale-of-measurement problem). Again we might agree that the two halves of figure 2.4 represent equally unequal distributions of chocolate; it is just that there is twice as much chocolate to go round in the bottom picture. But would we still say the same if we were told that the five dollars or chocolate bars in the first distribution were just on the borderline of survival? There may be alternative distributional principles that are reasonable.

To see the point, let us consider the property of *translation independence* which is seen by some as a viable alternative to the standard case. Figure 2.5 illustrates the basic idea; by contrast with figure 2.4 the 'new' distribution in the bottom half of the picture has been created from the 'old' distribution in the figure simply by shifting the block containing the distribution bodily to the right; this preserves the absolute differences between the incomes in the distribution (again you can interpret the diagram in terms of dollars or chocolate bars). There is nothing to say that scale independence is 'right' and translation independence 'wrong' in some prior sense: it all depends on how we view inequality comparisons when the size of the cake changes.[4] In our view it is an issue which deserves further investigation which we will undertake in chapters 4 and 6.

But what should happen to inequality comparisons when we consider communities of different sizes of population rather than different amounts of income? If we restrict attention to situations that involve a 'balanced' increase in the population, then it is arguable that a lot can be said. If we were to create a new

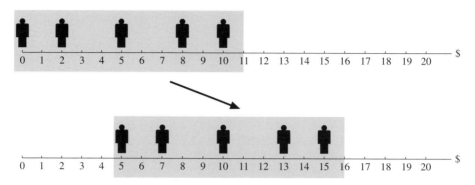

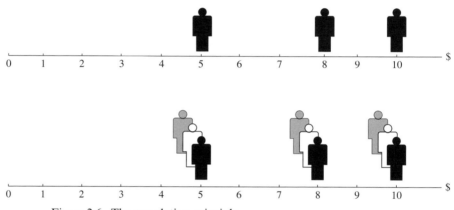

Figure 2.5. Translation independence.

Figure 2.6. The population principle.

distribution just by scaling up the population, then it may seem that nothing essential has changed in terms of the inequality of the distribution. This is what has come to be known as the *population principle*. The idea is very simple. Imagine that you replicate the economy by creating a set of clones for the whole population. Intuition suggests, perhaps, that the combined economy – the original and clones together – has the same inequality as the original distribution before the cloning. The argument can be extended to arbitrary numbers of replications. This is the point that is illustrated in figure 2.6. The bottom part of the diagram is a threefold copy of the distribution in the top of the diagram; for every one person with a given income in the original distribution, there are now three persons with that income.

Nevertheless, intuition may again be an unreliable guide. In the case of extreme inequality it is arguable that population replications are not neutral in terms of inequality. Consider figure 2.7, which shows two situations in which there is undoubtedly extreme inequality. The top half of the figure displays the case where this is one rich person, and a whole bunch of people clustered together at the

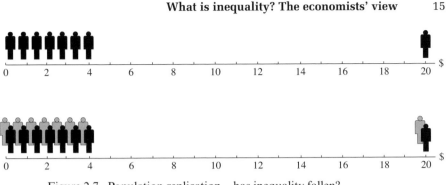

Figure 2.7. Population replication – has inequality fallen?

bottom of the distribution; the bottom half depicts the situation that would emerge if the population were simply cloned and merged in the way that we have just discussed. Notice that in the way the example has been constructed there was just one very rich person in the original distribution; the very fact that the cloning process implies that there are many enjoying a very high income, rather than just one individual, even though there are proportionately as many extra poor people, may suggest that inequality has actually fallen in the process. Again there is nothing inherently 'right' about the population principle as such; obviously it makes the analysis much simpler, but it may not happen to correspond with the way in which inequality comparisons are typically made; more of this in chapter 4.

2.5 Decomposability

Along with the transfer principle, the issue of decomposability is of tremendous importance in the standard approach to the measurement of inequality. Basically it involves the logical relationship between inequality in a whole population and inequality in each of a set of constituent groups in the population (males and females, age groups, ethnic groups, and so on). There are a number of different approaches to aggregation and grouping issues, most of which are very closely related. The principle that is relevant here is that, if inequality should increase in one subgroup of the population, then *ceteris paribus*, inequality would increase in the population as a whole. To explain what is involved we shall concentrate on just one of these.

To focus ideas let us extend the example of the pair of distributions that we recently considered in figure 2.3. Now consider merging each of these three-person distributions with an additional 'immigrant' group: the immigrant group is identical in each case. Let us simplify the problem yet further by supposing that this immigrant group has the same mean income as the original population. The principle of decomposability implies that inequality rankings before and after the merger should be identical.

In figure 2.8, the top pair of distributions – before the merger – represent the same situation as in figure 2.3 above. The bottom pair of distributions represent

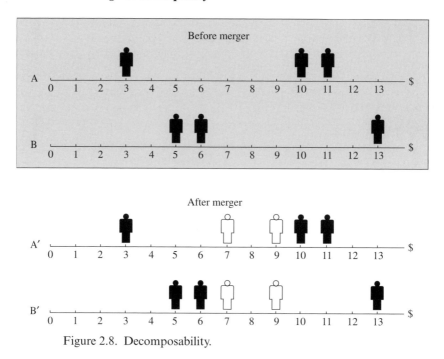

Figure 2.8. Decomposability.

the picture that would emerge if the immigrants were counted in with the rest of the population. The decomposability logic is as follows: the five-person population that we have in distributions A′ and B′ consists of a two-person group (the immigrants) combined with a three-person group (the original population), as shown by the shading; if overall inequality is consistently related to inequality in each constituent subgroup and inequality between the groups, then the ranking by inequality of distributions A′ and B′ must be completely determined by the original distributions A and B (after all, the distributions in the two-person immigrant group in A′ and B′ are identical and the two-person group and the three-person group have the same average income so there is no between-group inequality).

Notice that the principle of decomposability is independent of whether we are top-sensitive or bottom-sensitive in terms of inequality comparisons. As we noted in our discussion of figure 2.3, in the upper half of figure 2.8 a top-sensitive observer would rank A as being a more equal distribution than B; such a person should also rank A′ as being more equal than B′ in the lower half of the figure – if the principle of decomposability is to be accepted; a bottom-sensitive observer would come to the opposite pair of conclusions: B more equal than A and B′ more equal than A′. According to either view the pairs of distributions will be ranked consistently.

The practical importance of decomposability is considerable. If, for example, we try to set up some kind of coherent 'accounting framework' for changes in inequality of a country in the course of economic development – 'of the x%

inequality growth overall, $y\%$ is attributable to inequality change in the rural sector, $z\%$ to inequality change in the urban sector, and the rest to what happened to income differences between the sectors' – it is almost impossible to dispense with the decomposability principle. Similar considerations apply when one tries to break down inequality systematically in other complex heterogeneous populations. However, the principle imposes stringent limitations on the type of measurement tool that are available for constructing inequality orderings. Perhaps these restrictions are too stringent; this is something which we shall look into further in chapter 4.

2.6 Summary

In economic terms the question 'What is inequality?' resolves into the question 'How are inequality comparisons to be made?' Fancy statistical devices that might serve as inequality measures or other graphical tools for comparing distributions are given meaning by introducing a set of basic principles which embody ideas about what a 'more unequal distribution' connotes. The basis for these rules need be nothing other than 'that which is considered to be reasonable'. Who considers it to be reasonable is another matter.

We have had a brief look at some of the main principles that are commonly applied, explicitly or implicitly, in the standard approach to inequality comparisons. Later in the book we shall consider other principles, which have a special importance when inequality is interpreted in terms of welfare economics.[5] Two of the principles that we have introduced so far stand out as being of crucial importance. The principle of decomposability is required for a lot of the applications of inequality comparisons that empirical researchers would like to undertake. The transfer principle is even more fundamental; in fact this alone is often taken to be a defining characteristic of what is actually meant by an 'inequality measure' amongst all the various mathematical functions that might be defined upon the set of all possible income distributions. Nevertheless, along with the other principles reviewed above, we propose to subject the principle of transfers to further scrutiny.

Notes

1 For a detailed formal exposition of the axioms that appear in this and the following chapter, see appendix A.
2 A broader interpretation is given in Castagnoli and Muliere (1990).
3 For this reason some writers have appealed to additional principles such as 'transfer sensitivity' which impose an explicit view on the relative importance of transfers in different parts of the distribution (Kolm 1976a).
4 What we can be quite clear about is that – for meaningful inequality comparisons – they cannot both be true at the same time. If you are puzzled, see appendix A.
5 In particular we discuss the issue of 'anonymity' or 'symmetry' in chapter 5.

3 An investigative strategy

3.1 What are we investigating?

A glance ahead to the empirical chapters of this book will reveal that we concentrate heavily upon one particular investigative approach. Our approach may at first appear to be unconventional, and so one might well ask what it could achieve that cannot be covered by more conventional methods of economic investigation. Why go to the trouble of developing a specialised strategy for one specialised branch of welfare economics? The short answer is that what conventional methods can do inevitably misses a number of important issues completely: we show that our methodology fills a gap in the body of evidence about values and preferences in economics. We shall also argue that the approach can be useful in other branches of economics.

Consider the nature of 'evidence' in economics. The usual form of evidence is simply empirical corroboration – for example, in studies of consumer demand or of firms' costs. Obviously there is a variety of substantive issues to be addressed before accepting this sort of testimony in any economic debate: there are methodological issues about what constitutes a satisfactory 'test' of an economic theory; behavioural models may have to be put into desperately simple forms in order to be estimated empirically; particular data sets may have defects or even be downright shoddy. But it is usually assumed that these difficulties can be overcome, or can be accommodated to a sufficient degree, that other forms of evidence – such as that derived from experiments and surveys – is either superfluous or of inferior quality to data derived from real behaviour in real markets. Questionnaire or experimental methods may well suffer from the same sort of difficulties as do conventional behavioural estimation techniques, with some additional problems piled on top. More than that, the conventional wisdom appears to be that these alternative approaches could actually be misleading or dangerous: market research can be misdirected, people may lie to opinion polls or refuse to participate in official surveys. In sum, the conventional wisdom in mainstream economics appears to be that it is far better to judge people by what they actually do than by what they say that they would do.

However, an approach using behavioural evidence is simply inappropriate or irrelevant in the present case. After all, we are not dealing with a situation where the relevant concepts are traded in a market where individual values or tastes are translated into choices. Many people will have strongly defined views on inequality and welfare that will virtually never be translated into concrete actions. Even so, it might be argued that a counterpart to conventional evidence used in analysing the behaviour of consumers or firms is available in the field of applied welfare analysis. Politicians and other governmental agencies make decisions about allocation that reflect value judgments on inequality, inequity and poverty and so we might be able to use the outcomes of their choices to draw inferences about the basis on which they were made in a manner similar to that used in conventional consumer theory. However, this type of evidence runs into a number of special problems of its own. For a start the data base is always likely to be rather thin: there are not many agencies to observe and not many different 'cake-division' actions to observe. It is also reasonable to suppose that politicians will usually make decisions on the basis of a variety of criteria in addition to any specific coherent views about inequality; and of course they may not represent anyone other than themselves. Moreover, the outcome of the decision – which is all that we are likely to observe – will be influenced by a variety of factors that lie outside the government's control. We know for example that economic inequality rose substantially during the 1980s in a number of Western countries that had governments inclined toward the political right; how much those observed changes in income distribution are directly attributable to official policy is difficult to ascertain; still more difficult to ascertain from this evidence alone would be any specific views on the nature of economic inequality. In sum, it is unlikely that observing the outcome of distributional decisions in practice is going to address the sort of issue relevant to the subject matter of this book.

So if the problem in hand cannot make use of the conventional kind of behavioural data, what can be done? Considerable progress can be made in some branches of economics without calling on carefully documented evidence; a lot of economic models are based essentially on uncorroborated general appeal because they have an important story to tell – simple general equilibrium models and game theory. So why not just carry on with artificial models and assumptions in welfare economics? Furthermore where value judgments are involved there is a temptation to state *De gustibus non est disputandum* and move on to the next question. So why not just leave it at that? The *de gustibus* tag is virtually a truism, but it is perhaps an irrelevant truism. If the way that economists or other social scientists think about inequality is radically different from the way that it is perceived by others then there is good reason to think again – at least about the terms that we use. If we are concerned about the design of economic policy then it is important to consider the basis on which the objectives of the policy have been framed. For this reason we should perhaps be ready to consider alternative investigation techniques and information sources about perceptions of inequality and income distribution.

There is a practical alternative to the benign neglect of assumptions about preferences and values. It would be reasonable to consider analogous situations in related fields where behavioural data are unlikely to be available, or where the data are inadequate for the purpose of drawing conclusions about how economic agents act. There are many good examples of scientific approaches in economics which specifically address this sort of issue, including business games, income tax experiments, and surveys of investment intentions or consumer attitudes.

The closest of these to our present study are those that concern themselves with the analysis of individuals' attitudes to risk. A lot of information about people's willingness to take risks is available from observations on market behaviour – buying and selling of financial assets, insurance contracts, gambling – which will permit inferences to be drawn about the shape of people's preference maps. But usually these inferences require the prior acceptance of a system of behavioural axioms that cannot themselves be subjected to test by the evidence. For example, assuming that people's preferences can be adequately represented by von Neumann–Morgenstern utility functions one might be able to deduce something about the degree of risk aversion from their observed behaviour in selecting a portfolio or other actions (Levy 1994); but to investigate whether the von Neumann–Morgenstern structure is itself an appropriate way of modelling people's preferences in the face of uncertainty requires something more than just market data (Kahneman *et al.* 1982).

There is another practical lesson that can be drawn from the problem of investigating behaviour under uncertainty. There are a number of instances where data are, arguably, pathologically unreliable: even if data on choices were supposedly available, we might not want to trust them. A classic example of this kind of issue is the investigation of illicit behaviour, such as is required for the empirical estimation of models of tax evasion. Although it is of considerable interest to know the size of the underground economy and the behaviour of its participants, it appears that if one were to attempt to measure incomes flowing from illegal activity one would, almost by definition, end up measuring something else because if the activity could be quantified then it could not really have been 'underground'. If so, then there is little hope of using data from this source to get evidence on the patterns of preferences and the responses to incentives of those who engage in underground activities. What does the researcher do in such cases? Apart from the comparatively rare situations in which the tax authorities allow private individuals access to records of tax audits or otherwise confidential records, a common approach has been to rely on experiments, simulations and questionnaires (see Cowell 1990, ch. 6).

However, we have to admit, economists are often suspicious of this kind of approach and wary of the evidence that it provides. Why? Part of the reason could be that the techniques involved are perceived as principally belonging to other disciplines and that, on the whole, economists are fairly self-assured about the validity of their own methods: 'economists on the whole think well of what they do themselves and much less well of what their professional colleagues do' (Galbraith 1971). Nevertheless, if we as economists are to be involved in making policy recommendations on taxation or other measures that affect individual incomes, or if they are to interpret trends in income distribution, then we may just have to take on board methodologies that appear at first sight to be alien.

The approach that we develop in this book combines elements of these two techniques – experiments and questionnaires – which have become standard in some branches of economics and other social sciences. Let us briefly examine what is involved in each of them.

3.2 Experiments

It used to be conventional wisdom that, unlike the natural sciences, controlled experiments in economics are impossible. The economic history of the late 1980s and early 1990s may have given the lie to this: the drastic economic reforms in Eastern Europe, or the tinkering around with local taxation in the UK, seem to provide instances where economic advisers have been given a free hand to pursue the logical consequences and observe the practical implementation of a theory or doctrine. Attractive as the idea of a controlled economic experiment may be to some, to those who are unpersuaded of the doctrine or to observers who have watched some of the experiments go dramatically wrong, these developments are not strictly speaking 'experiments' in the conventional usage of the term.

Although there is some latitude in the interpretation of the term 'experimental method', experiments in economics usually have a number of elements in common, and these are discussed in the following paragraphs.

Theoretical base

The theoretical base for the experiment is essential in defining what its purpose is supposed to be and in interpreting the findings of the experiment. The point has been well made by John Hey (1991, p. 10): 'Consider, then what is being tested. There are two components . . .

1   that the theory is correct given the appropriate specification (that is, under the given conditions);
2   that the theory survives transition from the world of theory to the real world.

All too often the theorist . . . assumes that point 1 is true – usually without discussion. Thus attention focuses on point 2.' The theoretical base need not, of course, be a conventional model of utility- or profit-maximising agents; it could encompass other types of optimising behaviour, or situations where the notion of optimisation is irrelevant.

Rules of the game

The set of rules within which the experiment operates needs to be clearly specified and understood. This applies to all sorts of economic models that can be represented as games; it applies to the relationship between experimenter and experimental subject; and it even applies if we consider the real world as the outcomes of cosmic 'experiments'. It is an important step in defining what can be expected to be learned from the class of experiments of which the particular experiment in question is a part. In some instances the method of analysis delimits the sets of rules that could be considered within a particular experimental environment. We can illustrate this in the case of the board and counters used to play an ordinary game of draughts (checkers). The equipment comes with a set of rules for playing draughts, and we might imagine small variations in the rules which could make the game more interesting. We could even imagine generating a substantially new game with different rules: we could use the same counters and the same board to play a game like 'fox and geese'. What we do not allow is the opportunity for players to remake the rules as they go along, or just to kick over the board. So too with economic experiments: the 'rules of the game' define not just one particular experiment, but a class of experiments which could be run, and therefore a class of economic questions which could be addressed. The possibility remains that interesting questions on a particular topic could be ruled out by virtue of the class of rules of the experiment.

Control

The element of control is usually integral to the nature of economic investigations. For example, quantitative macro-models usually require the careful specification of a 'counterfactual' – a story of what would have happened otherwise – in order to appraise the worth of the model under consideration. The extensive Negative Income Tax experiments performed in the United States (Ferber and Hirsch 1982) went to considerable trouble to provide control groups of families who were not being confronted with the negative tax system of income support. In modern experimental economics it is common to provide the element of control through the setting in which the experiment takes place: this is conventionally described as a laboratory. The meaning of a 'laboratory experiment' in economics is simply that it takes place in a controlled environment – commonly a work-room equipped with computers for use by the experimental subjects – that is manifestly different from the real world. In this way some of the problems of human nature that confront the experimenter can be dealt with systematically. For example, the knowledge that you are actually part of an experiment may well affect your behaviour; so that, unless the experimenter is careful, misleading interpretations could be drawn from results in the laboratory; standard techniques can be applied to mitigate this problem – such as embedding the experiment that you are really interested in within the context of some other experiment, or providing experimental subjects with financial incentives that correspond to real-world gains and losses – but by the nature of the laboratory setting one can never be wholly free from it.

3.3 Questions

An important alternative approach to laboratory experimentation involves posing questions. This is an idea that, in this field, goes back at least to Cowell (1985). This can be done in a variety of formats, and we have to admit that questions bring their own problems. Some of these problems are familiar to those who run opinion polls and those who use them. Here is an abbreviated summary.

The 'framing' problem

Sometimes the responses to a question will be significantly affected by the way in which the question is phrased or the context in which it is placed.[1] One way of mitigating the problem is to ask about the same issue in a variety of forms. However, in some respects 'the framing problem' may not be a problem at all but rather a part of the design of the study, in that the particular way in which the questions are to be posed is intended to be significant. An important instance of this is where the researcher wants the respondent to make reference to a particular national or social context: examples are the subjective poverty-line questionnaires used by Hagenaars (1986) and others.

Misrepresentation

People have been known to tell the questioner what they think the questioner wants to know; or they tell tales to advantage if they do not want to look foolish or boorish in the eyes of the interviewer; or they simply lie. Although people may respond to a political pollster – with good motive – in one fashion, they may well do something rather different within the privacy of the voting booth. If they think that there is something to be gained personally from their response they may try to manipulate the system by choosing their answers appropriately.

Imprecision

Applied economists delight in precise numerical answers to precise questions; but if the questions are to be posed to individuals in questionnaires rather than being embedded in an econometric study, then a high degree of precision may be illusory or unattainable. On many important issues people may have clear and decided views but yet be unable to express them in a way that would satisfy the niceties of numerical representation that might be considered desirable in an empirical study. To try to force people's responses into a more 'precise' format might result in a spurious quantification which smacks of the 'how-upset-were-you' type of question that is sometimes posed by officious reporters to the grieving widow after a traffic accident.

All of these issues are relevant to a questionnaire investigation of people's attitudes to inequality but, as we shall see, they can be satisfactorily handled by working on a suitable design of the questions that are to be put.

3.4 A new approach

Our approach involves presenting individuals with questionnaires in a way that uses many of the features of experimental methodology reviewed above – for this reason we call it the questionnaire-experimental method. To understand the basis of the approach let us consider the way in which distributional judgments may be presented to people.

Imagine a society to be made up of 'identities' – labels, if you like – which can be adopted by the various people who are actually going to inhabit the society. The situation is a bit like the children's game with cherry stones: tinker, tailor, soldier, sailor, rich man, poor man . . . The various possible states of society can then be considered as systems of rights, rewards and privileges that are associated with each of these identities. In making judgments about alternative social states it is obviously of crucial importance to be clear about the relationship between the person or group of persons making the judgment and the set of identities making up the society. There are two distinct scenarios.

In the first scenario we make the assumption of Olympian detachment: we suppose that whoever it is making judgments about the society is an outsider who is not going to be involved in the society. It is perhaps like that of a representative of an international organisation such as the World Bank or the IMF who is reviewing alternative policies for some country of which he is not a national.

The alternative scenario, of course, is to suppose that the individual will be – *and knows that he will be* – allocated one of the identities in the society on which he is passing judgment. Instead of being a disinterested, albeit compassionate, observer of the scene, he is an insider who is going to benefit or suffer from the particular state of society that will be adopted. Rather than being a representative of the World Bank, he is the Prime Minister, a government adviser, a company executive or a trade union leader. At this point a second issue arises which can be explained by the use of a couple of simple diagrams.

Suppose the tinker-tailor-soldier-sailor identities are numbered $1, 2, \ldots, n$. What should one assume that the person (or persons) making the value judgments knows about his (their) identity? Following the work of Harsanyi (1955)

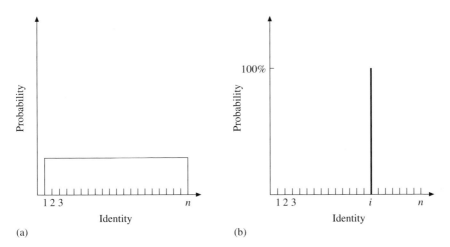

Figure 3.1. Two extreme approaches to identity in the distribution problem.

and Rawls (1972)[2] it is common to assume that welfare judgments are in effect made behind a 'veil of ignorance'; in other words, to suppose that the individual does not know which identity he or she will adopt. In its simplest form the position can then be represented as in panel (a) of figure 3.1. Here the assumption is that any one of the identities is equally likely, so that each person making a distributional judgment is faced with a rectangular probability distribution as to his own chances in the lottery of life (strictly speaking we should only draw a density like this if the collection $\{1, 2, \ldots, n\}$ were to be replaced by a continuum: let us ignore this technicality). The obvious alternative is where the person making the judgment knows *exactly* which suit of clothes he is going to put on in this society. This is represented in panel (b) in figure 3.1, where all the probability mass is concentrated at identity i.[3]

These two extremes by no means exhaust the possibilities. In practice the situation very often lies somewhere between them. The veil of ignorance may be replaced by the net curtain of partial ignorance in that you, as the person passing judgment, have some information but not complete information about the allocation of identities. For example, it could be you know that you probably belong to the rich set although you do not know exactly which member of the rich set you will be. Alternatively expressed, your prior distribution over the set of labels in society is not uniform (figure 3.2).

This type of issue appears to be commonly regarded as important in the design of rules and procedures that have to do with distributional fairness. On the whole, people regard with distaste the law-maker who profits personally from his privileged position when making laws. Recognising that you – the law-maker or social commentator – cannot be completely neutral if you are actually a member of the society, society will devise institutions and rules that limit your power to use your inside knowledge: conventions of public life may require that your business

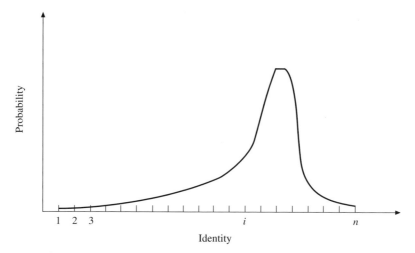

Figure 3.2. The identity problem with some information.

interests be handled by trustees during the tenure of political office; the law may limit the extent to which you can use patronage in providing 'jobs for the boys'. And just as the connection between self-knowledge and self-interest is perceived as important in real life we would expect it to be important in experimental situations as well.

It is clear that this second scenario of the relationship between the person making distributional judgments and the component identities of society is both more demanding in its basic assumptions (have the probabilities of individual identities been made clear to all concerned?) and perhaps sensitive to the context in which the questions are framed (the individual will be asking himself 'Where am I in this income distribution?'). For this reason the questionnaire-experimental method that we have adopted is designed so as to give the respondents the impression that they are making judgments about a society in which they themselves do not participate. In this way the issue of the alternative identity assumptions in figures 3.1 and 3.2 are sidestepped.

All of the work reported in this book conforms to the same general pattern: questions about income distributions in an abstract setting are presented to individuals in a controlled environment that is similar to a laboratory environment. Some of the advantages of this approach are immediately apparent. For example, because the topic with which we are concerned – the structure of inequality comparisons – is not principally behavioural, we do not have to worry about behaviour in reporting the results of our experiments. Moreover, the issues themselves are not of the 'what would you do if . . .', but rather of the 'what do you think of . . .' variety, we may reasonably assume that strategic decisions are not going to have a significant rôle to play in the pattern of responses; and because no decision is consequent upon the responses to the questions, or upon other related questions as in the cases of voting-intention opinion polls, there is reason to believe that the responses are relatively uncontaminated by people's desire to impress or mislead.

3.5 Implementing the approach

In chapters 4 to 8 we apply the principles outlined above to a series of interconnected investigations on inequality, social welfare and poverty. Within the questionnaire-experimental framework the issues could be put in a variety of forms; in particular, questions on comparisons of income distributions could be expressed numerically or verbally.[4] Consider the sort of arguments that might be used for or against either of these approaches.

- *Numerical dazzle.* A kind of number blindness may affect people when they see a problem put on paper. Reasonable people will sometimes wilt in the face of fairly elementary arithmetic when it appears printed in front of them. This effect is exacerbated when a whole mass of these problems appear together. So if numbers are to be used they should not be used *en masse*.
- *Careless calculation.* Few of us today are as practised as our parents in the art of mental arithmetic. The mistakes that are commonly made even in elementary operations such as counting or taking differences warn us to be cautious about numerical responses and suggests that verbal responses may be more reliable.
- *Tricky phrasing.* However, words have their own way of misleading. An inappropriate word or phrase can take respondents down the wrong track. This is particularly important for our work, which takes in respondents from several countries – things can get lost or modified in translation.
- *Word fatigue.* One of the problems of trying to be precise and unambiguous with words is that there is a natural tendency to verbosity in explanation. Even the most willing and co-operative respondent will get fed up with a questionnaire that runs over much more than half-a-dozen A4 pages or that takes more than twenty to thirty minutes to complete. There is a three-way trade-off amongst painstaking detail, broad-brush simplicity and the number of issues covered in one questionnaire.

Finally, let us mention a problem that can affect both numerical and verbal types of questionnaire, which we must always expect to find in an investigation of this sort.

- *The illusory quest for Truth.* Many respondents are likely to suffer from the deceptive notion that there is a 'right' answer lurking just underneath the question that sufficiently energetic application of standard methods will uncover.

Our principal strategy for avoiding the problems that we have just listed is to make use of both types of approach, numerical and verbal. All of the questionnaires that we have used in the work reported here essentially make a three-phase approach to the respondent, as follows.

(1) A series of numerical problems is presented. Each problem involves a pair-wise comparison, usually in terms of the apparent inequality of two simple distributions A and B. The respondent is asked to circle A or B or both A and B according to his own judgment.

(2) There then follows a series of verbal questions that closely match the preceding numerical problems. As the respondents quickly become aware, these verbal questions cover the same issues as were illustrated by the problems, and they appear in the same order. Almost always, the list of available reponses to the numerical questions includes a 'none of the above' option.[5]

(3) The final phase is merged with phase 2. After each verbal question the respondent is invited to reconsider the response that he made on the numerical problems. Now that he has had the problem explained in words, he might feel that he originally missed the point. Has he now 'seen the light'?

Of course we do not claim that this methodology is problem-free, although we have found that it is remarkably robust. Let us consider some of the obvious snags that may arise.

One of the problems of representing and capturing opinions about economic policies is that they tend to be both vague and rooted in the specifics of a particular respondent's experiences. Vagueness is essential because, if you go to a lot of trouble to specify the nature and context of the issues in painstaking detail, you run the serious risk of losing your audience before the questions are actually put. Furthermore, precise judgments about distributional issues might be strongly influenced by the context in which the issues are perceived; for example, if the question is put in dollars, is the American respondent going to make some connection with the situation in the USA?

With any direct approach to individuals the problem of manipulation may arise, as we have noted. However, using the questionnaire-experimental technique enables the researcher to build in a number of checks against the possibility of deliberate distortion, and making the approach anonymous reduces the problem of possible distortions in the responses as a result of the targeted individuals not wanting to look foolish and choosing their answers accordingly.

A major problem in implementing the technique is that there is a weight of standard practice in the subject area. Experts in inequality analysis – and even reasonably well-informed amateurs – are going to bring to the subject views that have been formed from an acquaintance with the conventional axiomatic systems. This is obviously not what we want. On the other hand, if we were to use lay people as respondents it might be that we would have to throw out a lot of responses simply because the respondents did not have the basic numerical skills to deal adequately with the experiments. Our compromise was to use university students. Obviously students possess the great advantage of eminent availability for academic researchers: it is a practical method of getting a respectably sized sample with a very good response rate. However, in the present case there is a deeper reason why using students may be a particularly good idea: if one targets those who are going to study the subject matter of the experiment, but *who have not yet studied the received wisdom* then one has a reasonable prospect of obtaining respondents of about the right sort: they will be about halfway between the unprejudiced but innumerate and the hidebound expert.[6]

Our students

The samples for our various questionnaires are detailed on pages 144–5 in appendix B (table B.1); in all we had about 4,000 respondents in eight countries.[7] One of the main features of our sample was that we tried to get students who had not yet taken courses that involved a substantial component of welfare economics or that explicitly dealt with inequality and income distribution (in some cases the teachers presented the questionnaire at the beginning of such a course before revealing the 'truth' in the main body of the lectures). In this way we sought to reduce the problem of received-wisdom bias amongst our respondents. However, there were some exceptions to this which, as we shall see, provided us with some interesting information. The sample included both economists and non-economists.

Format of questionnaires

Questionnaires were prepared and distributed on standard size paper during class or lecture time. The standard text of the questionnaires is presented in appendix B (pp. 146–72). However, some respondents did not see the questions in exactly this format. As a control we occasionally reversed the presentation of the pairs of problems in the numerical part of the questionnaire (switching the left and right columns) and we also tried rearranging the order of the numerical questions (top and bottom switches). These rearrangements of the questionnaire had no perceptible impacts on the responses.

Translation of questionnaires

In the course of the research programme which led to this book we were assisted superbly by colleagues who were willing to run our questionnaire experiments in their own universities and colleges around the world. Since we did not want to restrict our attention to the English-speaking world the issue of translation of the text of the questionnaires arose. This was treated pragmatically. In Germany and Sweden the text was left in English, but the Germans explained queries about the meaning of the questions in German where necessary. In Israel all questionnaires were translated by one of the authors (Yoram Amiel) into Hebrew.

3.6 Summary

The issue that concerns us in this book – the way in which inequality is to be perceived – is not something which is susceptible of analysis by the 'standard' approaches of applied economics. Conventional approaches to inference about people's preferences do not provide the right tools for the job in this case, and for this reason we have made use of the questionnaire-experimental technique.

However, we do not want the results to be a mere 'trick of the light'; otherwise the conclusions that we would try to draw from our questionnaire-experimental approach might be mere artefacts of the structure of the questionnaire. For this reason the multi-stage questionnaire seems to be the appropriate method of getting to the bottom of the way in which people conceive inequality comparisons.

The question arises why we, or economists in general, should care about other people's opinions on distributional orderings. In the light of this chapter's discussion there are two points to be made. Firstly, economists care very much about other people's orderings of entities such as commodity bundles; but in that case, of course, one has real market data to provide the information. Should one not be just as interested in situations where market data is not going to be available? Secondly, inequality analysis is not just for inequality experts. Judgments about inequality and income distribution affect policy issues that concern real people, and so it makes sense to know what real people 'see' when they think about this subject.

Notes

1 See, for example, Plous (1993, ch. 6).
2 See, in particular, Rawls (1972) pp. 137, 164. See also Dahlby (1987).
3 In related work Beckman *et al.* (1994) have explicitly compared this pair of extreme alternatives in an experimental setting.
4 The issues could be displayed graphically as well, of course. However, early experiments with conventional pie charts proved to be unsatisfactory (respondents found it difficult to distinguish the sizes of relative pie slices). The diagrams that we use extensively in this book were not invented until we had collected most of the evidence in numerical and verbal forms.
5 See Schuman and Pressler (1981, ch. 4).
6 In other types of questionnaire study on distributional issues, non-student opinions have been found to be consistent with the opinions of student samples; see Schokkaert and Capeau (1991), Schokkaert and Devooght (1995), Schokkaert and Lagrou (1983), Schokkaert and Overlaet (1989). Other questionnaire studies in the same spirit using student samples include Amiel *et al.* (1999), Ballano and Ruiz-Castillo (1992), Beckman *et al.* (1994), Yaari and Bar-Hillel (1984).
7 This is a subset of the sample of student respondents in our research programme. In all we have about 5,000 students in nine countries.

4 What is inequality? The students' view

4.1 Drawing an inequality map

In this chapter we undertake an empirical investigation of attitudes towards the basic principles of inequality comparisons, based on our purpose-built questionnaires. We will have a first attempt at answering the question of whether the standard formalisation of inequality comparisons – such as that outlined in chapter 2 – captures the picture of inequality rankings that may be in the heads of those who think about inequality without the benefit of studying the standard story first.

Not all of the questionnaire experiments were directly about inequality; some of them were phrased in terms of social welfare or poverty, which are to be discussed in later chapters. Right now we are going to focus on just the issues that were raised in the theoretical discussion of chapter 2; chapters 5 to 7 then take the approach on into three related areas of interest concerning distributional questions.

The views expressed could in principle be used to provide a type of inequality map of our student respondents' attitudes to inequality. Although this idea is simple in principle, drawing an inequality map in practice can be quite complex. Even if we had just three persons in the society we would need to construct a diagram such as that in figure 4.1. The income of each person is measured along one of the x_1, x_2, x_3-axes (x_1 means the income of person 1, and so on), and the shaded triangular area depicts all the possible distributions of a given total income (if no income is wasted in the distribution). Some income distributions are relatively easy to see on this map; for example, distributions that correspond to perfect equality must lie on the diagonal ray, and distributions where just one person gets all the income must be at one of the corners of the triangle $A_1A_2A_3$. However, most distributions are difficult to interpret. Moreover the iso-inequality contours that should be drawn in this diagram would themselves be three-dimensional surfaces. The problem of depicting income distributions and inequality maps is obviously augmented for larger populations.

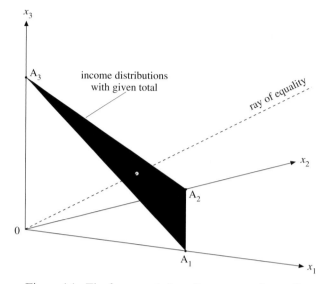

Figure 4.1. The framework for a three-person inequality map.

As far as possible we will seek to reduce the complexity of the diagram. We do this by presenting the evidence about the basic inequality axioms in terms of one of the simplest possible formal diagrams; the two-dimensional framework, set out in figure 4.2. Here the set of income distributions corresponding to perfect equality is a ray at 45° through the origin, and the set of all no-waste income distributions of a given sum is the line at right-angles (the set of all possible income distributions of a given total, including wasteful ones, is given by the shaded triangle bordered by this line). Figure 4.2 can be taken as a representation of the distributional possibilities in literally a two-person economy or, more interestingly, as a two-dimensional plan-form view of a many-person problem – the projection of the *n*-person case. This is the appropriate interpretation of its use here, and for this reason we have labelled the axes as x_i, x_j ('Irene's income', 'Janet's income') to emphasise that two arbitrarily chosen individuals from the population have their incomes depicted on the axes. As we shall see, some of the issues under consideration translate naturally into this simple framework, others less so. And it is usually precisely at the point in the argument where the two-person framework proves inadequate that the most interesting problems re-emerge from our questionnaire-experimental results.

4.2 An introduction to the questionnaires

The order of presentation of issues to our respondents in the questionnaires is not always the best order for presenting the results of the questionnaires for discussion. In designing the questionnaire we tried to avoid putting the apparently more complex questions in too prominent a position. It seemed better to start

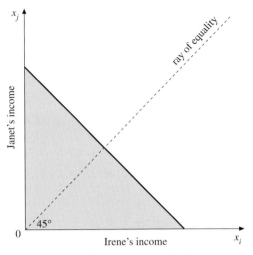

Figure 4.2. The framework for the two-person projection of the inequality
map.

with numerical questions, where the issue was relatively obvious, to reinforce the
message (which we tried to get across in the rubric) that there really were no
tricks; these issues were also ones that would be regarded as fairly non-con-
tentious. The questions that touched on deeper issues were usually packed somewhere in the interior of the questionnaire.

In the standard questionnaire design we also segregated the numerical problems and the verbal questions so that respondents would always be presented
with two distinct phases of the study to allow for reconsideration of the initial
responses: numbers first, then words. However, in discussing the results, it is more
illuminating to pair up each verbal question with the corresponding numerical
problems that preceded it. This rearrangement provides a good opportunity to
illustrate the interaction between numerical and verbal questions that formed a
feature of all of our questionnaires. Figure 4.4 shows the set of simple numerical
problems that were presented in our first main questionnaire in order to see how
people viewed the impact of changes in income and population totals on inequality. Although we shall present extracts from the questionnaires like this throughout most of our discussion, it may be helpful to take a look at the questionnaire
as a whole, which is reprinted in appendix B[1] in order to get a feel for the way it
would have appeared to the respondents. The corresponding verbal questions are
displayed in figures 4.3 and 4.5.

Notice that questions 10, 11 and 12 in these two figures closely mimic numerical problems 1, 2 and 3 in the numerical-problems panel. We thus get two parallel sources of information for views on scale transformations, translations of
the distribution and replications of the population.

The final sentence in each of the verbal questions provides us with a third
source of information on each of the three issues. This is designed to ensure – as

---

10) Suppose we double the "real income" of each person in a
     society, when not all the initial incomes are equal.

  a) *Each person's share remains unchanged, so inequality
     remains unchanged.*

  b) *Those who had more also get more, so inequality has
     increased.*

  c) *After doubling incomes more people have enough
     money for basic needs, so inequality has fallen.*

In the light of the above, would you want to change your answer
to question 1? If so, please write your new response - "A" or
"B" or "A and B" (if you now consider the two distributions to
have the same inequality):

11) Suppose we add the same fixed amount to the incomes of each
     person in a society, when not all the initial incomes are
     equal.

  a) *Inequality has fallen because the share of those
     who had more has fallen*

  b) *Inequality remains the same.*

  c) *Inequality has increased.*

Suppose instead of adding we deduct a fixed amount from each
person's income. Then inequality...

  a) *is the same*

  b) *increases*

  c) *decreases*

In the light of both of the above, would you want to change your
answer to question 2?   If so, please write your new response
("A" or "B" or "A and B") here:

Figure 4.3. Verbal questions on scale and translation independence.

far as we can – that the respondents did not let themselves be tripped up by some
unintended numerical illusion in the first part of the questionnaire; we wanted to
make it clear to the respondents that there were to be no tricks in the design of
the questionnaire-experiment, and we wanted them to be able to see the issue
clearly in both main parts of the questionnaire. As it happened, the instances of
respondents indicating a desire to change their answers on the numerical questions were relatively few, and so we did not tabulate them separately, but rather
incorporated them with the presentations of the numerical answers.

Of course, it is not to be expected that an exact match of the pattern of
responses to numerical problems and that of responses to the verbal questions

In each of the first nine questions you are asked to compare two distributions of income. Please state which of them you consider to be the **more unequally** distributed by circling A or B. If you consider that both of the distributions have the same inequality then circle both A and B.

1)   A = (5, 8, 10)   B = (10, 16, 20)

2)   A = (5, 8, 10)   B = (10, 13, 15)

3)   A = (5, 8, 10)   B = (5, 5, 8, 8, 10, 10)

Figure 4.4. Numerical problems on changes in income and population.

12)   Suppose we replicate a three-person society by merging it with an exact copy of itself (so that we now have a society of six people consisting of three sets of identical twins).

   a) *The income inequality of the six-person community is the same as that of the three-person community because the relative income shares remain unchanged.*

   b) *The income inequality of the six-person community is less than that of the three-person community because in the six-person community there are some people who have the same income.*

   c) *The income inequality of the six-person community is greater than that of the three-person community.*

In the light of the above, would you want to change your answer to question 3?   If so, please write your new response ("A" or "B" or "A and B") here:

Figure 4.5. The question on the population principle.

will occur: just as we may have different mental maps of a city in our heads according to whether we go around it on foot or by car, so it is reasonable to find slightly different pictures of the inequality map being revealed by the two different methods of presenting the issues. Nonetheless, it is interesting to see how often the numerical and the verbal responses do concur, and also how often responses to the same issue in different guises and separate questionnaire experiments concur, as we shall see in chapters 5 and 7.

4.3 Inequality and changes in income and population

As the extracts in figures 4.3, 4.4 and 4.5 indicate, we first asked students about simple across-the-board income changes in order to see whether their views

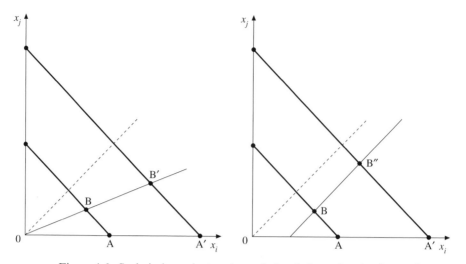

Figure 4.6. Scale-independent and translation-independent iso-inequality
lines.

corresponded to the standard view – scale independence – or to some other
coherent view, such as translation independence. In terms of the inequality map
these two special views on the relationship between overall income change and
inequality are illustrated by the two parts of figure 4.6. Suppose we start with
some arbitrary distribution represented by point B, with total income proportional to OA; now if we double total income to an amount proportional to OA'
the picture on the left-hand side depicts the distribution B' (with the new, higher
total) which would be regarded as 'equally unequal' in comparison with point B
under scale independence; and the picture on the right-hand side depicts the distribution B" (with the new, higher total) which would be regarded as 'equally
unequal' in comparison with point B under translation independence. In each
panel the line through B depicts income distributions that are just as equal as B
under each of the two assumptions.

Of course, the three-income distribution (5,8,10) used in the questionnaire-
experiment (see figure 4.4) cannot be fully represented in a diagram such as figure
4.6, but in this case the two-dimensional projection used there adequately captures the main idea, however many income receivers there may be in the distribution.

Just about half of the respondents appeared to concur with the proposition
that doubling all incomes leaves inequality unchanged in that they circled both
A and B in question 1 of the questionnaire (51% did so) or selected response (a)
in question 10 (47% made this selection). But more information can be extracted
from the responses to questions 1, 2, 10 and 11. To see this, inspect figure 4.7,
which is an enlargement of parts of figure 4.6. Suppose we are dealing with a true
two-person case: it is clear that if a person's inequality map exhibits the scale-
independence property, so that the line BB' forms part of an iso-inequality

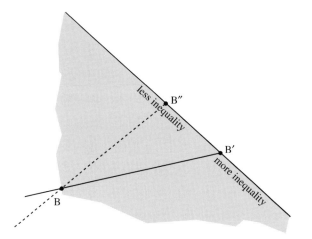

Figure 4.7. Deviations from scale transformation.

contour, then the points 'below' BB′ should represent greater inequality (they lie further away from the inequality ray) and the points 'above' BB′ should represent less inequality; in particular, point B″ should be regarded as less unequal than B′.

Taking this argument into account a person who circles both A and B in question 1 should circle just A in question 2 (see figure 4.4). The actual breakdown of attitudes to scale and translation changes amongst our respondents are summarised in table 4.1,[2] which shows essentially the same pattern of responses whether the issues are put in terms of numbers or words. There is still a clear preference for scale independence (the numbers in bold) with translation independence coming a rather distant second (the numbers that are underlined). Intermediate situations between these two cases are given by the (Up, Down) pair in row two, column 1 of each part of the table. The bracketed entries will be discussed later in this chapter.

This glimpse of the relationship between overall income levels and inequality rankings raises a number of further questions which our elementary questionnaire experiment A1 cannot answer by itself: is the relative support for scale independence as against translation independence sensitive to overall income levels? Is the choice between the two largely a function of the background of particular subgroups of our panel of respondents? We deal with these questions in chapters 6 and 8 below.

The counterpart to this investigation into income change is the examination of what happens when the population, rather than income, is changed. The bottom row of table 4.2 shows that both the numerical and verbal evidence is that there is substantial support for the population principle – that creating one distribution from another by the simple process of replication leaves inequality comparisons unaltered. This is fairly reassuring if we consider the way that students are

Table 4.1. *Inequality and proportionate and absolute income differences (percentage responses)*

		Numerical problems					Verbal questions		
		Add 5 units (q. 2)					Add fixed sum (q. 11)		
		Down	Up	Same			Down	Up	Same
	Down	8	(2)	(5)		Down	7	(1)	(4)
Double	Up	15	3	<u>17</u>	Double	Up	21	2	<u>17</u>
income (q. 1)	Same	**37**	(5)	(9)	income (q. 10) Same		**30**	(3)	(14)

Note: Results are based on responses to questionnaire A1 ($N = 1,108$).

Table 4.2. *The effect on inequality of cloning the distributions (percentage responses)*

	Numerical (q. 3)	Verbal (q. 12)
Down	31	22
Up	10	9
Same	58	66

Note: Results are based on responses to questionnaire A1 ($N = 1,108$).

usually introduced to practical aspects of income distribution analysis. Typically they are taught to construct relative frequency distributions and to use these as a basis for making distributional comparisons in terms of inequality; but this procedure will only be valid if the population principle holds, since it enables one to discard information about the size of the population. Nevertheless, it is worth noting that one-third or more of respondents feel that population size does matter when comparing distributions.

4.4 Transfers and the structure of inequality comparisons

The key questions in our first questionnaire were positioned in the middle of the list of numerical problems, and just after the middle of the verbal questions. The text of the relevant numerical problems and the corresponding verbal questions is reproduced in the figures 4.9 and 4.10; these focus upon the transfer principle and the principle of decomposability. We have segregated these two issues from the discussion of overall income and population changes because of their tremendous importance in the whole field of economics that makes use of distributional analysis.

First, consider the transfer principle. The argument for this principle in terms of the inequality map seems to be straightforward: in figure 4.10 an income transfer from rich Irene to poor Janet appears to move the distribution incontestably in the direction of greater equality; if B is the point corresponding to the

4)	A = (1, 4, 7, 10, 13)	B = (1, 5, 6, 10, 13)
5)	A = (4, 8, 9)	B = (5, 6, 10)
6)	A = (4, 7, 7, 8, 9)	B = (5, 6, 7, 7, 10)

Figure 4.8. Numerical problem on the transfer principle and decomposability.

13) Suppose we transfer income from a person who has more income to a person who has less, without changing anyone else's income. After the transfer the person who formerly had more still has more.

    a) Income inequality in this society has fallen.

    b) The relative position of others has also changed as a consequence of this transfer. Therefore we cannot say, a priori, how inequality has changed.

    c) Neither of the above.

•••　　　•••　　　•••　　　•••

14) Suppose there are two societies A, B with the same number of people and with the same total income, but with different distributions of income. Society A is now merged with C, and society B is merged with C' where C and C' are identical.

    a) The society which had the more unequal income distribution before the merger still has the more unequal distribution after the merger.

    b) We can't say which society has the more unequal income distribution unless we know the exact distributions.

    c) Neither of the above.

Figure 4.9. Verbal questions on the transfer principle and decomposability.

original distribution, then E is the point corresponding to equal shares with the same total, and any point in the interior of the line joining B and E – such as C for instance – would correspond to a partial equalisation between Janet and Irene.

However, it is important to grasp the status of the underlying concept. The argument of the preceding paragraph would be almost watertight if the economy consisted just of Irene and Janet. But the transfer principle purports to apply also in cases where figure 4.10 refers not just to a toytown Irene-and-Janet economy, but to any two-person projection of the inequality map of an *n*-person society;

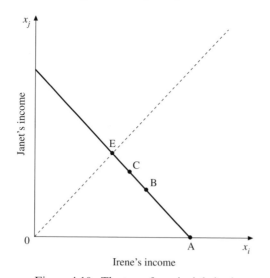

Figure 4.10. The transfer principle in the two-person projection.

we shall discuss this in more detail on page 46. Moreover, unlike scale independence where there is at least one very obvious alternative (and in fact an infinity of other compromise alternatives), the transfer principle is not usually treated as one of a range of possible assumptions that we might make about the structure of inequality comparisons. As we noted in chapter 2, for many researchers this is the defining concept for inequality analysis: explicitly or implicitly the transfer principle is invoked almost everywhere in theoretical and empirical analysis carried out in the area.

Yet it is clear from table 4.3 that a majority of our respondents reject the transfer principle when presented to them in the form of a numerical problem. Why? Notice that the hypothetical incomes involved are exactly the same as those used to construct the series of pictograms when we discussed the point in chapter 1 (compare the extract of question 4 in figure 4.8 with figures 1.1–1.3): the 'Agree' response here means that people checked the 'right' answer B (see figure 1.3). Comments provided by some of the respondents on their questionnaires reveal that rejection of the transfer principle *in this type of problem* was for exactly the reasons that we outlined in chapter 1: people are concerned about the overall structure of income differences and not just about the incomes of the particular individuals who are involved in the transfer. Had the numerical example involved either the richest or the poorest individual in the transfer a different answer might well have been obtained – we pursue this further in an experiment reported on page 46. Moreover, there are also problems with the response to the verbal part of the questionnaire on this issue – see the right-hand column of table 4.3. Although a much higher proportion (60%) respond in support of the transfer principle, the support is not overwhelming.[3] Furthermore, why, even after some of the respondents had reacted to the invitation to change, did the verbal and

Table 4.3. *The transfer principle (percentage responses)*

	Numerical (q. 4)	Verbal (q. 13)
Agree	35	60
Strongly disagree	42	24
Disagree	22	14

Note: Results are based on responses to questionnaire A1 ($N = 1,108$).
For interpretation of "Agree" and "Disagree", see text and note 3.

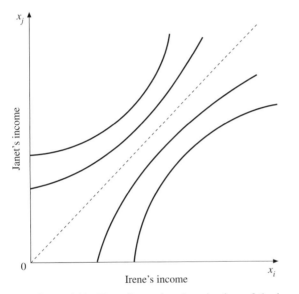

Figure 4.11. Two-dimensional projection of the inequality map.

numerical responses diverge? It may be that people find it difficult to translate an apparently appealing general verbal principle into concrete examples and, perhaps, into actual situations also. If so, then we should perhaps return to this issue later and take a closer look.

Now let us consider the issue of decomposability, again using the idea of the inequality map. Imagine a series of experiments with Irene's and Janet's incomes (keeping all the other incomes fixed) which enables us to draw an inequality map, perhaps something like that depicted in figure 4.11. Now imagine that the experiment series were to be done all over again but with the incomes of everyone else fixed at some other arbitrary levels: will we still get the same pattern of contours as that depicted in figure 4.11? If the principle of decomposability applies then we will indeed find this. Note, incidentally, that we are not requiring that the inequality levels associated with each contour should remain unaltered; just that the *ordering* of distributions should remain unaltered, irrespective of the *levels* at which all those other than Irene and Janet have had their incomes fixed.

Table 4.4. *Decomposability (percentage responses)*

	Numerical (q. 5 & q. 6)	Verbal (q. 14)
Agree	57	40
Strongly disagree	n.a.	45
Disagree	41	11

Note: Results are based on responses to questionnaire A1 ($N = 1,108$). For interpretation of "Agree" and "Disagree", see text and note 3.

There are also problems with the issue of decomposability, as we can see from the evidence displayed in table 4.4. Here 'Agree' on the numerical questions means that the ranking of distributions A and B was the same in question 5 and in question 6 (see again figure 4.4). Notice that the mean income in question 6 is 7 units (for both A and B) and that the two distributions in question 6 have been formed from those in 5 simply by merging each of them with two additional people with incomes of exactly 7 units. The decomposability principle then states that these merged incomes are irrelevant to the inequality ranking of A and B. Interestingly, in this case the respondents are less happy about the decomposability principle when it is presented to them in verbal form rather than implicitly in the numerical questions; see the right-hand column of table 4.4.

4.5 Do the answers make sense?

The results of the basic questionnaire experiment can be summarised in terms of a standard distributional tool, the Lorenz curve, an example of which is displayed in figure 4.12. This curve plots the proportion of total income (vertical axis) received by the bottom 1%, 2%, 5%, 50%, etc. against the corresponding population proportion (horizontal axis): so in figure 4.12 the bottom 40% of the population receive only about 15% of total income, the bottom 60% of the population receive about 30% and so on. The curve must pass through the two corners and be convex as shown, and in the state of perfect equality it would lie exactly along the diagonal.[4]

Some powerful theorems are available to interpret distributional rankings in terms of the Lorenz curve, as depicted in figure 4.13. According to this, distribution B appears to be more unequal than distribution A (the bottom 20% get less under B than under A; so does the bottom 80%; so too does any other 'bottom *x*%' of the population) and, as we explain formally in appendix A the powerful theorems we just mentioned establish that this intuitive ranking of distributions concurs with a broad class of formal tools for ranking distributions; but these results depend crucially on the acceptance of some of the specific axioms that we have been examining in this chapter.

To compare distributions in terms of the Lorenz curve we would need to invoke

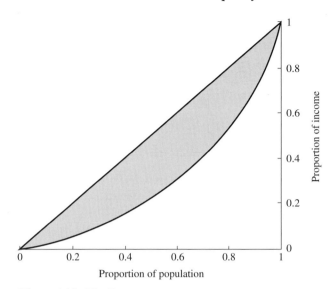

Figure 4.12. The Lorenz curve.

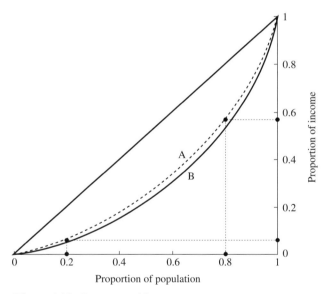

Figure 4.13. Lorenz ranking.

scale independence, the population principle, and the transfer principle. But if we were to look at the combined response to the relevant questions on these issues (questions 10, 12 and 13) we would find that 76% of the students reject the Lorenz axiom system. If we also include the principle of decomposability along with those in the Lorenz system (in other words we include question 14 along with 10, 12 and 13) then 84% reject the standard axioms. Our students' responses seem to

Table 4.5. *What happens to inequality if you add or subtract a fixed sum? (Percentage responses)*

		Deduct fixed sum		
		Down	Up	Same
	Down	4	53	1
Add fixed sum	Up	2	3	1
	Same	1	9	25

raise a serious question of whether the standard axioms for inequality comparisons are appropriate.

Now students, like other people, are fallible, and sometimes irrational and perverse: so of course we do not insist that our respondents display a degree of icy logic under all circumstances. Nevertheless, it is obviously reasonable to enquire whether the results that we have presented are internally consistent and broadly in accord with common sense. A pattern of results that is contaminated by carelessness or perversity is not going to be much of a guide to drawing an inequality map.

We have an obvious control built into the design of the questionnaire: since we cover the same issues in the two parts of the questionnaire – numerical and verbal – we can check for consistency between responses to questions. As we have seen the percentages for the responses to the two parts of the questionnaire are remarkably similar in the case of scale and translation changes. We can also examine the issue of whether respondents view upward and downward shifts of income antisymmetrically – see question 11 in the extract in figure 4.3 – although unconventional responses here do not necessarily imply inconsistency. As we can see from table 4.5, on the whole (80% of the sample) our respondents are conventional, in that they report increases of income as having the opposite effect upon inequality to decreases in income.

All the same, the sceptical reader might raise the question of whether this supposed check is in fact open to manipulation by the respondents. However, even if we disregard the numerical–verbal consistency argument we have further checks that are likely to be much less easily observable and thus less susceptible of manipulation by respondents. For example, if students were responding capriciously to the questionnaire experiment, we would not expect them to reveal a coherent ordering over distributions. But the evidence of all our questionnaire experiments reveals that they were not capricious: for example, cross-tabulations of responses to interrelated numerical problems such as questions 7, 8 and 9 (which focus on issues examined in chapter 6 below) reveals that only 11% of the A1 sample violated transitivity;[5] nor did any respondent indicate that it was impossible to make the comparisons that were presented.

One might also wonder whether those who expressed minority views – for example, those who did not give the conventional view of population replication in table 4.2 – simply failed to understand the questions or the underlying issues. Although we cannot answer that directly, as we have seen, it can be shown that the respondents' answers were, on the whole, not self-contradictory. But we can say more than that. Our questionnaire allows people to indicate whether they want to change their responses to numerical problems once they have thought through the answers on the related verbal questions. On the 'second thoughts best' principle we should find that where the respondents took advantage of this they moved in the direction of rationality. This is what we find: after they had been allowed to have second thoughts, just under 4% of the sample indicated both 'up' on q. 3 and 'down' on q. 12 or vice versa, as against the figure of just under 5% on the first pass through the numerical problems. So we seem to have an acceptably small proportion of respondents who give meaningless answers.

4.6 More on the transfer principle

Another way in which we might have interpreted the question 'Do the answers make sense?' would be to query whether the more surprising results are robust. The results on the principle of transfers demand special consideration: they suggest that there is a substantial body of opinion which rejects the principle in its pure form, although, of these, many were prepared to go along with the 'borderline' view that a rich-to-poor transfer might leave inequality unchanged. As we discussed in chapter 1 this is exactly the opposite to the 'right' view of inequality rankings as conventionally understood in the inequality literature.

This issue is so special and so far-reaching in its implications that it warrants further investigation. It would be reasonable to investigate whether the conclusion is sensitive to alternative questions about income transfers. One way of doing this would be to try to present the question in a different format in order to control for the 'framing problem' that we referred to in chapter 3. This could be done in two ways.

Firstly, the issue could be put in a different context from that of direct questions about income inequality. To anticipate our argument slightly we did this by incorporating the transfer principle into separate questionnaires that focused on *social welfare* or *poverty* rather than inequality, so as to dress the same issue up in a different guise. The results of these experiments are discussed in detail in chapters 5 and 7 respectively, but the main conclusion is that changing the context of the distributional issue does almost nothing to increase support for the principle – in the case of poverty the transfer principle was rejected overwhelmingly.

Secondly, the language of the inequality comparisons could be kept unchanged, but the details of the question could be altered to see whether there was something critical about the particular income distribution that was specified in the original questionnaire experiment. We did just this with a further

Table 4.6. *Agreement with the transfer principle for different types of transfer:*
numerical responses (percentages)

			Is A more unequal than B?		
		Agree	Strongly disagree	Weakly disagree
(q. 1) A=(2, 5, 9, 20, 30)	B=(2, **6**, **8**, 20, 30)	37	23	39
(q. 4) A=(2, 5, 9, 20, 30)	B=(2, **10**, 9, **15**, 30)	61	31	8
(q. 3) A=(2, 5, 9, 20, 30)	B=(2, **6**, 9, 20, **29**)	67	17	16
(q. 2) A=(2, 5, 9, 20, 30)	B=(**3**, 5, 9, 20, **29**)	78	11	11
(q. 5) A=(10, 10, 10, **10**, **30**)	B=(10, 10, 10, **20**, **20**)	70	24	5

Note: Results are based on responses to questionnaire A4 ($N=358$). Q. 1, . . ., q. 5 refer to the
question numbers as they appear in the questionnaire. 'Agree' mean 'A more unequal than B',
'Strongly disagree' means 'B more unequal than A', and 'Weakly disagree' means 'A and B have the
same inequality'.

Table 4.7. *Verbal agreement with the transfer principle (percentages)*

Suppose we transfer income from a person who has more income to a person who has less,
without changing anyone else's income. After the transfer the person who originally had
more income still has more.

(a) Income inequality in this society has fallen if the ranking of the income of all the people
remains the same. If there is any change in the rank of all the incomes then it is possible that
income inequality increases or remains the same.   11

(b) If the transfer was from the richest to the poorest, and after the transfer the richest
remains the richest and the poorest remains the poorest, than income inequality has fallen.
In other cases we cannot say *a priori* how inequality has changed.   32

(c) The relative position of others has also been changed by the transfer. So we cannot say *a
priori* how inequality has changed.   10

(d) Inequality in this society has fallen, even if there is a change in the ranking of the income
of people as a result of this transfer, and even if the transfer is not from the richest in the
society to the poorest.   31

(e) None of the above.   4

Note: Results are based on responses to questionnaire A4, q. 6 ($N=358$).

questionnaire experiment run on the same rules, the results of which are reported
in tables 4.6 and 4.7. The experiment (labelled A4) is described in appendix B
(p. 143). The idea of the numerical part of the questionnaire is to present the
respondents with a variety of income distributions in which, implicitly, a pure
income transfer between a pair of individuals takes place; this is done at various
income levels and covers both important subcases: those where only 'middle'
incomes are affected, and those where an extreme income is involved. To make

interpretation easier the rows of table 4.6 have been arranged in a different order from the corresponding questions in A4 (in the experiment we deliberately shuffled the questions around so as not to give a strong hint at a supposedly 'right' answer). Each row gives the income distributions that the students were asked to compare, and the overall proportions of responses in each category. If one follows the pairs of incomes highlighted in bold down the first four rows of the table, the underlying structure soon becomes clear: we move the transfer progressively 'outwards' towards the case of 'richest poorest' (in each of rows 1 to 4 the total income is the same). In view of this, it is reasonable to expect that agreement with the transfer principle would increase as we move down the table. This is precisely what we find: the proportion of 'Agree' responses is initially at the level of the first experiment (A1) and then increases uniformly; however, the ratio of 'Weakly disagree' to 'Strongly disagree' responses does not change monotonically. In row 5 of table 4.6 we give an 'out-of-sequence' example which confirms the conclusion drawn from the first four rows: since one 'extreme' income is involved in the transfer we would have expected the proportion of agreement with the transfer principle to be relatively high, and it is.

This remarkable conclusion about the pattern of agreement with the transfer principle is also borne out by the pattern of verbal responses. A glance at the last-but-one row of table 4.7 shows that less than one-third of our respondents agreed with the transfer principle, as stated in its standard form; there were significant minorities who said either that the answer depended on the rank of everyone in the population (11%) or on the relative positions of others (10%). But we also find that when the richest and the poorest are involved then there is strong support for the transfer principle (an additional 32%). This result is not so puzzling if we look at what is happening to income differences as opposed to simple levels of income. In the case of a small (order-preserving) transfer from the richest to the poorest, it is clear that some of the *differences* decrease and all the others remain unchanged, but of course this is not the case for other types of income transfer. So if people evaluate income inequality in terms of income differences rather than in terms of incomes directly we would expect to get the pattern of responses indicated in table 4.7.

The 'headline results' of our first sounding of opinion on the inequality axioms are summarised in table 4.8. These make it fairly obvious that there is a substantive divergence between the views expressed by our initial batch of respondents and the standard story of how income distributions should be compared in terms of inequality. It is of course important to look behind the headlines, as we have done in this chapter, and as we shall do further in subsequent chapters.

As we have emphasised, the status of the transfer principle is rather different from those of the others: unlike each of the other axioms there is in the literature no obvious alternative assumption to be invoked if the transfer principle were to be abandoned. As we have seen, the results on the attitudes to inequality comparisons exhibited by our joint sample of students are sensitive to the type of

Table 4.8. *Agreement with basic axioms: summary (percentage responses)*

	Numerical	Verbal
Scale independence	51	47
Population principle	58	66
Transfer principle	35	60
Decomposability	57	40

Note: Based on summaries of responses to questionnaire A1. Questionnaire A1 gave only a limited set of alternative verbal responses on the question relating to the transfer principle. When the richer set of alternatives of questionnaire A4 is allowed for the verbal responses, support for the transfer principle falls to 31% (see table 4.7).

transfer involved: it is this which gives a clue to an alternative way of looking at the logic of income distribution comparisons in terms of inequality. Instead of basing inequality comparisons just on individual income levels it may make sense to recast the problem in terms of income *differences* in the community: as the discussion on page 47 showed, the two approaches need not coincide in their rankings of distributions.

In tackling the question of 'What is inequality?' from a questionnaire-experimental point of view, the analysis of this chapter has raised other questions about the basis on which people form ideas about ranking income distributions. Since there appears to be a good *prima facie* case for challenging the validity of some of the basic tenets of the standard approach to the subject it seems appropriate to move beyond the examination of simple static inequality comparisons set within the context of pure inequality analysis and to examine these issues as they emerge in three related areas: social welfare, inequality and the process of income change and poverty. We shall find that the same sorts of techniques that have been introduced here can be usefully deployed in these other fields.

Notes

1 This extract is from questionnaire A1 (pp. 146–9).
2 Throughout this book results are given as percentages. In many tables the reported figures do not sum to 100%: the missing percentage points being attributable to cases where there was no clear answer or no answer at all and also to rounding errors.
3 Here, and in table 4.4, the verbal response 'Strongly disagree' means that students chose the response (b) which indicates that other incomes matter in the inequality comparison; 'Disagree' means that people checked the response 'Neither of the above'.
4 For more detail on this see Cowell (1995, pp. 19, 20).
5 This issue is discussed further in chapter 5, see (p. 49).

5 Income and welfare

5.1 What is welfare?

The meaning of welfare is a bit like the meaning of life: most people are delightfully vague about it; some logical purists will question whether there is any meaning to be given to it; the zealot can interpret it in as narrow a fashion as he wishes. The welfare of an individual obviously depends on a variety of features of the social and economic environment in which he finds himself and a variety of individual characteristics and circumstances. Each of us will probably give different degrees of emphasis to these various features depending upon our backgrounds and prejudices. Each of us will probably have a pet idea on how to incorporate these features into a specific theoretical or empirical model of individual welfare.

Even if we were to narrow the issue to one of *economic* welfare, or of utility – as it is conventionally interpreted by economists – problems would still remain. A person's utility is usually regarded as being determined by his own income or resources and his tastes, but in principle there is an enormous range of other possible factors that could be taken as determinants of a person's welfare; for example, it might be affected by other people's income or utility. Apart from these factors there is a complex of market forces, institutional provisions and individual constraints which will influence his economic opportunities. However, there is a danger that in trying to adopt a very general approach one might not be able to say anything useful at all. So we are going to simplify the situation radically and focus on the use of income as a yardstick of a person's well-being, and take the list of people's incomes as the basic element in our discussion.

Of course, the problems do not get any easier once we try to move from the concept of individual welfare to social welfare. If we assume that social welfare depends upon individual welfare then it is going to inherit the problems of individual welfare. Furthermore, even if we were to wave these problems airily away – as we have just done – then there would still be a number of other problems associated with the specific issue of extrapolating from individual welfare analysis to social welfare analysis. These issues have deservedly been accorded entire books of their own, but it is useful to summarise them briefly here.

- *The conflicting priorities problem.* Because of the variety of personal preferences, as well as the variety of economic goods, there are substantial problems in aggregating views on issues which are regarded as affecting the well-being of a community. Of the extra $10 million saved by defence cuts you may consider that the proceeds ought to be used to improve public transport, your next-door neighbour may think that it ought to go on the health service, while your other next-door neighbour may think that it should instead go towards reducing taxes on the private sector.
- *The 'Where am I?' problem.* An individual's perception of where he is personally located in the distribution may strongly affect his own ranking of social states. As we discussed in chapter 3 (p. 18) it may be possible to sidestep this issue by placing the issues within an artificial framework rather than within a specific national or historical context.
- *The 'there-is-no-such-thing-as-society' problem.* In one sense this is a perfectly valid objection, and may even be taken to be the most difficult of the three problems that we have chosen to highlight. The essence of it is that even if all economic goods could be represented as chocolate bars (which in part disposes of the first problem), and individuals were somehow unaware of their position in the pecking order within the candidate distributions that they are comparing (which disposes of the second problem), there could still be no coherent 'social ordering' of distributions. The reason is that each member of the society could individually have a different ranking of an income distribution in terms of perceived welfare.

We are not going to involve ourselves further with these difficulties, but will instead sweep them away with an unsatisfactory but appealing assumption. The assumption is that although it may be impossible to draw up a coherent 'social' evaluation system that is systematically linked to the views about distribution of each member of the community, it is actually possible to ascribe coherent views about social welfare to each of those members. Although people may act in a venal, self-seeking fashion in their workplace or their private life, nevertheless they are capable of disinterested judgments about distributional questions. These supposedly coherent views will be taken to form the basis for the meaning that we want to give to the concept of social welfare.

5.2 Social welfare

Imputing to individuals this kind of coherence of view about social welfare means that it does at least make sense to talk about welfare comparisons of income distributions. Then the problem of giving meaning to the concept of social welfare

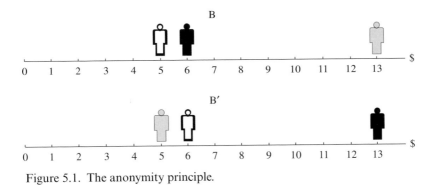

Figure 5.1. The anonymity principle.

can be treated in much the same way as the approach we used in chapter 2 to focus upon the meaning of inequality. As counterparts to inequality rankings and inequality measures we can work with welfare rankings and social welfare functions.

The idea of a social welfare ranking is closely analogous to that of an inequality ranking: it is a systematic chaining of pairwise welfare comparisons (where they can be made) that satisfy the principle of transitivity. A social welfare function is just a formula which aggregates all the information about an income distribution into a single numerical welfare index. Both these concepts will again require a system of axioms – basic assumptions – which give meaning to the concepts when they are applied to distributional questions. Some of these axioms carry over from the discussion of inequality rankings that we had in chapter 2. In particular, we shall again have occasion to make reference to the transfer principle and to the principle of decomposability, which again have an important rôle to play in standard social welfare analysis. In addition we shall need to examine more closely the issue of anonymity, and to refer to three other important principles known as monotonicity, dominance and the Pareto principle.

Anonymity

As with the discussion of inequality, the principle of anonymity means that the identities attached to a list of incomes in any given income distribution have no significance whatsoever for welfare comparisons. This might appear to be so compelling as to be blindingly obvious. For example in figure 5.1 distribution B is based on the second of the two distributions displayed in figure 2.3 (p. 11), and distribution B' is achieved by a trivial rearrangement of the personnel in distribution B. One might be forgiven for thinking that there is little more to be said. But further thought suggests that there may well be a substantive issue to be considered here.

Examine figure 5.2, and consider the top pair of distributions, A and B; then decide which of the two has greater inequality. Now consider the bottom pair of

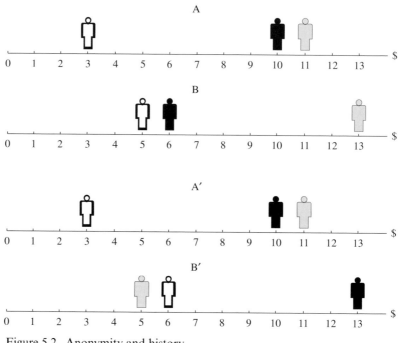

Figure 5.2. Anonymity and history.

distributions, A′ and B′: a quick visual check confirms that the positions of the incomes in these two distributions are exactly the same as in A and B – in terms of where the incomes are located on the line – but that the shading of the persons differs. Now, if the shading of each icon is again used as a means of identifying a particular person we can see that there is important contrast between the two pairs of distributions. In the top pair of distributions, a movement from distribution A to distribution B would leave each of the persons in the same rank-order within the community, whereas (in the bottom pair) going from distribution A′ to distribution B′ would involve a substantial reordering of the individuals in the distribution. Some people might argue that if A′ corresponds to the distribution on Monday and B′ to that on Tuesday then they cannot represent situations of equal social welfare because of the personal losses and gains that seem to have occurred on Monday night. A tender-hearted observer might argue that one should give greater weight to the losses rather than the gains and so judge that social welfare in B′ was less than that in A′. Someone else with a sense of retributive fairness might claim that welfare had gone up on Monday night, along the lines of the 'the-first-shall-be-last' principle. Of course, others will insist that this reordering is irrelevant to an assessment of inequality or of welfare – that the anonymity principle should be applied irrespective of individual personal histories.[1]

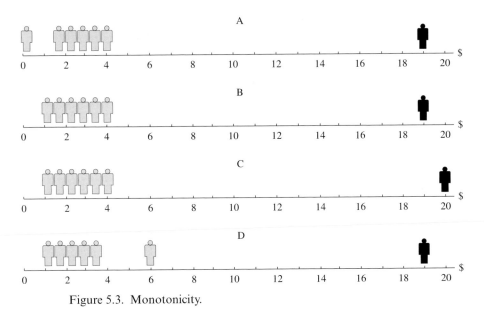

Figure 5.3. Monotonicity.

Monotonicity, dominance and the Pareto principle

The property of monotonicity implies that if the income of any one individual increases (and no one else's income decreases) then social welfare must have increased. The basic idea is depicted in figure 5.3 where we take the distribution A as a reference point. It is clear that if we compare distribution B with A then all the people's incomes remain unchanged except for the bottom person whose income has moved upwards: it seems reasonable to suppose that this change is indeed one that increases social welfare. But what about comparing distribution B with distribution C? Again one and only one person is made better off but on this occasion it happens to be the richest person in the community. Some people might feel that this sort of change cannot represent an increase in social welfare: although no one is made worse off in absolute terms by going from B to C, the worsening of the relative position of the poor as average income rises may seem so overwhelmingly unattractive that the increase in inequality outweighs the overall gain in mean income. Some people may also feel that a switch from B to D does not increase social welfare, in that there is again a rise in inequality which offsets the income gain of the single individual. However, if we are to accept the principle of monotonicity then all these changes – A→B, B→C and B→D – are to be counted as welfare increases.

Dominance refers to the comparison of two anonymous distributions rather than to what is happening to one or more selected individuals in the population. Suppose you plot distribution A as a series of uniform blobs on the income line that we have drawn as in our earlier figures. Now look at another distribution B plotted on the same line; if it looks as if distribution B could have been derived

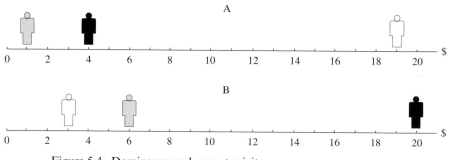

Figure 5.4. Dominance and monotonicity.

from distribution A by moving some of the blobs in A to the right, and none to the left (because the blobs are uniform there is no way of telling whether this is the way that B was actually derived), then we say that distribution B *dominates* distribution A.[2] If our criterion of social welfare comparisons is such that, given that distribution B dominates distribution A, we always accord higher welfare to B than to A then we say that the social welfare ranking has the dominance property.

The concept of monotonicity is closely related to, but not identical with, the concept of dominance in social welfare rankings.[3] Figure 5.4 makes clear why this is so. First of all, ignore the shading of the figures and consider the two distributions just as anonymous lists of incomes: clearly the highest income in B lies to the right of the highest income in A and the same applies to a comparison of the second-highest incomes and to the lowest incomes in the two distributions: so distribution B is 'better than' A in terms of the dominance criterion. Now let us use the shading of the icons as indicators of identity in the two distributions. Then we can see that in going from A to B two persons have experienced an increase in their incomes, but one person (the unshaded character) has had a huge income decrease: B would not be ranked as preferable to A in terms of monotonicity.

Furthermore, the monotonicity principle has also to be distinguished from a third well-known concept: the Pareto principle. The Pareto principle simply states that if at least one person is made better off and no one is worse off then social welfare must increase. The essential difference between this and monotonicity lies in the distinction between a person being 'better off' and a person experiencing an increase in income. This is not mere logic chopping. It is perfectly reasonable to suppose that just as a person's state of well-being may be affected by things that he does not purchase or consume directly, such as pollution, traffic congestion and crime – 'externalities' in the economics jargon – so his well-being may be affected by other people's incomes.[4] Feelings of altruism or envy may legitimately interpose themselves in the relationship between a person's income and the benefit that he experiences from it.

The distinction between the two criteria can be important, because they may lead to quite different stories about the kind of changes in income distribution which make a society 'better off'. For example, a social welfare function may satisfy the Pareto principle and yet violate monotonicity. To see that this is so, take the case where social welfare is just the sum of everyone's utility, but each person's utility is determined by his own income minus the average income of everyone richer than himself. Now give $1 to the richest person: this raises the utility of the richest person, but lowers the utility of everyone else and, if there are more than two persons in the society, social welfare will fall; monotonicity has been violated. Likewise, the social welfare function could satisfy monotonicity and yet violate the Pareto principle. Again this can be seen by an example: suppose that social welfare is simply 'national income' – the sum of everyone's incomes – but that some rich people are altruistic in that their utility is increased by any income gains of the poor. Then it may be possible to take $2 off a rich person, throw away $1 and give the other $1 to the poorest person and thereby increase the utility of both rich and poor: social welfare falls even though no one's utility has fallen, and some people's utility has risen. Only in the case where everyone's utility is a (strictly increasing) function of his own income and is independent of anybody else's income will monotonicity and the Pareto principle coincide.

As with anonymity, the issue of monotonicity of social welfare orderings is something for which we could, in principle, investigate whether the assumption 'more income to one person and no income loss to anyone else means higher social welfare' is a reasonable one. This could be done using the same kinds of techniques that we presented in chapter 4. Looking back at the formulation of the problems and questions that we used for the empirical investigation it is clear that many of the same issues that we originally discussed in terms of inequality could usefully be rephrased in terms of social welfare.

Relationship to inequality

In fact we can do more than that. Given the heroic over-simplification of the problem of social welfare that we introduced earlier, a neat analogy with chapters 2 to 4 suggests itself. Social welfare – defined on income distributions – is to be regarded as a Good Thing, and inequality – again defined in terms of income distribution – is to be regarded as a Bad Thing. If there is some consistency of view between the way alternative distributions are perceived in terms of social welfare and the way they are perceived in terms of inequality, then there ought to be a straightforward connection between the two concepts. We might expect that if, in going from distribution A to distribution B, inequality falls and average income remains the same, then social welfare should rise; if average income rises and inequality stays the same then we again might expect social welfare to rise.

Symbolically we would then have some kind of functional relationship f linking our inequality index and our welfare index, thus:

$$\text{welfare} = f(\text{inequality, mean income}) \tag{5.1}$$

Let us suppose that this is so. Then, granted some not particularly demanding mathematical conditions, we should be able to invert the relationship f – that is turn (5.1) around – to give

$$\text{inequality} = g(\text{welfare, mean income}) \tag{5.2}$$

where g is a function which has the property that if welfare increases while mean income stays constant, then inequality must fall. If this process of inversion is valid, then we can take a further step.

The significance of relationship (5.2) is that we should be able to infer inequality rankings from welfare rankings, as long as we restrict attention to distributions that all have the same mean. In other words we have two routes by which to investigate people's attitudes to inequality and the meaning that they attach to inequality comparisons:

- The *direct* approach is that which we adopted in chapter 4: the issues are presented to people explicitly in terms of inequality (whether this is done by numerical example, verbal question or by some other means).
- The *indirect* approach involves presenting issues to people in terms of social welfare (again by numerical example or verbal question) and then, for cases where mean income is held constant, using relationship (5.2) to infer attitudes about inequality comparisons.

So it would be interesting to compare evidence on social welfare rankings with the results of chapter 4 to see whether this indirect approach to inequality orderings does in reality match up with inequality orderings obtained by the direct approach.

The analogy between the two systems of analysis of income distribution is not perfect. Although, as we have seen, the axioms that are usually invoked for welfare comparisons correspond closely to those required for inequality comparisons for cases where only distributions with a given total income are to be compared, there are notable divergences elsewhere. In particular, when we consider changes in the distribution that affect mean income, the standard axioms that are used for inequality analysis focus principally on changes that affect all incomes simultaneously: for example, a uniform scaling-up of all incomes, or a uniform translation of all incomes; but the welfare axioms focus on what happens to individual incomes or the income of individuals – the ideas of monotonicity or dominance, or the Pareto principle. For this reason the arrangement of the problems and questions had to be rather different from that used in the inequality questionnaire experiments.

In Alfaland two economic programmes are proposed. It is known that both programmes will have the same effect on the population except on their incomes and all the people are identical in every respect other than income.

In each of the first ten questions there are given two alternative lists of incomes A and B (in Alfaland local currency) which result from these two programmes respectively. Please state which programme you consider would make the community of Alfaland better off by circling A or B. If you consider that each of the programmes is just as good as the other then circle both A and B.

1)   A = (1, 4, 7, 10, 13)   B = (1, 5, 6, 10, 13)

2)   A = (4, 8, 9)   B = (5, 6, 10)

3)   A = (4, 7, 7, 8, 9)   B = (5, 6, 7, 7, 10)

Figure 5.5. The setting for the social welfare numerical problems.

5.3 Empirical results

Despite these differences, the approach and the main structure of the social welfare questionnaire study were similar to those described in previous chapters: a set of numerical questions, followed by a set of related verbal questions, and after each verbal question an opportunity for individuals to change their minds if they so wished.

An extract from the main questionnaire used to investigate welfare issues[5] is shown in figure 5.5 which shows the preamble used to give a setting for the numerical questions and the particular examples used to investigate the issue of the transfer principle and decomposability (these examples use exactly the same numbers as in the corresponding inequality questionnaire).

We now give an overview of the findings from the social welfare experiment. Our purpose is twofold. Firstly, we want to see whether the assumptions mentioned on pages 51–5 are reasonable. This step is crucial to the standard approach to applied welfare analysis: for example, the transfer principle and the principle of decomposability together imply that the contours of the social welfare function in figure 5.6 must be convex to the origin, like indifference curves in conventional elementary economic theory. Secondly, we want to compare, where appropriate, the results presented here with what was found from the direct approach to inequality adopted in chapter 4. To make this comparison easier we will also use results from an additional inequality questionnaire[6] that pursued further some of the issues raised by the social welfare investigation.

But before we get into a detailed discussion of each property of a social welfare function, it would be a good idea to see whether the empirical evidence supports the basic idea of such a function as a tool of distributional analysis. Specifically let us see whether it is reasonable to suppose that people's views are capable of

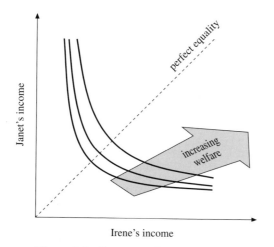

Figure 5.6. Contours of a standard social welfare function.

being represented by a well-defined ordering of distributions. In chapter 4 we noted that the responses to a subset of the numerical problems in the inequality questionnaire A1 indicated that respondents' views on income distributions were transitive (p. 45). This is borne out by the special supplementary inequality questionnaire (A2) in which we investigated this property explicitly: see the top row of table 5.1 which shows that 79% of our respondents agreed with the principle verbally, and only 18% rejected it.[7] It is interesting to note that although agreement with the transitivity principle is rather lower according to the social welfare question (70% – see the bottom row of table 5.1), the proportion of those disagreeing with transitivity is almost the same as in the case of inequality; there is just a larger proportion of 'don't knows'. This result is one example of a rather lower agreement with the principle according to the indirect approach to inequality (bottom row in table 5.1) than according to the direct approach (top row), a point to which we return below.

Now we can go on to investigate the axioms about welfare and inequality comparisons individually.

Anonymity

We begin with the assumption that it seems almost obvious to make and perhaps not worth testing. Even though we have no suggestion for respecifying the anonymity axiom or replacing it by some other principle, it seems to be a good idea to investigate whether people's ranking of distributions do actually accord with the principle. The top row of table 5.2 shows that, in the case of inequality comparisons, agreement with anonymity is very clear: 83% of the numerical responses are in accordance with it and only 12% of the responses violate it; 72% of the respondents agree with anonymity verbally. In terms of the social welfare

Table 5.1. *Agreement with transitivity of inequality and social welfare orderings (percentage responses)*

	Agree	Disagree
'If inequality in Alfaland is higher than inequality in Betaland and inequality in Betaland is higher than inequality in Gamaland then inequality in Alfaland is higher than inequality in Gamaland.'	79	18
'If society is better off under A than under B and is better off under B than under C, then it must be better off under A than under C.'	70	19

Note: Inequality response to questionnaire A2, q. 8 ($N = 181$); social welfare response to questionnaire B1, q. 15 ($N = 620$).

Table 5.2. *The anonymity principle (percentage responses)*

	Agree	Disagree
The distributions (7, 5, 10, 9) and (9, 5, 7, 10) are seen as equivalent . . .		
. . . in terms of inequality	83	12
. . . in terms of social welfare	66	32
If we permute the incomes of people who are identical in every respect other than income then . . .		
. . . inequality remains the same	72	19
. . . social welfare remains the same	54	33

Note: Inequality response to questionnaire A2, q. 7 and q. 10 ($N = 181$); social welfare response to questionnaire B1, q. 10 and q. 16 ($N = 620$).

approach (the bottom row of table 5.2), we still find two-thirds of the numerical responses in accordance with the principle, but – perhaps surprisingly – we find that the verbal agreement decreases to a level of only 54%.

Notice that for either the direct (top row) or the indirect approach (bottom row), agreement with the principle of the axiom appears to be higher when the issue is presented numerically then when it is presented verbally. There appears to be an obvious explanation of this phenomenon. As far as the numerical questions are concerned respondents are faced with a simple list of incomes, and the order of appearance of the incomes (the order of the components of the income vector) should not matter either in respect of inequality or in respect of social welfare: the layout of the numerical section of the questionnaire is probably so simple that the order of appearance does not matter much in respect of people's perceptions of the situation either. However, when the issue is presented to people verbally, it is natural that respondents should pause and ask themselves a few extra questions about the situations that they are being asked to compare. Although we took care to qualify the question by inserting the phrase 'people who are identical in every respect other than income' it may be natural for

Table 5.3. *The transfer principle again: numerical responses (percentages)*

Is (1, 4, 7, 10, 13) more unequal than (1, 5, 6, 10, 13)?

	Inequality (direct)	Social welfare (indirect)
Agree	35	47
Strongly disagree	42	21
Disagree	22	30

Note: Inequality response to questionnaire A1, q. 4 ($N = 1,108$); social welfare response to questionnaire B1, q. 1 ($N = 620$). For interpretation of 'Agree' and 'Disagree', see text and note to table 4.6.

respondents to introduce further, unstated qualifications of their own – 'What about the history of these individuals?', 'What about the possibility that these persons have different family circumstances?' – which do not spring to mind when just comparing lists of numbers. Whatever the reason for the phenomenon the results suggest that our respondents are uncomfortable with anonymity or symmetry as a principle of social welfare judgment when this issue is presented to them in plain language.

The transfer principle

In chapter 4 we raised some doubts about this principle, doubts which were raised by successive numerical and verbal questionnaire results, and which were strengthened following our analysis of respondents' comments arising from the questionnaires. As we have suggested, calling into question the transfer principle raises problems from the point of view of social welfare analysis. If social welfare is defined in terms of individual incomes and the contours of the social welfare function have the standard convex-to-the-origin shape depicted in figure 5.6 then the transfer principle is bound to hold.[8] But, although the Irene-versus-Janet contours look reassuringly conventional, why should we accept the assumptions that conventionally shaped contours are appropriate to welfare comparisons in practice?

Our numerical investigation of this point mimicked the approach of the first inequality questionnaire reported in chapter 4. We asked respondents to compare exactly the same pair of income distributions as appear in the extract in figure 4.8. Table 5.3 reports the new results from the social welfare questionnaire alongside the earlier results for comparison purposes. To make the comparison easier table 5.3 paraphrases the question that was put, but remember that the respondents saw it in the form depicted on page 157 (question 1). It appears from the first row of table 5.3 that when the numerical problems are interpreted in terms of social welfare rather more are inclined to respond in line with the transfer principle (47%) than in the numerical responses on the original inequality question-

Table 5.4. *Transfer principle: verbal responses on social welfare questionnaire (percentages)*

Irene is richer than Janet. Under programme A Irene would have $1 less than under B, and Janet would have $1 more under A than under B.	
Programme A would make the community better off	33
Programme B would make the community better off	19
We can't say, because the relative position of others are different	23
None of the above	18

Note: Responses to questionnaire B1, q. 12 ($N=620$).

naire (35%). But this finding is not borne out by the results from the accompanying verbal questions.

The presentation of the verbal question in the social welfare questionnaire was different from that of the corresponding question in the inequality questionnaire. In the social welfare questionnaire we asked respondents to compare two situations which are appropriate for illustrating the transfer principle, while in the inequality questionnaire we asked them about a specific transfer of income – an income change. The reason for this difference in the formulation of the question is that there might be a status quo bias were the social welfare issue to be presented in terms of changes: some people may reasonably take the view that every transfer decreases social welfare *per se*, irrespective of from whom or to whom the transfer may be. Putting the question 'even-handedly', as the choice between two hypothetical programmes, is a way of getting around that bias. A paraphrase of the question appears at the head of table 5.4 (the original is in appendix B, p. 143).

We can see from table 5.4 that the implied verbal agreement with the transfer principle in the responses to the social welfare questionnaire is only 33%. Such a result is remarkable in that it corresponds almost exactly with the degree of support found for the transfer principle in the detailed inequality question reported in table 4.7 (p. 46), and corroborates our finding from the numerical questions on inequality comparisons also discussed in chapter 4. It calls into question even more strongly this fundamental axiom of welfare analysis.

Table 5.4 also reveals the sort of reservation about the transfer principle that attracted substantial minority support. The third row of the table shows that almost a quarter of our respondents took the view that the relative position of other people in the distribution is also relevant to the ranking of the two distributions. As we noted in chapter 4 this modification of the strict interpretation of the transfer principle is actually consistent with the views originally expressed in Pigou (1912).[9]

Table 5.5. *The effect on social welfare of cloning the distribution (percentage responses)*

	Numerical (q. 11)	Verbal (q. 17)
Better	26	22
Worse	5	9
Same	66	53

Note: Results are based on responses to questionnaire B1 ($N = 620$).

Principle of population

As we discussed in chapter 4 this principle makes the inequality comparisons and the formulation of specific inequality measures much simpler; it is obviously also extremely useful in simplifying the structure of social welfare contours in a multi-person community. All the same, we ought perhaps to have some reservations about applying it uncritically *a priori.*[10] As it happens, when we investigate people's views using questions about social welfare, the results are similar to those of the inequality questionnaire. This can be seen from the results in table 5.5: two-thirds of the numerical responses are in accordance with the principle, while over half of the sample agree verbally. Whichever way you put it – as direct or indirect inequality comparisons – there is reasonable support for the population principle but a substantial minority who view population replication as a means by which inequality is reduced.

Decomposability

The issue of decomposability can be tackled using exactly the same methods as we adopted in the questionnaire on inequality discussed in chapter 4. Interestingly we get almost the same answer as before: it does not matter whether the issue is put directly in terms of inequality comparisons, or indirectly through the medium of social welfare comparisons of income distributions.

The results for the social welfare questionnaire are given in table 5.6: 58% gave the same ranking in each of the two numerical questions, which means agreement with the axioms (57% in the inequality questionnaire). Only 37% accept the axiom when presented verbally (40% in the inequality questionnaire) while 45% strongly disagree and 11% disagree, which are exactly the same percentages as in the inequality questionnaire. Thus we can conclude – as in our investigation of inequality – that our students reject decomposability as a principle of distributional comparisons. One of the implications of this is illustrated in figure 5.7: it is possible that if social welfare is not decomposable by population subgroups then the Irene-versus-Janet contours could be non-convex (to check that the con-

Table 5.6. *Decomposability of social welfare?*
(Percentage responses)

	Numerical (q. 2 & q. 3)	Verbal (q. 13)
Agree	58	37
Strongly disagree	n.a.	45
Disagree	39	11

Note: Results are based on responses to questions 2, 3 and 13 of
questionnaire B1 (*N* = 620 for verbal responses; *N* = 409 for
numerical questions – no data were available from the University of
Bonn). For interpretation of 'Agree' and 'Disagree', see text and
note to table 4.6.

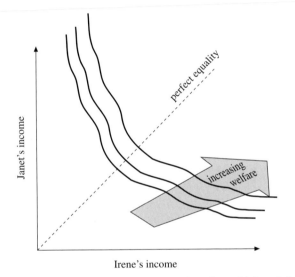

Figure 5.7. A social welfare function which satisfies the transfer principle, but
not decomposability.

tours do nevertheless satisfy the transfer principle, superimpose them on figure
4.10 and follow through the discussion on page 38).

Additions to incomes

All the issues that we have examined thus far have virtually parallel axioms for
the direct and indirect approaches to inequality. But the situation is rather
different regarding the issue of additions to incomes. The direct approach to
inequality usually addresses the very specific case of additions to all incomes
simultaneously, as we discussed in chapter 4. This may be expressed in terms
either of equal absolute additions, or of equal proportional additions, or of some

Table 5.7. *Agreement with monotonicity: numerical questions (percentage responses)*

			'B better than A'	'A&B equivalent'	'B worse than A'
(q. 4)	A = (5, 5, 5, **5**)	B = (5, 5, 5, **10**)	64	1	33
(q. 6)	A = (4, 8, **9**)	B = (4, 8, **20**)	59	1	39
(q. 5)	A = (5, 5, 5, **5**)	B = (5, 5, 5, **30**)	54	1	44

Note: Results are based on responses to questions 4, 5 and 6 of questionnaire B1 ($N = 620$).

compromise between the two. This is something that we take up in more detail in chapter 6 where we discuss the different ways in which this simultaneous increase can be interpreted in terms of a 'direction' of income change.

By contrast, the indirect approach to inequality focuses upon the impact on distributional comparisons of altering just one person's income at a time or, by extension, of altering the incomes of any arbitrary collection of persons. This, of course, is exactly the approach of the monotonicity axiom, which states that a *ceteris paribus* addition to one or more persons' incomes will increase social welfare.

Here we will concentrate on the results for the indirect approach to inequality comparisons. As we have explained, the monotonicity axiom is closely related to the Pareto principle. While the monotonicity axiom is usually put in terms of persons' incomes, the Pareto principle is typically expressed in terms of utility. We did not postulate any explicit relationship between income and utility in our questionnaires,[11] so here we focus our discussion on monotonicity as one part of the results from our comprehensive experiment.

People would very probably agree that an addition to the income of a poor person is welfare-increasing; but at the same time it is possible that they might reject the notion that an income addition to a rich person is welfare-increasing if the addition were also to increase the gap between rich and poor.[12] However, we should remember that the meaning of the monotonicity axiom is that every addition to any person's income, including a bonus to the richest person, will increase social welfare. Once again we check support for the axiom both verbally and numerically. For the numerical investigation we present different additions to the richest person using three questions.[13] Table 5.7 shows that the greater is the addition to the rich, the higher is the proportion of the respondents who consider that social welfare decreases as one moves from distribution A to the higher-income case B.

We now consider for the results from the verbal questions, presented in table 5.8. Once again the heading of table 5.8 contains a paraphrase of the issue put to the respondents, and the exact wording of questionnaire B1 should be checked in appendix B. Just over half the respondents agreed with monotonicity, but a

Table 5.8. *Agreement with monotonicity: verbal questions (percentage responses)*

If programme B yields more income for someone than programme A, does it, *ceteris paribus*, make the community better off?	
Programme B would make the community better off because no one is worse off and someone is better off	55
Relative positions of others are also different as between A and B, so we can't say which programme is better	23
Neither of the above	14

Note: Results from questionnaire B1 q. 14; $N = 523$ (the sample is smaller because we have no results on this question for the Stockholm School and for one group from Koblenz).

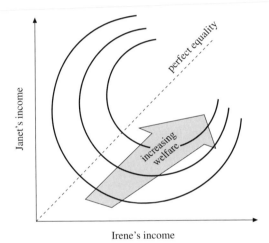

Figure 5.8. Contours of a non-monotonic welfare function.

further quarter of the sample indicated that the relative positions of other individuals in the distribution are important in assessing the impact on social welfare of an income increase to one person. It is reasonable to conclude that, although this axiom receives more support than, say, the transfer principle or decomposability, monotonicity is indeed in dispute as a general principle of welfare analysis.[14] One implication of the sort of rejection of monotonicity that we have encountered in our questionnaire responses is illustrated in figure 5.8: the contours are consistent with the transfer principle, but where they 'curl up' at the ends (in contrast to the standard case in figure 5.6) we find that giving more income to an already-rich person would lead to lower rather than higher social welfare.

Table 5.9. *Agreement with basic axioms on social welfare: summary (percentage responses)*

	Numerical	Verbal
Monotonicity	54*	55
Population principle	66	53
Transfer principle	47	33
Decomposability	58	37

Notes:
Results are based on responses to questionnaire B1 ($N = 620$).
* Based on question 5.

5.4 Summary: welfare judgments and inequality comparisons

In passing from the topic of inequality to the topic of social welfare much more is involved than just replacing a negative with a positive. As we mentioned in the introduction to this chapter, there is the difficult problem of the lack of social consensus whether from the political right ('what this country wants') or from the left ('for the good of the people'). In addition to the issue of consensus there is the question of whether the views of any one person or group of persons can adequately be represented by the sort of assumptions that are commonly made in applied welfare economics.

We have not attempted to address the question of consensus, much less resolve it: that is a matter which is likely to be specific to culture and historical circumstance.[15] But the second question is of central importance to the main theme of this book, in that economists have often appealed to social welfare concepts when thinking about inequality. In tackling this question we have been working on three things simultaneously. Firstly, we have tried to replicate our earlier results on inequality rankings when set in a different context. Secondly, we have attempted to get at inequality issues through the route of social welfare comparison, even where there was no direct counterpart in the direct approach to inequality discussed in chapter 4. A summary of the outcome of these components of the chapter is presented in table 5.9,[16] and should be compared with the 'headline results' on inequality (p. 48). Thirdly, we have been able to go a small way towards addressing the question of whether it is reasonable to imagine that there could be a coherent social ordering. Our investigation of the question of transitivity of inequality comparisons and of social welfare comparisons is fairly reassuring on this point. People may well form coherent views about the ranking of income distributions in terms of social welfare, but we should not expect those views to conform closely to 'standard' patterns.

Two major implications of the social welfare investigation stand out. The first is that there is broad consistency between the direct and indirect approaches to inequality comparisons. Support for the anonymity principle and the population

Table 5.10. *Support for basic principles of inequality comparisons (percentage responses)*

	Direct	Indirect
Anonymity	72	54
Population principle	66	53
Transfer principle	31	33
Decomposability	40	37

Note: All results are based on verbal responses to questionnaires. For the direct approach, anonymity responses are based on questionnaire A2 and the transfer principle responses are based on questionnaire A4. All social welfare responses are based on questionnaire B1.

principle is lower, but appears to be very close on the issues of the transfer principle and decomposability – see table 5.10.[17] The second is that if we take seriously the possibility that monotonicity and the transfer principle will have to be ditched, then some of the familiar basic tools of applied economics may have to be ditched with them too. Ordinary 'Benthamite' social welfare functions will not do.

Notes

1 People in the last group could at least claim to be consistent: those arguing that social welfare falls if A′ is followed by B′ would also have to say that welfare falls if B′ is followed by A′; likewise, those who argue that welfare increases under the reordering.
2 In the jargon this is known as *first-degree dominance*.
3 See Amiel and Cowell (1994c).
4 For examples of this approach, see Arrow (1981), Boskin and Sheshinski (1978), Brennan (1973), Duesenberry (1949), Hochman and Rodgers (1969), Kapteyn and van Herwaarden (1980), Layard (1980), Morawetz (1977) and Oswald (1983).
5 This is questionnaire B1 (appendix B, pp. 157–60).
6 This is questionnaire A2 (appendix B, pp. 150–2).
7 Here and elsewhere we have simplified the presentation of the verbal responses by including a paraphrase of the question in the table. Appendix B should be consulted for the exact wording and layout of the question.
8 The reverse is not true: acceptance of the transfer principle does not imply that the contours have to be convex to the origin. See Rothschild and Stiglitz (1973) and figure 5.7 below.
9 On this question there was a small change of response in favour of the conventional view (B) after the students had responded to the verbal question. Sixteen changed their answers in this way on questionnaire B1 (3.9% of respondents), whilst three changed their answer in the opposite direction to A (0.7%) and seven changed to A&B (1.7%).
10 See the discussion of this point in chapter 4 (p. 38). The numerical and verbal questions in the social welfare questionnaire (B1) were designed to be as similar as possible to those of the inequality questionnaire (A1).

11 The Pareto axiom has previously been investigated experimentally by McClelland and Rohrbaugh (1978) who formulated their questions in terms of utilities.

12 See Dagum (1990).

13 These are questions 4, 5 and 6 in questionnaire B1. Notice that the questions appeared in a different order in the questionnaire from that reported in table 5.7.

14 On this issue, two features of the responses deserve special mention. Firstly, the differences here between the results for different university subsamples is very striking, and is in sharp contrast with the results for the other axioms discussed: see note 16 below and chapter 8 (p. 114). Secondly, there was a noticeable change of mind recorded by the students after they had tackled the verbal questions. On question 4, eight students switched their answers to B (the conventional view), eight switched to A, and two switched to A&B. However, on questions 5 and 6, where the recipient was richer, the switch in favour of the conventional view was more pronounced: sixteen switched to B on question 5 and fourteen switched to B on question 6. (The corresponding switches to A were four in the case of question 5 and three for question 6. The corresponding switches to A&B were two in the case of question 5 and three for question 6.)

15 An interesting example of this type of approach is found in Brittan (1973).

16 We carried out a further study (B2) on social welfare questionnaires to check whether students' responses were influenced by the order of presentation of the questions. This check was carried out on LSE and Israeli economics students only. In the B2 sample there was higher agreement with monotonicity (67% on numerical questions, 68% on verbal questions) and decomposability (64% numerical, 51% verbal) but lower agreement with the population principle (60% numerical, 50% verbal); agreement with the transfer principle was lower on numerical questions (44%) and higher on verbal questions (50%). For details of the B2 control see appendix B (p. 143).

17 Notice that in Amiel and Cowell (1994a) there is a similar table where the percentage reported for verbal support for the transfer principle refers to questionnaire A1 (a higher value). This is also what is presented in table 4.8. Here we report for the more extensive questionnaire A4 which was run after preparation of Amiel and Cowell (1994a) and is reported in Amiel and Cowell (1998a). See also page 122 below.

6 Income change

6.1 Introduction: comparing cakes

Up to now we have given only scant attention to the size of the economic 'cake' or 'pie' – in other words, to income *levels*, as opposed to income *distribution*. The principal exceptions to this were our questions concerning scale versus translation independence in chapter 4 and the case of the monotonicity principle which we considered in chapter 5. But what has been lacking in all this is a systematic treatment of the way in which distributional judgments may change when income levels and the extent of inequality are varied jointly.

There are several reasons why income levels might affect people's views on inequality. For example, it could be that people's 'taste' for equality, like their taste for butter, guns or other economic goods, depends on income in the sense that the amount of other things that they are prepared to see sacrificed for the sake of marginally greater income equality is income-dependent. This income dependence could be related to the person's own income, or the average income in the community, or both. This point alone raises issues that can be quite important for policy-makers: because people's views on the relative urgency of income inequality may be determined by the average living standard, or of their perceptions of it, the income-growth-versus-equality trade-off may be resolved in different ways in economies at different levels of economic development.

However, there is a deeper question that is particularly relevant to the things that we have discussed in earlier chapters. The size of the cake can affect the meaning of inequality *rankings* as well as the equality–efficiency or equality–growth trade-off. Suppose we think about the inequality comparisons illustrated in figure 6.1. In this picture it is clear that A and A′ represent the same *distributional shares* or proportional divisions, since in each case the pie has been cut into pieces at the same angles; likewise, B and B′ represent identical slices, but different slices from A and A′; finally, A and B represent the same smallish total income while A′ and B′ represent the same largish total income. If we were to

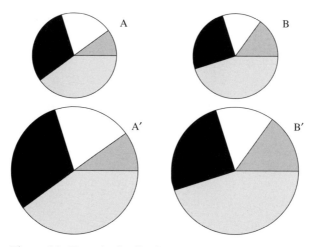

Figure 6.1. Two pie distributions, before and after income growth.

respond to this picture unreflectively we might assert that 'of course' A and A′ are equally unequal and 'of course' B and B′ are equally unequal. But we know from the discussion of chapter 4 that many people, quite reasonably, assert that inequality *increases* as all incomes are scaled up proportionately (see the responses to the question in table 6.1 on page 77).[1] Even if we were more cautious in replying, we might yet imagine that the rankings somehow 'ought to' stay the same: if A is regarded as more unequal than B, then A′ should be more unequal than B′. But there is no necessity for this to be so: it is perfectly logical to allow for the possibility that as income grows the ranking of a particular pair of distributional shares changes. The same individual could rank A over B at low incomes, B′ over A′ at higher income levels, and perhaps A″ over B″ at very high incomes.

As we shall see in this chapter there is a variety of ways in which we could approach this issue. It is important to go into some detail on this because each of these ways has an impact upon how we think about inequality. We have simplified by aggregating the various approaches into two principal categories:

• *Uniform enrichment.* In this case there is a systematic increase in everyone's incomes. However, there are several views on what constitutes an appropriate definition of a 'systematic' increase. More of this in a moment.
• *Unbalanced enrichment.* In contrast to the case of uniform enrichment we assume that income growth occurs individually: income increases accrue to each of the members of a primordially equal population in turn, thus automatically creating inequality along the way. In this specific model of inequality, income inequality is a transitional state between two notional states of equality before and after income growth.

Each of these two broad types of approach has something to say regarding the meaning of inequality and its relationship to the size of the cake. We have incorporated them explicitly in our series of questionnaire experiments. We begin with a discussion of the more standard approach.

6.2 Uniform enrichment

We asserted in the introduction that there is more than one meaning to be given to the concept of systematic income increases when comparing income distributions. We have already introduced two of these when we discussed scale independence and translation independence in chapter 4 (see figures 2.4 and 2.5 on pages 13 and 14 and also figure 4.6 on page 36).

These basic concepts can be generalised in a number of interesting ways. For example, we could replace the idea of independence as we have interpreted it so far: a standard approach is to consider scale or translation invariance. Scale invariance means that when you multiply up or down everyone's income in any set of income distributions by a common factor the ranking of the distributions remains unaltered even though the measured inequality level may change. As a simple example of this consider the variance, as conventionally defined in statistics: if the variance of distribution A is greater than that of distribution B then, on scaling up or down all the incomes by the same factor to produce distributions A' and B', we will find that the variance of A' is always greater than that of B', so that the ordering of distributions remains invariant under transformations of scale; but it is well known that if you double everyone's income the variance will increase fourfold, so that the level of inequality in this case is not scale-independent. We could have also carried out the same sort of intellectual exercise with translation independence and translation invariance: in this case if the variance of distribution A is greater than that of distribution B then adding a constant to all incomes to produce distributions A' and B' will mean that the variance of A' will be the same as that of A, and the variances of B' and B will also be equal. Furthermore it is clear that, whether we consider scale changes or translation changes, the property of independence implies invariance but not vice versa.[2] For many results on inequality measurement, invariance rather than the stronger form of independence is all that is required.

An alternative approach to the generalisation of scale and translation independence retains the idea of independence but applies it in a different 'direction'. Instead of discussing just changes of income-scale on the one hand or of changes of income-origin on the other we can consider a general scale-and-origin transformation as a description of inequality-invariant income growth. It is this approach that is particularly appropriate for analysing the effect of uniform enrichment. To make the generalisation of scale and translation changes more precise it is useful to introduce a couple of further concepts:

- *The transformation type.* Type 0 will be used to denote the translation-independence case, and type 1 the scale-independence case. Other, intermediate cases can be characterised by values of t lying between 0 and 1.

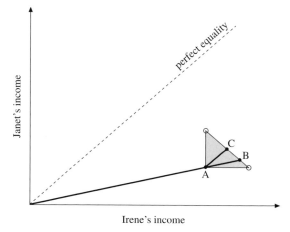

Figure 6.2. Additions to Irene's and Janet's incomes.

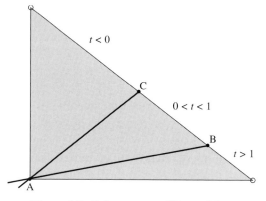

Figure 6.3. Enlargement of figure 6.2.

- *The transformation direction.* This is derived from the transformation type and will usually depend upon the status quo distribution of income.

We can illustrate it in the elementary diagram of figure 6.2. Plot the incomes of Irene and Janet on a graph as in figure 4.2: point A in figure 6.2 and the enlarged figure 6.3 (as in chapter 4, we happen to have assumed that Irene is richer than Janet, but this is not important for the analysis). Now let us suppose that there is an extra $10 to be given to them: it could go to just one person – the circled points at each end of the line through B and C – or it could be split between them. The distributions that we can reach with the extra $10 are illustrated by the shaded triangle: but which of these distributions would result in the same level of inequality as the starting point A? If we insist that full scale independence is required (see page 12) then point B is just as unequal as A: points A and B lie on the ray through the origin, so Janet and Irene's incomes under B are

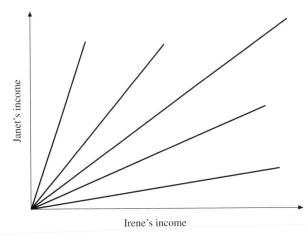

Figure 6.4. Scale independence.

in exactly the same ratio as they were under A. If we go along with translation independence, then distribution C is regarded as just as unequal as distribution A: the line AC is at an angle of 45° which means that each person gets exactly $5, irrespective of her original income.

Of course, there might be a variety of intermediate cases which could also represent interesting ways of dividing the $10 that – in some people's opinion – leave inequality unaltered. These intermediate types can be characterised by a simple index t of the transformation type. If Irene and Janet are the only two persons in the community and if x_i and x_j denote their respective incomes respectively, then a transformation of type t means that inequality remains unchanged if the $10 are split y_i to Irene and y_j to Janet where

$$y_i = \frac{\$10}{2} \times \frac{x_i t + 1 - t}{\frac{x_i + x_j}{2} t + 1 - t} \tag{6.1}$$

$$y_j = \frac{\$10}{2} \times \frac{x_j t + 1 - t}{\frac{x_i + x_j}{2} t + 1 - t} \tag{6.2}$$

The transformation direction is the direction on the diagram from the point (x_i, x_j) to the point $(x_i + y_i, x_j + y_j)$.[3] Whether $t = 0$ or $t = 1$ or is equal to some other value in the range illustrated in figure 6.3 we just do not know, even though the usual assumption in the economics literature on inequality is overwhelmingly in favour of scale independence (the AB solution). However, if the transformation type were everywhere uniform we could envisage a simple inequality map drawn on a diagram like figure 6.2.

For example if $t = 1$, the case of scale independence, we would get a map that looks something like figure 6.4. The way to read figure 6.4 is this. The lines on the diagram represent 'iso-inequality' contours: as we move along any one of these,

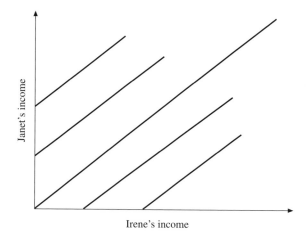

Figure 6.5. Translation independence.

inequality remains constant. Because (in this case) the contours are rays through the origin, the 'inequality map' of figure 6.4 implies that inequality remains unchanged under uniform proportional additions to, or deductions from, each person's income.

Alternatively, if we take the assumption of translation independence ($t=0$) as standard then the corresponding map will be that illustrated in figure 6.5, where the contour lines of the map are all at 45°. As an experiment pick a point on any one of the lines; then displace the point by the same number of millimetres in the Irene direction and the Janet direction; the new point should be on the same line. The economic meaning of this is that adding the same number of dollars to Irene's income and Janet's income leaves inequality unchanged; likewise for deductions of the same absolute amount.

In view of our previous discussion the contour systems of figures 6.4 and 6.5 do not exhaust the possibilities of drawing interesting inequality maps: we could also consider an intermediate case where the transformation direction lies between that of translation independence and scale independence ($0<t<1$): this is illustrated by the inequality map in figure 6.6.[4] We could even consider cases that correspond to $t<0$ or $t>1$, although the applicability of these is necessarily more restricted.[5]

So suppose we were to apply here the same sort of techniques that we have used before on questions about inequality and welfare: we would extend the elementary map-drawing that we carried out in chapters 4 and 5 to examine in more detail how the inequality terrain looks at different income levels. The principal issue to be investigated appears to be: what is the appropriate value of t? But this begs a more fundamental question, namely: is the transformation direction constant in practice? This second question raises an issue which deserves more detailed discussion.

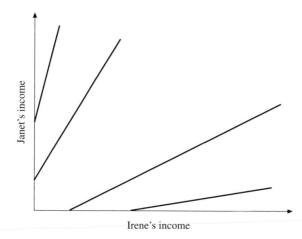

Figure 6.6. Intermediate-type independence.

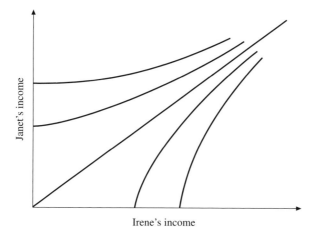

Figure 6.7. Transformation direction dependent on income (1).

6.3 The dependence hypothesis

We have already had a preview of the meaning of 'dependence' in the present context. The idea is that the transformation direction depends upon the level of income at which you start. A simple example of this is illustrated in figure 6.7. In the particular case that we have drawn, consider what happens to inequality if all incomes increase by a uniform absolute amount. Start at some low income point that is off the diagonal ray of perfect equality and then move outwards at 45°: at low and moderate income levels the movement increases inequality ($t < 0$), and in the limit (at indefinitely large income levels) it would leave inequality unchanged ($t = 0$).

Of course, there are many other possibilities for which the transformation

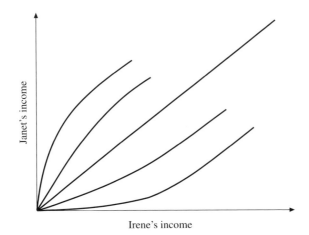

Figure 6.8. Transformation direction dependent on income (2).

direction depends on the income level: figure 6.8 illustrates the case where an across-the-board income increase would reduce inequality at low income levels ($0 < t < 1$), and would leave inequality unchanged at high income levels ($t = 0$). Figure 4.11 (p. 41) goes one stage further than figure 6.7: as one progressively moves outwards from the origin a uniform absolute increase in all incomes would first of all increase and then reduce inequality.

The questionnaire results that we have already presented provide empirical evidence on the relationship between distributional judgments and the reference level of overall income. As we have just explained, the issue that we want to examine is whether these people's judgments about the structure of inequality conform to a particular transformation direction. In this case it makes sense to present the results in the opposite order to our usual practice of looking first at the responses to numerical problems and then at those to verbal questions.

Table 6.1 provides a succinct summary of the main result.[6] The first row corresponds to the map in figure 6.4 and the second row corresponds to the map of figure 6.5. Obviously scale independence receives more support than does translation independence (interestingly the support for these two principles when expressed in the format of questionnaire A3 is very similar to that we discovered in questionnaire A1, reported in table 4.1). It is also obvious from table 6.1 that the response 'depends on the income level' (third row) gets almost as much support as the first two conventional cases taken together. So the evidence suggests that the income level is crucial to an assessment of the transformation direction. But in what way?

To address this question we may look at the responses to the numerical problems included in questionnaire A1. To make the issue of the income level meaningful we have to give some sort of frame of reference to the respondents about

Table 6.1. *What income change will leave inequality unchanged? (Percentage responses)*

The same proportionate amount added to all incomes	32
A fixed sum added to all incomes	11
Depends on the income level	41
None of the above	9

Note: Results are based on responses to questionnaire A3 ($N = 186$).

In Alfaland there are some areas with different levels of income. All areas have the same number of people which are identical except in their incomes. In each area half of the people have one level of income and the other half have another level of income. The average income in Alfaland by local currency is 1000 Alfa-dollars and the income which ensures a supply of basic needs is 400 Alfa-dollars.

In each of the following questions you are asked to compare two distributions of income - one per each area. Please state which of them you consider to be the more unequally distributed by circling A or B. If you consider that both of the distributions have the same inequality then circle both A and B.

Figure 6.9. Introduction to questionnaire A3.

what the units of income in the problems are supposed to be 'worth'. We do this by postulating an imaginary country, Alfaland, with an imaginary currency, and putting a brief story in the preamble to the questionnaire (see figure 6.9). Notice two things: firstly, the income distributions to be compared are presented as those corresponding to different regions in Alfaland; secondly, the implicit value of the Alfadollar is suggested in two ways – we mention the average income in Alfaland and the 'basic needs' income level. Further elaboration seemed to us to be superfluous and probably confusing.

The relationship between the verbal and the numerical parts of the questionnaire was essentially the same as in all the others that we have discussed and we find, once again, that the responses to the numerical problems are in line with those made to the verbal questions.

The issue of the transformation direction was investigated using a series of questions that appear on the left-hand side of table 6.2. Although the questionnaire posed the question in terms of the comparison of the income distributions in two equal-sized regions of the country, named A and B, we have taken the liberty of paraphrasing and presenting each question as though it were an evaluation of a change of income distribution from case A to case B. Also, for clarity, we have rearranged the order of presentation of the questions so as to group them into three principal transformation types: absolute income changes (first group), proportional income changes (last group) and intermediate or compromise changes (middle group). The transformation direction can be inferred from the

Table 6.2. *What happens to inequality when you increase people's incomes?* *(Percentage responses)*

	'Inequality decreases'	'Inequality increases'	'Inequality stays same'
Adding a fixed absolute sum			
(q. 1) (200, 400) → (400, 600)	78	10	11
(q. 4) (600, 900) → (900, 1200)	55	18	23
(q. 7) (1200, 1800) → (1800, 2400)	51	24	23
Adding a compromise* sum			
(q. 2) (200, 400) → (400, 700)	68	28	3
(q. 5) (600, 900) → (900, 1300)	40	52	6
(q. 8) (1200, 1800) → (1800, 2550)	41	52	5
Adding a fixed proportionate sum			
(q. 3) (200, 400) → (400, 800)	40	29	28
(q. 6) (600, 900) → (900, 1350)	24	53	22
(q. 9) (1200, 1800) → (1800, 2700)	16	59	24

Notes:
* 'Compromise' means 'between absolute and proportionate'.
Results are based on numerical responses to questionnaire A3 ($N = 186$).

direction in which inequality is reported to change under each income transformation.

Table 6.2 reveals a consistent pattern of views about the effect of income growth on inequality. As we move from relatively low incomes (the first row in each group) to relatively high incomes (the third row) there is, with one exception, a switch away from the view that an across-the-board addition to income (for any of the transformation types covered in table 6.2) will reduce inequality as one looks at successively higher income levels. In fact, for proportionate or compromise additions to income, the majority view is that at low income levels an income addition will reduce inequality, whereas at moderate or high income levels the same type of income additions will increase inequality; on the other hand, the 'median voter' view implicit in table 6.2 would be represented by a set of contours similar to those in figure 6.8.

6.4 Unbalanced enrichment

As we mentioned earlier in the chapter there is an alternative approach to inequality and income growth. This owes much to the work of the philosopher Larry Temkin. The Temkin approach is founded on the notion of an individual's *complaint* in income distribution: he has a complaint if he finds that his income falls below that norm to which he might reasonably be entitled. These complaints can be aggregated up over the community – what Temkin refers to as the *additive principle* – so as to generate a measure of inequality inherent in the set of com-

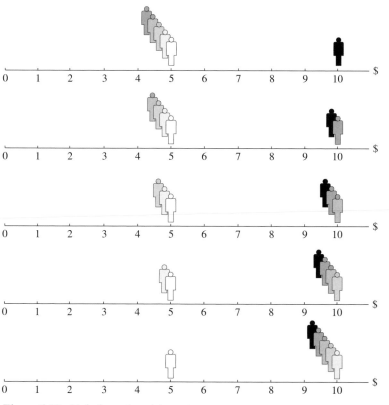

Figure 6.10. Unbalanced enrichment.

plaints. In order to see the main thrust of the Temkin approach it is useful to run through a story which (almost) paraphrases Temkin's exposition.

We qualify the last remark with 'almost' because we are actually going to tell Temkin's story in reverse: Temkin (1986) actually discusses the problem of defining inequality change in a depressing model of unbalanced immiserisation, but our modified tale is one with a happy ending. Imagine a population of n people who are alike in virtually every respect: in this case all except one also have the same income, but the one exception enjoys a higher income. Now let the remaining $n-1$ individuals in the population start jumping to this higher income level one by one. Go on until $n-1$ are on the upper income level and one has been left behind on the original low income level. The process is illustrated in figure 6.10. What happens to inequality along the way?

There are several stories that could be told here, but let us focus on two opposing arguments, each of which appears to have some force:[7]

(1) As the process continues it appears to be more and more the case that just one person is being especially victimised by the situation. As we move towards the situation with $n-1$ people on the upper level and one person left

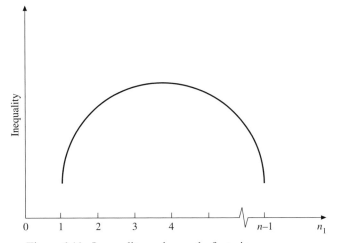

Figure 6.11. Inequality and growth: first view.

behind it appears that the entire burden of the inequality is to be borne by the one lone remaining member of the worse-off group, and it may seem both that he has a very large complaint, and that the inequality is especially offensive.

(2) If we take on board the additive principle, the inequality in this tiny world is measured by summing each of the complaints that the members have. On that view, all but one of the members start out with the same size of complaint; but fewer and fewer people will have this complaint as unbalanced enrichment continues; and, according to the additive principle, the fewer people there are with a given amount to complain about, the better the situation is with respect to inequality.

We may suspect that both story 1, which sees inequality rising as total income grows through unbalanced enrichment, and story 2, which gives the opposite reasoning, contain elements of 'the truth'. We might conjecture that an appropriate amalgam of these will come close to a consensus view of the relationship between inequality and income group. If so, then there are two principal shapes which the relationship could adopt. The first of these is illustrated in figure 6.11: the inverted U-shape means that inequality is at a maximum when exactly $n/2$ persons are at each of the two income levels.

But what are we to make of the alternative view illustrated in figure 6.12? Here we find a logical problem which is readily apparent if we modify the Temkin story somewhat further in one respect: begin one step further back where no one has the higher income and carry the story on one step further so that at the end of the process all n persons enjoy the higher income level. Then it is obvious that the extended story takes the society from a state of primordial complete equality (at a low income level) to a terminal state of complete equality (at a high income

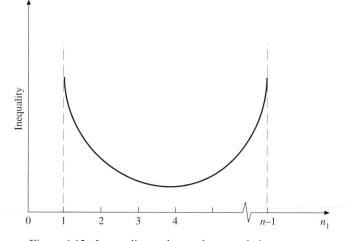

Figure 6.12. Inequality and growth: second view.

15) Suppose there is a society consisting of n people. There is
one rich person and n-1 identical poor people. One by one,
some of those who were poor acquire the same income as the
rich person, so that eventually there are $n-1$ (identical)
rich people and just one poor person. Please circle the
appropriate response:

a) *Inequality increases continuously.*

b) *Inequality decreases continuously.*

c) *Inequality at first increases and then decreases.*

d) *Inequality at first decreases and then increases.*

e) *Inequality remains the same throughout.*

f) *None of the above*

Figure 6.13. Extract from questionnaire A1.

level). So for inequality statements to have any meaning it must be the case that inequality increases at some point during the process of unbalanced enrichment and decreases at some later point. This may mean that there is a discontinuity at each end of the relationship between the number of high-income individuals and the perceived degree of inequality. Although it may seem less likely than the case illustrated in figure 6.11 we should not rule it out as a logical possibility.

Once again it is interesting to check for empirical evidence on the structure of people's inequality judgments. We included questions on these issues right from the earliest of our questionnaire experiments. Two extracts from the first of these (questionnaire A1) appear in figure 6.13. Some of the issues raised by respones to this questionnaire were pursued further in questionnaire A2, which we will discuss further in a moment.

Table 6.3. *Perceived inequality change in the growth process of figure 6.13 (percentage responses)*

	Questionnaire A1		Questionnaire A2
	Numerical (qq. 7, 8, 9)	Verbal	Verbal (q. 9)
Inequality . . .			
increases continuously	8	7	4
decreases continuously	8	20	8
first increases then decreases	26	19	54
first decreases then increases	42	35	3
remains the same	3	11	8
does none of the above	1	4	18
No transitive answer	11		
Partial or no answer	1	4	5

Note: Based on responses to questions 7, 8, 9 and 15 of questionnaire A1 ($N = 1,108$) and question 9 of questionnaire A2 ($N = 186$).

The main results are summarised in table 6.3 which enables a comparison to be made of the numerical and verbal approaches, and of the results from the two separate questionnaires. First of all, notice the fairly low proportion of intransitive answers (which we commented upon on page 45 in chapter 4) and the overall agreement between the numerical and the verbal approaches to the issue as presented in questionnaire A1 (the first two columns of table 6.3). Now consider the responses in the light of the Temkin questions that we described earlier. It is clear that there is little support for the view that inequality increases monotonically as people get richer, nor (as far as the numerical questions are concerned) for the view that inequality decreases monotonically; these conclusions are also borne out by the A2 questionnaire (the third column in table 6.3). Columns 1 and 2 (the A1 questionnaire) indicate that more respondents think that inequality first decreases and then increases during the poor-to-rich migration sequence (42% for the numerical questions and 35% for the verbal question) than the opposite (26% and 19% respectively).

However, the third column (questionnaire A2) seems to tell a rather different story from the other two. There is a simple reason for this. As the extract in figure 6.14 shows, questionnaire A2's implied sequence of problems starts and finishes with perfect equality – (5, 5, 5, 5) and (10, 10, 10, 10), and the corresponding verbal question is worded so as to reflect this. In the light of this it seems natural that the support of the first and second views in table 6.3 should be lower according to questionnaire A2 than according to A1. Moreover, the fourth row of table 6.3 is also readily explained by this fundamental difference between the two questionnaires: if someone were to support the fourth option presented in questionnaire A1 ('inequality at first decreases and then increases') then logically he should support the last option in questionnaire A2.

1) A = (5, 5, 5, 5)   B = (5, 5, 5, 10)

2) A = (5, 5, 5, 10)   B = (5, 5, 10, 10)

3) A = (5, 5, 10, 10)   B = (5, 10, 10, 10)

4) A = (5, 10, 10, 10)   B = (10, 10, 10, 10)

5) A = (5, 5, 5, 5)   B = (10, 10, 10, 10)

6) A = (5, 5, 5, 10)   B = (5, 10, 10, 10)

    • • •   • • •   • • •

9) Suppose there is a society consisting of n persons. All of
    them are identical poor people. One by one each person
    receives in turn an identical large bonus and thus becomes
    a rich person: so eventually there are n identical rich
    people. Please circle the appropriate response:

    a)   Inequality increases continuously

    b)   Inequality decreases continuously

    c)   Inequality at first increase and then decrease

    d)   Inequality at first decrease and then increase

    e)   Inequality remains the same throughout

    f)   None of the above

Figure 6.14. Extract from questionnaire A2.

The same reasoning may also explain the different degree of support for the third and sixth options. But another possible explanation may be the phenomenon of 'framing' (Tversky and Kahneman 1981): it is well known that the presentation of a questionnaire may elicit different answers, depending on the way in which certain pieces of information appear in the question. Now we suggested (on page 80) that it may be reasonable to suppose that inequality is a continuous function of n_1/n as indicated in figure 6.11, but the format of questionnaire A1 left out the end cases, $n_1 = 0$ and $n_1 = n$. So it may be that respondents failed to take account of these cases and their implications when replying 'inequality at first decreases and then increases' to questionnaire A1, and overlooking the possibility of a discontinuity (such as that displayed at each end of the graph in figure

Table 6.4. *Comparing extremes in the growth process (percentage responses)*

Compare the distributions A = (5, 5, 5, 10) and B = (5, 10, 10, 10) . . .		
	Questionnaire	
	A1	A2
A is more unequal	22	18
B is more unequal	23	19
Inequality in A and B is the same	53	62

Note: Based on question 9 of questionnaire A1 ($N = 1,108$) and question 6 of questionnaire A2 ($N = 181$).

6.12). The format of A2, on the other hand, forced the issue of the end points to the respondents' attention.

The issue is important because, as Fields (1987) has pointed out, although there are many inequality measures which would exhibit the kind of behaviour typified by figure 6.11, there is virtually no commonly used inequality measure which would exhibit figure 6.12 as the outcome of the Temkin process. The responses to the two inequality questionnaires may reveal not only the broad pattern of people's perceptions of inequality, but also the validity of certain specific inequality measures implied by those perceptions. If we are to take the responses to the A2 questionnaire (which covers the extended sequence including the end points) as definitive then it appears that some sort of measure that has continuity at the end points would be appropriate. But we can say more.

The respondents also exhibited an interesting 'symmetry' in their evaluations of the process, as we can see in table 6.4: notice that more than half of the respondents consider inequality to be identical in the two cases where $n_1 = n - 1$ and $n_1 = 1$. There are several points to be made concerning this symmetry phenomenon.[8]

In the first place it rules out the Gini coefficient and most of the standard mean-independent inequality indices that are used in the literature. This is illustrated in figures 6.15 and 6.16 which depict the outcome of two versions of the simple process in figure 6.10. In figure 6.15 we have a situation similar to the experiment reported in table 6.3:[9] there are two income levels ($5 and $10) and people progressively migrate from the lower to the higher income; as this process occurs, mean income rises (horizontal axis) and inequality, measured by standard indices, at first rises then falls (vertical axis). Figure 6.16 shows what would have happened had the income growth been greater – incomes rise from $1 to $10 in this case. In each case, results are presented for the Gini coefficient and six members of the class of Atkinson indices: notice that only for the one Atkinson index where inequality aversion equals 2 do we get the symmetric pattern suggested by our questionnaire responses.[10] If we were to take this finding as evidence of our respondents' attitudes towards different types of income transfer, then it would suggest quite a high sensitivity to incomes at the bottom of the dis-

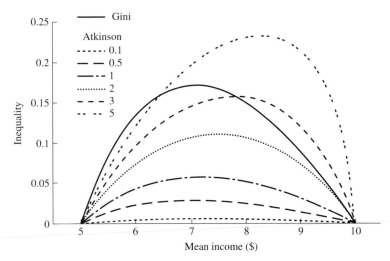

Migration of 50 persons from $5 to $10

Figure 6.15. Mean income and inequality as incomes grow from $5 to $10.

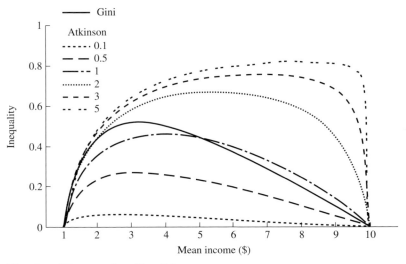

Migration of 50 persons from $1 to $10

Figure 6.16. Mean income and inequality as incomes grow from $1 to $10.

tribution: if Irene has $100, Janet has $10 and Kate has $1, then transferring just 5¢ from Janet to Kate is regarded as having the same impact as transferring $5 from Irene to Janet. However, this conclusion is predicated on the assumption of scale independence, which we know to be inappropriate as a general assumption because of the earlier discussion about the transformation direction. Were we to adopt the opposite polar assumption of translation independence, we would then find that Gini's mean difference and the variance (the translation-independent counterparts of the Gini coefficient and the Atkinson coefficient respectively) also exhibit the symmetry property.

The unbalanced enrichment story – or the 'reverse-Temkin' process – reveals useful supplementary information for our understanding of the inequality maps people have when they compare income distributions. Respondents to our questionnaires indicate that the general shape of the inequality path in the growth process may be regular – the classic inverted U – but that its precise form is either one that represents quite high inequality aversion or one that is inconsistent with scale independence and decomposability.[11]

6.5 Policy appraisal

As we have seen in this chapter, the structure of inequality comparisons across situations where total income differs is more complicated than the simple alternatives which we outlined in chapter 2. We will summarise the principal points of this chapter by examining two issues that are particularly relevant to applications of inequality analysis to the making and assessment of economic policies.

Fairness, comparability and income levels

First, we touch on issues of fairness or comparability of income structures at different income levels. Scale and translation independence are not the only options, nor necessarily the best options, when looking for an appropriate assumption about the relationship between inequality maps at different income levels. However, we can now throw some light on the relative merits, according to our respondents, of two simple propositions concerning fairness in income growth or, turning the process around, fairness in income sacrifice. The two propositions could be crudely stated thus:

- *Fair shares.* Fair treatment requires that the gains from economic growth, or the sacrifices required by taxation, should be proportional to a person's means.
- *The Duke and the Dustman.* Fair treatment requires equal monetary gains (or sacrifices) for all. Whether the person's resources place him in the top 0.1 per cent (the Duke) or amongst the poorest paid (the Dustman) it is argued that the same absolute payment to all – or absolute sacrifice by all – is a just way of transforming the income distribution. This has actually been argued as a principle of fair taxation in justifying the brief and inglorious system of local taxation in the UK known as the 'poll tax' (or, formally, the Community Charge).

The questionnaire evidence reveals that neither principle is regarded as overwhelmingly appropriate in all circumstances. However, the responses indicate more than a simple 'don't know' or 'can't say'. The evidence from the questionnaires is that there is a systematic link between views of what constitutes fair treatment in dividing the cake and the size of the cake itself (see table 6.1). The higher is the 'reference income level' that is relevant to the distributional comparison, the weaker is the perceived inequality-reducing effect of an across-the-board absolute income increase; and although an across-the-board proportional increase is perceived to reduce inequality at low income levels, it is perceived to increase inequality at high income levels.

The implications of these findings emerge more starkly if we turn them around and translate them into perceived inequality effects of an income reduction – a tax. An equal absolute sacrifice (the poll-tax type) would be regarded as inequitable (inequality-increasing) for all income distributions, but particularly so for cases with a small total income. A proportional tax would be regarded as inequitable (in the sense just explained) in a low-income economy but equitable in a high-income economy.[12]

Inequality and growth

The second area concerns a relationship that is central to a variety of research questions that are of current concern. In the context of economic development this relationship is commonly addressed in the form of a trade-off epitomised by the question 'how much inequality is to be anticipated as a concomitant of economic growth?' In this chapter we have looked at another type of trade-off: in a sense we have turned the question around so as to focus on 'how much inequality is to be tolerated as a concomitant of economic growth?' Our questionnaires did not put the issue in this form, but it can be inferred from questionnaire A2 which investigates the way in which people appear to view changes in inequality as incomes grow.

The stylised story that has been set out in figures 6.10 to 6.12 can be applied directly to inequality tolerance. One way of describing the relationship between growth and inequality in the course of economic development is as a 'migration' process: workers and their families move from a relatively low-income sector (the country?) to a relatively high-income sector (the city?), and so the unbalanced enrichment story of section 6.4 may be represented as a type of unbalanced economic growth. Must unbalanced income growth imply a growth in inequality too? Or could there be a fall in inequality as one group of the population moves ahead leaving others behind? One argument for this apparently controversial view has been neatly characterised by Hirschman and Rothschild (1973) as the 'traffic in the tunnel' problem: those left behind, on witnessing the income gains of others, experience a rise in their utility because of their expectations about a future rise in their own incomes, much as somebody stuck in traffic may be heartened by seeing the beginnings of movement in other lanes of vehicles. Whether the income inequality associated with the intermediate stages of a growth process is perceived to be rising or falling may depend upon each person's expectations about his own income, and those expectations in turn will depend upon his evaluation of other people's incomes. Once again 'externalities' – the dependence of one person's utility on another person's economic circumstances – play a central role in perceptions of income inequality.

One important lesson has emerged from both main parts of this chapter: the dependence of inequality rankings on the income level at which the distributional comparisons are made. The issue of a reference income level will emerge at the centre of the discussion in the next chapter.

Notes

1 The original distributions were A = (1, 2, 3, 4) and B = (1.5, 1.5, 2.5, 4.5). Notice that this means that neither can be derived from the other in terms of a sequence of richer-to-poorer transfers, so that A and B cannot be compared on the basis of the transfer principle alone, for example.

2 Notice that, whilst a measure cannot display the properties of scale independence and translation independence at the same time (as we pointed out on page 13), the variance is a nice example of a measure that happens to satisfy scale and translation invariance at the same time.

3 The argument generalises to the n-person case. Corresponding to equations (6.1) and (6.2) the critical proportions for dividing the sum $\$Y$ in this case would be given by

$$y_i = \frac{Y \, x_i t + 1 - t}{n \, \mu t + 1 - t}$$

where $Y = \Sigma_{i=1}^{n} y_i$ and $\mu = (1/n)\Sigma_{i=1}^{n} x_i$.

4 See Bossert and Pfingsten (1990).

5 The reason for this is that these cases cannot be applied to maps that have a coverage of all positive incomes without generating a logical contradiction.

6 Once again, although we provide within the table a summary of the questions posed, the original wording should be consulted in appendix B (p. 143).

7 These are freely adapted from Temkin (1986, pp. 108–10). Remember that we are retelling his story 'backwards'. See also Temkin (1993).

8 One small point on terminology should be noted. The anonymity principle that we have discussed extensively in chapter 5 is sometimes referred to as the 'symmetry assumption', because of the mathematical property of the social welfare function that this principle implies. This, of course, has nothing to do with the symmetry property that we are talking about here.

9 The only difference is that to make the diagram smooth both figures have been drawn for the case where there is a much larger number of persons: $n = 50$.

10 In this case the inequality measure would be given by

$$1 - \frac{n}{\sum_{i=1}^{n} \frac{\mu}{x_i}}$$

See appendix A for general definitions.

11 Notice that there are some scale-independent non-decomposable indices which exhibit the symmetry property, for example the Gastwirth index (appendix A, p. 136).

12 Although in this questionnaire we did not test whether individuals regarded the implications of income reduction in a way consistent with those of income growth, this point was checked in questionnnaire A1 (see chapter 4).

7 Poverty

7.1 Introduction

Thinking about inequality usually invites, at least in passing, thinking about poverty. It seems reasonable to suppose that people who are sensitive to inequality are not going to be indifferent to the existence of poverty, nor vice versa. This suggests that there may be considerable advantage in pursuing an approach to the analysis of poverty comparisons that is similar to those of inequality or social welfare comparisons. In this chapter we will examine how the issue of poverty may be addressed using the techniques that we applied to the subject of inequality in chapter 4. Two steps are involved.

First we need to make precise what we mean by 'poverty' in principle. As with the theoretical approach to inequality that we described in chapter 2 this step resolves into imputing meaning to a type of distributional comparison. To do this, we again introduce a system of axioms by which such comparisons may coherently be made, in this case the axioms that are sometimes used to provide a formal basis for commonly used poverty measures. Once this system of axioms is established we examine some basic propositions about poverty comparisons using this system.

The second step is to investigate whether the standard approach, based upon these axioms, appears to give a 'reasonable' picture of poverty comparisons, one that is in accord with the way poverty judgments commonly appear to be formed. As with chapters 4 to 6 we shall again examine the problem of framing a questionnaire investigation on this subject and report on our respondents' views about poverty.

7.2 What does 'poverty' mean?

The question 'What is poverty?' is virtually as large and as unwieldy as the question 'What is inequality?' which underlay the discussion of so much of the previous chapters. Some of the insights of the analysis of the previous chapters on inequality and social welfare can be used to make the question less unwieldy and to provide a coherent account of the issues involved in ranking income distributions according to poverty criteria. But more is involved.

In the real world, inequality and poverty are often found in the same places, have similar underlying causes, and grow or diminish together. However, in principle, inequality and poverty are two different things: the presence of the one does not logically imply the presence of the other.

Of course, it is true that in *some* respects inequality and poverty will touch on issues in common. The two types of analysis draw upon similar ethical concerns and logical problems, and in many cases raise similar issues of comparison of income distributions. Furthermore, in the modern literature on the analysis of income distribution, similar types of statistical tools have been developed for poverty and for inequality analysis, based on similar sets of axioms. But even where there is common ground, there may be a fundamental difference between the bases for interpretation of income distributions in terms of poverty and in terms of inequality. For example, in a large population take two poor persons whose incomes are different. If the two poor persons were to pool their incomes and share equal misery we might argue that inequality has decreased, and perhaps that poverty has decreased too. On the other hand, if the income of the 'richer' of these two is just brought down to the level of the other, then it is arguable that while inequality may have fallen, poverty has increased.

Given this sort of clear difference in interpretation of the facts about income distribution it is a good idea to take a look at the principles of poverty measurement, independently of our previous discussion of inequality analysis.[1] The essential components of poverty measurement can be reduced to three:

- the fundamental partition of the population into the poor and the non-poor;
- the way in which persons are to be identified individually as poor or non-poor;
- the way in which information about the income distribution of the poor and the non-poor is to be used.

Each of these steps has an influence on the way in which we modify the questionnaire approach to deal with this economic issue. Let us look at them in turn.

Partitioning the population

The first step is illustrated schematically in figure 7.1. Imagine that the population is arranged according to one or more observable personal attributes: these attributes could include various indicators of resources and of needs. In principle, we could partition the population according to any of those attributes (males-versus-females, different regions or occupational groupings and so on), and then adopt an approach similar to the kind of 'accounting' framework for the analy-

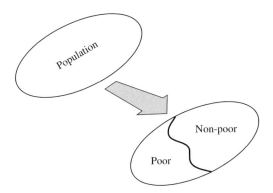

Figure 7.1. A fundamental partition of the population.

sis of inequality that we discussed on page 16. However, more importantly, we could try to choose a fundamental partition of the population that, according to the resources and needs attributes that we have selected, will neatly categorise every actual or hypothetical member of the population as 'poor' or 'non-poor', according to his economic status and other relevant characteristics.

Identifying the poor

Once the criterion for dividing up the population is determined then any one person's poverty status can be determined. Here it is useful to use a small amount of mathematical notation to introduce a key concept of individual poverty, the income gap. This is illustrated in figure 7.2. As in chapter 4, let x denote a person's income, measured in whatever units of currency are appropriate, so that, for our two arbitrarily chosen members of the population, Irene's income is x_i and Janet's income is x_j (in this case we shall assume that they are both poor). We shall write the poverty-line income as z and average (arithmetic mean) income as μ, where both of these are measured in the same currency units as before. If Irene's income is below the poverty line then the poverty gap for her income is just the difference between her income and the poverty line ($g_i = z - x_i$); and if Irene's income is on or above the poverty line then her gap is counted as zero ($g_i = 0$): the gap can never be negative. There are then three basic ways of characterising an individual's poverty status:

- a simple 'yes/no' as to whether the person's income x falls short of z;
- the person's actual income x;
- the poverty gap for the person, g.

Using information about the distribution

In principle, each of the three pieces of information about the person's status could be incorporated into the final step of poverty measurement. This involves

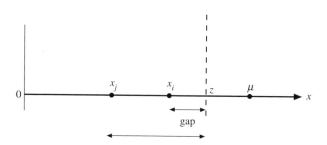

Figure 7.2. The poverty line, incomes and poverty gaps.

some type of aggregation rule covering the poverty status indicators for each member of the population.

So why does poverty analysis raise complicated questions? The answer to this can be found in the three-stage breakdown of the problem that we have just reviewed. Firstly, the partition itself may be ambiguous: there is considerable room for debate as to what should determine the poverty line, in principle, and how it should be adjusted through time. Secondly, it is not always very clear what should be the appropriate choice from the information that is available in practice about each person: should we use income or expenditure, or perhaps some measure of personal wealth, for the categorisation of each individual? Thirdly, although there seems to be an obvious 'solution' as to how to aggregate information about individuals, the answer is in fact not obvious at all.

Let us take this last point a little further. The main point at issue is: how should we count the poor? We might be tempted to brush aside the question and say that the way to count the poor is just to count the number of mouths to be fed or bodies to be housed. This line of thought is illustrated in figure 7.3: on the vertical axis we have a simple scale used to evaluate poverty for each person; the evaluation is done on the simple 'yes/no' basis, so that if the person's income falls below z the evaluation is 1, otherwise it is 0. If we work out the overall poverty count in the population using this approach, then the exercise yields a well-known poverty index, the simple (normalised) *head count*:

$$\text{head count} = \frac{\text{number of the poor}}{\text{population}}$$

But it is also a valid position to say that, in counting the poor, proper attention should be given to the depth of poverty of individual poor people, not just to the fact of whether they are poor or not.[2] This approach then counts the poor by evaluating each person's poverty in proportion to his poverty gap (see figure 7.4). Following this route yields the *poverty deficit* as a measure of overall poverty:

$$\text{poverty deficit} = \frac{\text{average poverty gap}}{\text{poverty line}}$$

It is not difficult to see that the two different ways of counting the poor represented by figures 7.3 and 7.4 can lead to contradictory results: if an 'anti-poverty

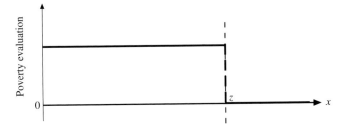

Figure 7.3. Counting the poor (1): all the poor are equal.

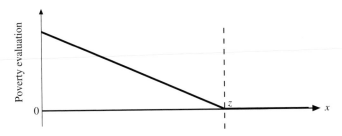

Figure 7.4. Counting the poor (2): poverty is proportional to poverty gap.

programme' lifts the incomes of a very few from just below the poverty line to just above the poverty line, while at the same time cutting the incomes of a large number of the very poor by a substantial amount, then the head-count measure will decrease (poverty falls?) while at the same time the poverty-deficit measure will increase (poverty rises?).

However, that is not the end of the matter. There may also be a case for a more complicated method of counting the poor: one that takes into account the dispersion of incomes amongst the poor. This can be done by evaluating the poverty status of each person i in a way that is dependent on either the person's income x_i or the poverty gap g_i, but which is not proportional to the poverty gap. One particular example of such a scheme is illustrated in figure 7.5, but in principle there are indefinitely many ways of drawing such a 'counting-the-poor' scheme.

Obviously all this is bound to introduce further complexity, so why do it? The short answer is that the two standard approaches that we have considered – the head count and the poverty deficit – suffer from what may be a conceptual flaw. Irrespective of whether they contradict each other in practice, they unquestionably provide only *ad hoc* answers to the question 'What is poverty?'. It has been argued that, as with inequality, a more reasonable approach to the subject would be to found the analysis explicitly upon a set of axioms that give meaning directly to poverty comparisons:[3] then a poverty-count scheme such as that depicted in figure 7.5 will not be something that has just been pulled out of the air, but will be derived directly from the agreed set of poverty axioms.

This argument suggests two things. Firstly, the welfare criteria that we explained and discussed in chapter 5 will also apply here, with the proviso that

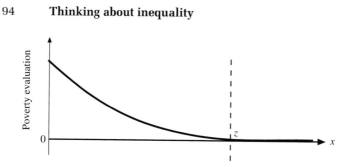

Figure 7.5. Counting the poor (3): sensitivity to inequality amongst the poor.

the scope of their application may be affected by the fundamental partition. Secondly, as we have suggested earlier in this chapter, the suitability or otherwise of these axioms may be susceptible of investigation using the same methodology as that which we outlined in chapter 3.

7.3 The poverty questionnaires

Because the modern approach to poverty measurement is founded explicitly upon an axiomatic base, it makes sense to use this base in designing a question-naire approach to poverty comparisons. As with the studies of inequality and social welfare in chapters 2 to 6 we sought to clarify whether the formal approach to the subject that has become received wisdom corresponds well with the way lay people perceive poverty. The next step is obviously to consider whether there are any special difficulties which have to be surmounted in trying to interpret poverty issues through a set of attitude questions.

There are two particular problems which cannot be avoided. The first is central to the questionnaire study of poverty, as opposed to inequality. It is that a frame of reference has to be given to those who are invited to make judgments or com-parisons. The reason is that at the heart of the poverty comparison is the funda-mental partition of figure 7.1 which requires the specification of some level of personal or family resources in order to construct the poverty line. This could be comparatively simple – for example, a rule-of-thumb poverty line of \$1 a day is sometimes used to motivate international concern for the poor (World Bank 1990) – or it could be based upon detailed budget studies of particular groups in the target population[4] or upon an analysis of the economic and social functions that are permitted by low incomes in a variety of economic circumstances.[5] Alternatively the criterion for the poverty line may be determined by reference to some statistic of the whole distribution: for example, the threshold level of income could be tied to some proportion of mean or median income.[6] Finally, rather than singling out one particular poverty line, it may be appropriate to specify just a range within which we are confident that the poverty line lies, as illustrated in figure 7.6, where $(\underline{z}, \bar{z})$ are the end points of an 'interval' of possible values within which the unspecified, or unspecifiable, poverty line z is supposed to lie.[7]

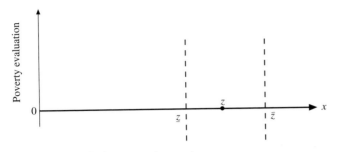

Figure 7.6. A poverty interval.

The second problem is that amongst the collection of axioms that has appeared over the years as being reasonable properties for poverty measures there are a number of internal contradictions: it has been shown that it is just not possible to produce a coherent poverty ordering that simultaneously respects all of the supposedly basic criteria for poverty comparisons. In this respect the position is different from that of inequality analysis where the transfer principle is usually taken as basic, and then the class of inequality measures is narrowed down by invoking a number of other not quite so basic criteria: decomposability, the population principle, scale or translation independence, and so on. The implication of this is that either one has to work with a variety of measures that maybe mutually contradictory in their poverty diagnosis, or one has to drop one or more of the 'basic' criteria and work with a specialised subclass of poverty measures.

One further issue should be mentioned. The relationship that may exist in principle between poverty and inequality raises the question of whether people perceive the common ground of the two subjects in the same sort of way. So, where practicable, it is a good idea to present the poverty and the inequality questions in a format that permits easy comparison[8] of the responses.

In view of the central importance of the partitioning of the population at the poverty line, there are two fundamental types of question to be investigated. We have used a specialised questionnaire for each of them:

- Questions relating to alternative distributions relative to a given poverty line. These are dealt with in questionnaire P1 (appendix B, pp. 164–7).
- Questions relating to the nature of the poverty line itself. These are dealt with in questionnaire P2 (appendix B, pp. 168–70).

We will deal with each of these in the next two sections.

7.4 Income distributions and poverty

Once again we have a problem of how to compare income distributions. We need to look afresh at some of the principles that we have encountered before in this

```
     In Alfaland there are two regions which have different
     levels   of  income.   All  the people of Alfaland  are
     identical in every respect other than their incomes. The
     level of income which ensures a supply of basic needs
     anywhere in Alfaland is 15 Alfadollars.

     In each of the ten following questions you are asked to
     compare two distributions of income - one for each region.
     Please indicate the region in which you consider poverty to
     be greater by circling A or B. If you consider that poverty
     is the same in the two regions then circle both A and B.

1)   A = (4,8,12,30,40,50,66)        B = (4,9,12,30,40,50,66)

2)   A = (4,8,12,30,40,50,66)        B = (4,9,11,30,40,50,66)

3)   A = (4,8,12,30,66,50,40)        B = (12,8,4,30,40,50,66)

4)   A = (4,8,12,30,40,50,66)        B = (4,4,8,8,12,12,30,30,
                                          40,40,50,50,66,66)

5)   A = (4,8,12,30,40,50,66)        B = (5,6,13,30,40,50,66)

6)   A = (4,7,8,12,30,40,50,53,66)   B = (5,6,7,13,30,40,50,53,66)

7)   A = (4,8,12,30,40,50,66)        B = (4,8,12,30,140,150,166)

8)   A = (4,8,12,30,40,50,66)        B = (4,8,12,20,30,40,50,66)

9)   A = (4,8,12,30,40,50,66)        B = (4,8,12,30,40,50,66,100)

10)  A = (4,8,12,30,40,50,66)        B = (4,8,12,14,30,40,50,66)
                                                \...Continued
```

Figure 7.7. Numerical problems in the first poverty questionnaire.

book, but that should now be reinterpreted in the context of poverty. Because most of the principles will be reasonably familiar from the discussion of chapter 2 and chapter 5 it is not necessary to discuss them exhaustively. So what we shall do is introduce each one, explain the relationship (if any) to the principles of social welfare and inequality analysis, and then examine the results from the P1 poverty questionnaire. As we have just mentioned, for the moment we set aside the problem of the poverty line itself.

Figure 7.7 shows how the issue was presented to the respondents and the numerical problems that were used to draw inferences about their views on some of the basic principles of poverty analysis. Notice the preamble which specifies a 'basic needs' income level which can serve as a *de facto* poverty line. In this way we sidestep the issues of partitioning the population into poor and non-poor and of identifying which individuals are in poverty. This is considered further later.

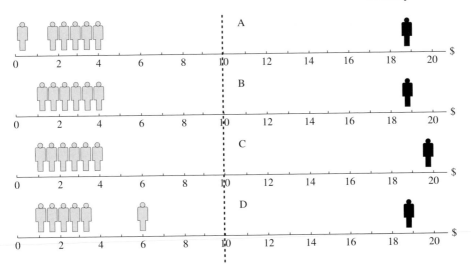

Figure 7.8. Weak monotonicity (note: B→C is irrelevant).

Monotonicity

We have already encountered this principle in chapter 5 (p. 49), but now we have to rephrase it slightly: in the context of poverty this refers to the issue of what happens to measured poverty when the income of a *poor person* is increased. Income increases amongst the rich are not relevant to the specification of this axiom, but we shall have more to say about them when we come to the 'Focus' axiom below. We could illustrate this schematically by modifying figure 5.3 so as to get figure 7.8.

In order to sharpen the analysis we have concentrated upon a particular version of the axiom – 'weak monotonicity' – in which we restrict attention to cases where the recipient of the income increase remains poor after his income has been increased: we do not attempt to investigate the case where the income increase is so great as to lift the person's income above the poverty line *z* (in figure 7.8 none of the persons crosses the heavy broken line). In this way we obtain a clear view of the distinction between cases such as figures 7.4 and 7.5, where the monotonicity axiom applies (increasing the income of any poor person will, by itself, reduce poverty) and the case of figure 7.3 where increasing a poor person's income only reduces poverty if the person crosses the poverty line.

The numerical problem that focuses on this issue is question 1 (see the extract in figure 7.7). The verbal question is given in figure 7.9. Notice that we posed it in the form of a comparison of two regions, rather than as a 'before-and-after' question involving time, to try to avoid the problem of status quo bias: this setting seems to be important.

The responses to the two types of question are presented in table 7.1. In this and other tables we have used a shorthand for presenting the answers to the

11) Suppose there are two regions A and B which have almost
     identical income distribution;the only exception is that a
     particular person *i* in region B has a higher income than
     the corresponding person *i* in region A. In both regions
     the income of person *i* is less than the level that ensures
     a supply of basic needs.

   a)   *Poverty in region A is higher.*

   b)   *The relative position of other people is also different in
          A and B; therefore we cannot say, a priori, in which
          region poverty is greater.*

   c)   *Neither of the above*

In the light of the above would you want to change your answer to
question 1? If so, please note your new response ("A" or "B" or "A
and B") here:

Figure 7.9. The monotonicity question.

numerical questions; so the response 'the distribution in A exhibits higher poverty than the distribution in B' is summarised as 'poverty falls'. The way to read table 7.1 is as follows: the right-hand column gives the percentages of the three different types of response that could be made to the numerical problem; the bottom row gives the percentages for the various responses to the verbal question. The cells in the main part of the table give the detailed breakdown by both numerical and verbal responses: so, for example, 17% of the combined sample indicated both that poverty was higher in distribution A than in distribution B (numerical part) and that the result of an increase in the income of a poor person would depend on the incomes of others (verbal part). As far as the numerical questions are concerned the main point that emerges is similar to the result that we found repeatedly in the case of the transfer principle in the inequality and social welfare contexts (chapters 3 and 5). In comparing distribution B with distribution A the addition to incomes in the numerical example was not made to the poorest individual. So the income gap between the poorest and some other poor people would actually increase under a hypothetical change from distribution A to distribution B. It is perhaps not surprising, therefore, to find that 30% of the respondents indicated that this change in the distribution leaves poverty unchanged. When verbal responses are considered the picture becomes more complicated: a smaller proportion of the population concurs with the monotonicity principle when it is stated verbally rather than numerically (44% as against 64%) but this is not surprising because of the role of the extra option provided for the verbal responses. It appears from the top centre of table 7.1 that 17% of the whole sample considered that although poverty fell for the particular numerical example given in question 1 of the questionnaire, the issue of whether an income increase reduces poverty generally would depend on the income of others. As a general rule, therefore, the monotonicity principle does not receive overwhelming support.

Table 7.1. *What happens to poverty if a poor person gets $1 more income?*
(Percentage responses)

| | | Verbal (q. 11) | | | |
		'Poverty falls'	'Depends on others'	'Stays the same'	All
Numerical (q. 1)	'Poverty falls'	35	17	11	64
	'Poverty rises'	2	2	2	6
	'Stays the same'	7	11	11	30
	All	44	31	24	

Note: Results are based on responses to questions 1 and 11 of questionnaire P1($N=486$).

The transfer principle

We have, of course, encountered the transfer principle many times before; but once again the interpretation of this principle in the context of poverty analysis has to be modified somewhat from the way in which we encountered it in chapter 2. The idea is that if there is a small income transfer from Irene to Janet, then measured poverty falls as long as (a) Irene is richer than Janet and (b) Irene was poor before the transfer took place. This assumption is intimately associated with the shape of the poverty evaluation curve that we introduced in figure 7.5. To see why, consider figure 7.10 which takes figure 7.5 one stage further. Consider the evaluation of the economic positions of Irene and Janet with incomes x_i and x_j (which can be read off the vertical axis in figure 7.10) before and after an equalising income transfer. The average of their poverty evaluation is given by 0B before the transfer takes place, and by 0A after the transfer takes place. Obviously a convex evaluation curve such as that depicted in figure 7.10 implies that poverty falls if there is a richer to poorer transfer amongst the poor. Spreading the misery of poverty equally reduces poverty.

Once again we focus upon a 'weak' version of the transfer principle in that, as with our approach to the monotonicity axiom, we do not consider income comparisons in which the implied income transfer causes an individual to cross the poverty line; this means that both donor and recipient are poor before and after transfer.

It is clear from table 7.2 that agreement with the transfer principle is lower – about a quarter – than in the case of inequality analysis or social welfare. There are sound theoretical reasons for expecting this to be so. Atkinson has pointed out that the case for applying the transfer principle to poverty analysis is not clear-cut because of the possibility of alternative interpretations of the meaning of poverty.[9]

From the right-hand column of table 7.2 we can see that 'poverty stays the same' was the clear winner amongst the responses to the numerical question (62%). About a quarter of the population agreed with the transfer principle when

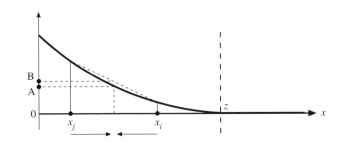

Figure 7.10. Income transfers and the poverty count.

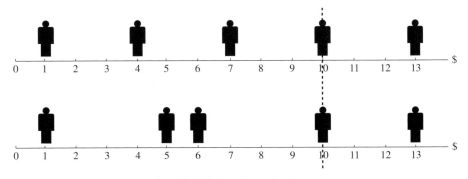

Figure 7.11. Transfer principle (weak version).

stated in terms of the numerical problem and only 22% of respondents supported the principle in the verbal part of the questionnaire; these proportions are very much lower than for the comparable issue posed in the context of income inequality (see chapter 4) or of social welfare (chapter 5). Furthermore only 11% agree with the transfer principle expressed in both its numerical and its verbal forms; and on this issue it happens that the proportion of respondents who changed their minds was very low. It seems fair to say that the transfer principle is decisively rejected as a principle for poverty measurement.

Anonymity

The interpretation of the anonymity axiom is virtually the same as that used in the discussion of social welfare and inequality – see page 51 in chapter 5. In other words, relabelling of the individuals in the population should have no effect on measured poverty. However, one should note that the implications of the axiom are somewhat stronger in the poverty case than in the discussion of social welfare: acceptance of the anonymity axiom implies that 'history does not matter', so that after a permutation of incomes we should be unconcerned about the relative positions before the permutation, *even if some individuals cross the poverty line during the permutation.*

Remarkably the numerical support for the anonymity principle in the context

Table 7.2. *What happens to poverty if $1 is taken from fairly poor Irene and given to very poor Janet? (Percentage responses)*

| | | Verbal (q. 12) | | | | |
		'Poverty falls'	'Poverty rises'	'Depends on others'	'None of these'	All
Numerical (q. 2)	'Poverty falls'	11	2	7	4	26
	'Poverty rises'	2	2	4	1	11
	'Stays the same'	9	3	29	19	62
	All	22	8	41	25	

Notes:
'Others' here means 'non-poor'. The 'none of these' column is required because the labelling of the first three columns is a simplification of the question put: in each case a specific reason for the change in poverty was suggested. Results are based on responses to questions 2 and 12 of questionnaire P1 ($N=486$).

Table 7.3. *If we permute the incomes, does poverty stay the same? (Percentage responses.)*

| | | Verbal (q. 13) | | |
		'Agree'	'Disagree'	All
Numerical (q. 3)	'Agree'	48	31	82
	'Disagree'	3	12	16
	All	53	44	

Note: Results are based on responses to questions 3 and 13 of questionnaire P1 ($N=486$).

of poverty is almost exactly the same as it was in the case of inequality (82% as against 83%) – see table 7.3. It is also clear from table 7.3 that agreement with the principle falls off dramatically when we move from numerical representation to stating the issue verbally;[10] also that fewer than half of the respondents agree with the principle both numerically and verbally. This pattern of responses is understandable given the way in which we posed the questions: the numerical questions depicted a rearrangement of incomes *among the poor*, and *among the non-poor*; the verbal question placed no restriction on the possible permutations, and so allowed for the possibility that people cross the poverty line as well as being reranked in the distribution. So if people are concerned about poverty histories rather than just poverty snapshots, we would expect them to respond in this way.

Population replication

The idea of the population principle is inherited directly from the analysis of inequality and of social welfare. However, in this context the *a priori* basis for the principle is less clear: one could plausibly argue that if the distribution is

Table 7.4. *What happens to poverty if we clone the economy? (Percentage responses)*

| | | Verbal (q. 14) | | | |
		'Poverty falls'	'Depends on others'	'Stays the same'	All
	'Poverty falls'	4	6	7	18
Numerical (q. 4)	'Poverty rises'	3	15	12	31
	'Stays the same'	2	7	38	49
	All	9	29	57	

Note: Results are based on responses to questions 4 and 14 of questionnaire P1 ($N=486$).

replicated (so that there are exactly double the numbers of poor and non-poor) then poverty is doubled. The issue is essentially whether poverty comparisons are to be made in relative or absolute terms with respect to the size of the population.

As we can see from table 7.4, support for the population principle is rather lower when expressed in terms of poverty rather than inequality (49% agreed with the principle when the issue was presented numerically in the poverty context, whereas 58% agreed when the issue was presented numerically in the context of inequality; when the issue was presented verbally we obtained 57% agreement in the poverty context and 66% in the inequality setting).[11] The interpretation of this seems to be that in assessing poverty – as opposed to inequality – people think much more in absolute rather than relative terms.

Population decomposability

The interpretation of decomposability is essentially the same as that which we explained in chapters 2 and 5 in connection with inequality and social welfare. Briefly the idea is that if we say that distribution A exhibits more poverty than another distribution B (with the same mean and the same number of persons) then we should say that distribution A' exhibits more poverty than another distribution B', where A' is formed by merging A with distribution C that has the same mean and B' is likewise formed by merging B with C. In addition we require that A, B and C all have the same poverty line.

Remarkably, once again we find the '60–40' pattern of support for the decomposability axiom that we found in the cases of inequality and of social welfare analysis. However, in the context of poverty the level of agreement with the principle is somewhat higher.

The focus axiom

The issue raised by the focus axiom is this: should the concept of poverty be sensitive to information about income distribution amongst the non-poor? Assume

Table 7.5. *Population decomposability (percentage responses)*

| | | | Verbal (q. 15) | | |
		'Agree'	'Disagree: depends on the distribution'	'Disagree: some other reason'	All
	'Agree'	31	17	8	62
Numerical (q. 5, q. 6)	'Disagree'	15	14	6	37
	All	46	32	14	

Note: Results are based on responses to questions 5, 6 and 15 of questionnaire P1 (*N* = 486).

Table 7.6. *What happens to poverty if the 'rich' get richer? (Percentage responses)*

| | | Verbal (q. 16) | | | | |
		'Poverty falls'	'Poverty rises'	'Stays the same'	'None of these'	All
	'Poverty falls'	9	18	17	4	55
Numerical (q. 7)	'Poverty rises'	2	10	3	1	16
	'Stays the same'	2	3	18	3	28
	All	13	31	38	8	

Note: Results are based on responses to questions 7 and 16 of questionnaire P1 (*N* = 486).

that the distribution of income below the poverty line is fixed, and that the number of persons on or above the poverty line is fixed: if the incomes of those on or above the poverty line were to change, should this affect the level of poverty, or poverty comparisons? Supporters of the focus axiom would argue not, but there are grounds for challenging this position. Do the poor compare themselves with all others, including those who are above the poverty line? Should the size of the poverty gap be compared with total income in the economy? Is it relevant to consider the proportion of income of the non-poor that would be required to eliminate the poverty gap? If the answer to any of these questions is 'yes' or 'maybe', then we are calling into question the focus axiom.

In presenting the issue in the questionnaire we took care to specify that the assumed poverty line rose along with the increase in income experienced by some of the non-poor. The views of our respondents, summarised in table 7.6, are clear. Support for the axiom was very weak: 28% on numerical questions alone, 38% on verbal questions alone, and 18% for both numerical and verbal questions together. The view that the poor compare themselves to all others was supported by 31%. We may conclude that information about the 'rich' does matter when assessing the extent of poverty.

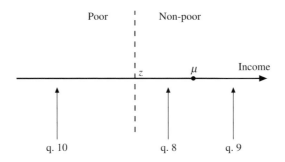

Figure 7.12. Positions for an additional population member.

New population members

Now for an issue for which there is no clear counterpart in the conventional approach to the analysis of economic inequality and social welfare: what happens if the population grows, not through balanced replication, nor by merging with another multi-person distribution, but by the introduction of a single individual at some point in the distribution? Two sub-issues immediately arise: the impact on perceived poverty of a new poor person and the impact of the addition of an individual amongst the non-poor group. We then further subdivide this second issue so as to distinguish between new individuals who have an income above the poverty line z but below mean income μ (in our numerical exercise the mean equals the median which is 30 Alfadollars), and those whose incomes are greater than μ – see figure 7.12.

It is commonly suggested that a poverty index should have the property that adding new members with incomes below the poverty line should result in an increase in measured poverty, and that adding new members with incomes above the poverty line should decrease measured poverty. However, this is not self-evident; for example, one could imagine a good case being made for the measured level of poverty being insensitive to additional members of the non-poor. What of the views of our student respondents?

The responses to the numerical questions are shown in table 7.7. Notice the close match between the responses when the question was framed firstly in terms of individuals whose incomes were above the poverty line but below the average (middle row) and secondly in terms of individuals whose incomes were above the average (bottom row). On the basis of the numerical responses there is clearly reasonable support (about half of the sample) for the view that the 'immigration' of non-poor people should reduce measured poverty. However, the responses to the corresponding verbal question (table 7.8) show considerable dispersion: respondents seemed to be less confident of this principle when expressed in words rather than a numerical example.

Now let us look at the effect of introducing an additional poor person to the population. The results appear to be straightforward, in terms of both numerical

Table 7.7. *The effect of introducing one new person (percentage responses)*

What happens if the person's income is . . .	'Poverty falls'	'Poverty rises'	'Poverty stays same'
below z (q. 10)	27	57	14
above z, below μ (q. 8)	46	19	34
above μ (q. 9)	53	17	28

Note: Numerical responses only. Based on responses to questions 8, 9 and 10 of questionnaire P1 ($N = 486$).

Table 7.8. *What happens to poverty if there is one more non-poor person?* (*Percentage responses*)

Suppose a person whose income is above the basic needs level is allowed to immigrate to a region, that there is no change in the incomes of all others and that the basic needs level in this region remains unchanged.

Poverty goes up	14
Poverty goes down	18
Poverty remains the same	38
We cannot say whether poverty goes up, goes down or remains the same unless we know the exact income distributions	14
None of the above	4

Note: Based on responses to question 17 of questionnaire P1 ($N = 486$).

Table 7.9. *What happens to poverty if there is one more poor person?* (*Percentage responses*)

		Verbal (q. 18)		
		'Poverty rises'	'Depends on distribution'	'Neither of these'	All
	'Poverty rises'	37	8	5	57
Numerical (q. 10)	'Poverty falls'	14	6	4	27
	'Stays the same'	7	4	2	14
	All	59	19	10	

Note: Results are based on responses to questions 10 and 18 of questionnaire P1 ($N = 486$).

responses (top row of table 7.7) and verbal responses (bottom row of table 7.9): almost 60% of the respondents agree that doing so would increase measured poverty. However, the proportion of the population which express the view that adding to the numbers of the poor increases poverty both in their responses to numerical problems and in the verbal part of the questionnaire is rather modest (37%) – see the top left entry in table 7.9.

In Alfaland there are two regions A and B. All the
people of Alfaland are identical in every respect
other than their incomes. The people of region A
consider that the level of income which ensures a
supply of basic needs in their region is 10 Alfa-
dollars, and the people of region B consider that the
basic-needs income level in their region is 20 Alfa-
dollars. Prices in A and in B are the same.

In each of the three following questions you are
asked to compare two distributions of income - one for
each region. Please indicate the region in which you
consider poverty to be greater by circling A or B. If
you consider that poverty is the same in the two
regions then circle both A and B.

1)   A = (4,8,12,20,24,32,40)   B = (4,8,12,20,24,32,40)

2)   A = (4,8,12,20,24,32,40)   B = (8,16,24,40,48,64,80)

3)   A = (4,8,12,20,24,32,40)   B = (14,18,22,30,34,42,50)

Figure 7.13. Numerical problems in the second poverty questionnaire.

Poverty perceptions and the poverty line

Thus far, all of the issues that we have considered – all of the problems that we have set the respondents, and all of the questions that we have posed – have been predicated on the assumption that the 'basic needs income level' (which may be interpreted as a poverty line) is fixed and that all the action in the income distribution comparisons takes place below that income level. This has been done so as to integrate the discussion of poverty analysis closely with that of inequality and social welfare analysis. It is time to move on from this assumption to a more basic question about the nature of poverty.

When implementing the questionnaire approach in the context of the poverty line we face an obvious problem: how much of a hint to give to the respondents about the nature of the poverty line. After all, one of the things it would be nice to know from the respondents is the concept of the poverty line that they would use if invited to make poverty comparisons. We certainly want to know whether it is viewed as appropriate to shift the poverty line as all incomes grow.[12] Ideally these views should emerge as general principles, not as particular reactions to a special set of political circumstances: it is important not to put the poverty comparisons within a specific historical or social context, as we discussed in chapter 3 (p. 26).

These considerations shaped the design of our specialised poverty questionnaire that focused on poverty issues with a variable poverty line.[13] Extracts from it are presented in figures 7.13 and 7.14: as can be seen, the respondents were

4)   Suppose two regions A and B have the same income
       distribution. Suppose the level of income which
       ensures a supply of basic needs is higher in region B.

       a)   *It is clear that poverty in B is greater than in A.*

       b)   *The basic-needs income level does not effect the level
             of poverty. So poverty is the same in A and B.*

       c)   *Neither of the above.*

       ...   .

5)   Suppose the real income of each person and the basic
       needs income level are doubled

       a)   *Poverty increases*

       b)   *Poverty decreases*

       c)   *Poverty remains the same*

       d)   *The direction of change of poverty depends on   initial
             and final levels of real income.*

Figure 7.14. Extract from the verbal questions in the second poverty
                            questionnaire.

introduced to the idea of a specific 'basic needs' income level but were not
prompted as to whether this income level corresponds to a poverty line z. Once
again we examined the issues both in terms of the respondents' assessments of
simple numerical examples and of their answers to multiple-choice verbal questions, and have cross-tabulated the responses to the numerical and verbal questions on each issue. The presentation of the results follows approximately the
form of the questionnaire with which the respondents were presented.

What happens if basic needs increase?

Perhaps the first question that ought to be asked is 'how can basic needs
increase'? Evidently there could be physical changes in the technology of the
economy, or its environment – for example, affecting the climate, or the costs of
shopping – which might impinge on the resources required to achieve any given
standard of living. Alternatively these changes might be in the assessment by
society of the money income or resources required to meet the required living
standard irrespective of any physical changes. Evidently, too, these changes could
occur independently of any change in the incomes of individuals.

   We did not attempt to spell this out in detail in the wording of the questionnaire, nor did we attempt to describe a process of change of basic needs. In questions 1 and 4 respondents were asked to judge the two situations in which there

Table 7.10. *What happens to poverty when the basic needs income level increases?* *(Percentage responses)*

| | | Verbal (q. 4) | | | |
		'Poverty rises'	'Basic needs irrelevant'	'Can't say'	All
Numerical (q. 1)	'Poverty falls'	4	1	4	9
	'Poverty rises'	44	5	10	60
	'Stays the same'	15	6	8	30
	All	64	13	23	

Note: Results are based on responses to questions 1 and 4 of questionnaire P2 ($N = 340$).

was the same list of personal incomes (x_1, x_2, x_3,...) but two different 'basic needs' income levels, as considered by people in regions A and B of the mythical country Alfaland. The right-hand column of table 7.10 reveals that whilst a majority of respondents agrees that the higher basic needs level implies higher poverty there is a substantial dissenting minority who appear to think that changing the basic needs level should not affect measured poverty. The responses to question 4 (bottom row of table 7.10) throw some light on this: here respondents were asked directly whether a higher basic needs income level implies, *ceteris paribus*, higher poverty. Where respondents had doubts they were expressed in terms of the 'neither of the above' responses which may indicate that more information would be required before an explicit judgment could be offered.[14]

The question arises as to why people might say that increasing the poverty line does not change poverty. Presumably the answer is that respondents are looking at poverty in some kind of absolutist or existentialist terms; in other words, judgments on poverty are perceived as separate from the administration that happens to measure poverty and to announce the poverty line. According to this view, raising the poverty line is a mere artefact of official policy or of social convention that has little bearing upon the reality of the human condition. On this evidence alone it may be the case that some people view poverty in statistical terms, and they do not read poverty along the lines of the 'basic needs' view; but we have more to say on this below.

As a final point on the responses to the matched questions 1 and 4, notice that there is little difference between the numerical and the verbal responses considered separately, although if we consider the responses together only 44% of the sample agreed both numerically and verbally with the proposition that a higher basic needs level implies higher poverty.

What happens if basic needs and incomes increase?

We now consider what happens to poverty if all income values in one distribution are scaled-up values of another distribution. In question 2, distribution B

Table 7.11. *What happens to poverty when you double incomes and basic needs?*
(Percentage responses)

		Verbal (q. 5)				
		'Poverty falls'	'Poverty rises'	'Stays the same'	'Depends on inc. levels'	All
Numerical (q. 2)	'Poverty falls'	3	8	21	6	38
	'Poverty rises'	1	2	7	1	12
	'Stays the same'	2	4	36	6	48
	All	7	14	66	13	

Note: Results are based on responses to questions 2 and 5 of questionnaire P2 ($N = 340$).

had a list of incomes ($x_1, x_2, x_3, \ldots$) that were exactly double those that appeared in distribution A, and a basic needs value that was also double that of A; question 5 put the issue in words (again see the extracts in figures 7.13 and 7.14). The results are reported in table 7.11.

In the numerical version of the question (right-hand column of table 7.11) nearly half the respondents felt that a simple doubling of all incomes and the basic needs level left measured poverty unchanged; but there was a substantial minority view (38%) that poverty decreases. From the verbal responses (bottom row of table 7.11) it appears that the reported responses come more into line with what may be considered as the 'conventional' view, in that the dissenting minority (those who think that doubling both incomes and basic needs will lead to a fall in poverty) becomes smaller when the issue is put in terms of words. However, note also from table 7.11 that the view that whether poverty has gone up or not must depend on the income level receives almost as much support as the dissenting minority view that poverty must fall.

Again, as with the results of questions 1 and 4, it is tempting to characterise the majority view as evidence of support for the Eurostat view of the poverty line (see note 6 above) whereby poverty is viewed as being linked to the population mean or some other statistic of the whole distribution. However, as argued below, this conclusion may not be legitimate.

As a final numerical experiment we considered two lists of individual incomes and basic needs levels that differ in terms of some absolute amount. Economic intuition does not provide an unambiguous suggestion as to the impact of such a shift on poverty: if $10 is added to basic needs and you give the $10 to each poor person, each poor person remains poor but has a higher percentage of total income; if the $10 were also given to each non-poor person this might be considered to be irrelevant from the point of view of the perception of poverty.

The issue addressed in question 3 and in the two parts of the related question 6 (call the second part 'question 6''')[15] is related to the concept of monotonicity, which we discussed earlier (see page 96). It is interesting to note that the verbal

Table 7.12. *Shifting incomes and the poverty line by a fixed sum (percentage responses)*

Compare A = (4, 8, 12, 20, 24, 32, 40) B = (14, 18, 22, 30, 34, 42, 50)	
Poverty higher in A	58
Poverty higher in B	22
Poverty is the same	17

Suppose we add/deduct a fixed sum to/from all incomes and the poverty line?		
	Add	Deduct
Poverty falls	9	22
Poverty rises	22	8
Poverty remains the same	62	60
Depends on initial and final income levels	7	8

Note: Results are based on responses to questions 3 and 6 of questionnaire P2 ($N = 340$).

responses to questions 6 and 6′ are reassuringly consistent in that we get almost the same percentage responses for adding or deducting $x to both incomes and the poverty line (see the bottom half of table 7.12). This implies that in making poverty comparisons *where individuals' relative positions and poverty statuses do not alter*, history does not matter.[16]

However, the results from the verbal questions do not appear to be consistent with the corresponding numerical question 3 (compare the upper and lower halves of table 7.12). In this case, eleven respondents announced a change of mind about their response to the numerical question 3, so it does not seem that misperception or misunderstanding of the question accounts for the discrepancy. However, it may be attributable to fundamental differences in view about the nature of the poverty line.

The definition of the poverty line

The discrepancy between the numerical responses to question 2 and the verbal responses to the corresponding question 5, and the discrepancy between question 3 and the corresponding questions 6 and 6′ may be explained partly by the context of the questions. The numerical questions were expressed in terms of two regions A and B with different basic needs levels, while the verbal questions spoke of income change. Other things being equal, if our respondents have a 'statistical' view of poverty then this should have yielded broadly similar results to the two types of question, whereas an absolutist approach need not have done.[17]

For this reason the responses to the final question on our questionnaire, reported in table 7.13, are particularly interesting. Here the agreement with 'basic needs' rather than the 'statistical' approach to the poverty line appears persua-

Table 7.13. *What is poverty? (Percentage responses)*

Poverty is a situation where incomes are . . .	
not enough for a supply of basic needs	72
below a level which is relative to the income distribution	
(for example 50% of the median income)	11
Neither of the above	10

Note: Results are based on responses to question 7 of questionnaire P2 ($N = 340$).

sive – 72%; the response 'related to income distribution' (the Eurostat view) scores almost the same as the response 'neither of the above'.

7.5 Conclusions: the approach to poverty comparisons

This chapter has focused upon the analysis of one of the most pressing economic and social issues of our time. It is an issue which in the real world demands prompt attention by policy-advisers and policy-makers and where questions of measurement might seem to be relatively less urgent. However, to dismiss issues of definition and measurement as unimportant would be a mistake, in that clear-sighted assessment of the nature of poverty helps in clarifying what needs to be done and the priorities to be attached to different manifestations of poverty in different circumstances.[18] If economists are to offer advice on the measurement of poverty, let alone practical help in quantifying it or in attempting to combat it, then it is as well that their theoretical and empirical constructs should be informed by some understanding of the concept of poverty as it is generally perceived.

So how should we measure poverty? As we have seen there are two types of answer to this question. The first assumes that we have an agreed poverty standard and that we know how to categorise people as poor or not poor, and then concentrates upon the way in which information about the poor is to be aggregated into a single indicator. The second focuses precisely on the issue of who is to be counted as being poor – how the line is to be drawn between the poor and the non-poor. Both types of answer have been addressed in our questionnaire studies.

The first type of answer to the question 'How should we measure poverty?' picks up some threads of thought that have run through the last few chapters, because several of the basic principles of distributional analysis are commonly applied to all three problems: inequality, social welfare and poverty. Conventional wisdom has it that the way we should measure poverty – the way we should make poverty comparisons – is essentially similar to the way we should measure inequality or social welfare. What do the responses from our questionnaires reveal in this regard? It appears that some of the standard axioms that are

Table 7.14. *Support for standard axioms in inequality, social welfare and poverty analysis (percentage responses)*

	Inequality		Social welfare		Poverty	
	Num.	Verbal	Num.	Verbal	Num.	Verbal
Monotonicity	—	—	54	55	64	44
Transfers	35	31	47	33	26	22
Anonymity	83	72	66	54	82	53
Population	58	66	66	53	49	57
Decomposability	57	40	58	37	62	46
Scale independence	51	47	—	—	48	66
Translation independence	31	35	—	—	17	62

Notes:
(1) Sources as for tables 4.8, 5.2, 5.9 and 7.1.
(2) For scale and translation independence the results for poverty are evaluated for the case where the poverty line is changed along with all other incomes.
(3) For verbal question the translation independence result refers to what happens if an addition is made to income. There is lower agreement with the principle is a deduction from income is made (28% in the case of the inequality questionnaire, 60% for the poverty questionnaire).

held in common with inequality and welfare analysis receive weaker support when presented in the context of poverty analysis: this is true of the central issues of anonymity and the transfer principle; see table 7.14. However, decomposability is more widely supported in the case of poverty than for inequality. This is perhaps not surprising since there is at the heart of the problem of poverty measurement the idea of a fundamental decomposition between the poor and the non-poor.

The second type of answer – the type that deals explicitly with the rôle of the poverty line – is by its nature rather more difficult. Where an official or other independently specified poverty line is known and recognised the issues involved in poverty comparisons can be made much more approachable. But, as we mentioned above, there are practical situations where this luxury is not available or ambiguous; the problem is particularly acute when making poverty comparisons between countries, or poverty comparisons over long periods. In such cases it might appear that the only thing to do in practice is to take a simplified relativist approach to specifying the poverty, $x\%$ of the mean or $x\%$ of the median, for example. There are obvious practical problems in implementing this approach – for example, it is often crucial what value x takes and whether the median or the mean is used. However, over and above these problems our results suggest that simple relativism may miss something essential in the underlying concept. People appear to perceive poverty and poverty comparisons in the abstract in a way that does not fit well into the $x\%$-poverty-line approach.

Notes

1 For surveys of the standard approach see Callan and Nolan (1991), Hagenaars (1986), Ravallion (1994), Seidl (1988).

2 See, for example, the recommendations in Panel on Poverty and Public Assistance (1995).

3 See, for example, Sen (1976).

4 See, for example, Panel on Poverty and Public Assistance (1995).

5 See, for example, Atkinson (1995) or Sen (1983).

6 In its comparative studies of poverty in Europe, Eurostat takes 50% of mean income as the criterion for the poverty line.

7 See, for example, Atkinson (1987).

8 Problems arise when the hypothetical income change implied in a comparison of two distributions would involve some person crossing the poverty line – see Kundu and Smith (1983).

9 'Do we wish to impose the Dalton transfer principle? Here views may differ. For those who see a minimum income as a basic right, the . . . transfer principle . . . may be irrelevant. On the other hand those viewing poverty as a continuous gradation may find the transfer principle quite acceptable' (Atkinson 1987, p. 759).

10 Cf. table 5.2. The proportion of agreement with the anonymity principle in the context of verbal questions (53%) is very similar to the corresponding figure in the social welfare study (54%), where again re-ranking seems to matter to our respondents. Notice that one group in our study is an exception; see page 120 in chapter 8.

11 For social welfare, 66% numerically, 53% verbally (see tables 4.2 and 5.5 on pages 38 and 62 respectively).

12 The issue of how the poverty line should change over time can be treated separately from the issue of whether poverty should be viewed as an absolute or a relative concept – see Sen (1983).

13 The results relate to poverty questionnaire P2 (appendix B, pp. 168–70).

14 Elsewhere when the 'neither of the above' response was explicitly offered (question 7) it did not receive such support.

15 A summary of question 6 appears in table 7.12; for full details see appendix B (p. 170).

16 Notice that the results for adding or subtracting a fixed amount here are closer than in the corresponding case of inequality; see table 4.5 on page 44.

17 For further details, see Amiel and Cowell (1997b).

18 Cf. the remark by Aldi Hagenaars (1986, p. ix): 'Poverty measurement is an important first step in a program aimed at reducing poverty; however the choice of the definition of poverty as a relative or an absolute concept may result in different measurement methods and hence different values of indices that measure the extent of poverty. A definition of poverty hence is essential for the results of poverty measurement.'

8   A cross-cultural perspective

8.1 Introduction

We have seen that the thinking about inequality practised by the economics profession may differ significantly from the thinking about inequality that is practised by others. But we might wonder whether there are substantial differences amongst people on this subject according to some criterion other than whether or not they are professional economists. For this reason it is appropriate to look at some aspects of the structure of the responses in the questionnaire-experiment studies that we have been discussing in chapters 4 to 7. As the title suggests, this is a more specialised chapter and can be skipped without loss of continuity of the argument in the rest of the book.

What do we mean by the grand term 'cross-cultural perspective'? This is just a shorthand for a systematic approach to the interpersonal and intergroup differences underlying our questionnaire-experiment programme. Obviously views about the meaning of inequality will differ according to the type of person, as will views about most things, but in addressing the question 'What determines attitudes to inequality?' it is not obvious what sort of determinants it would be reasonable to specify.

What kind of characteristics can be usefully considered in this sort of study? We might conjecture that background – such things as income and wealth, social position – is a significant aspect of 'culture' and has a role to play in determining attitudes to distributional questions. Some of these background characteristics are obviously very personal, and personalised data can be problematic. One of the main problems with personalised data in this context is that it may cause people to alter their responses if they know that they are going to be identified and that their responses will be subject to scrutiny. However, it may well be useful to look at characteristics of groups to which individuals belong, and this is why we have focused on the concept of 'culture'. Of course 'culture' is a nebulous expression, but we could try to narrow its meaning down to something specific.

The reason that this is important is that there appears to be a widespread notion that culture does matter when it comes to the consideration of distributional issues. Sometimes 'culture' is tacitly identified with 'country': for example, Ballano and Ruiz-Castillo (1992) in running a questionnaire investigation similar to our own focused principally on the comparison of the results for Spanish students with those in Amiel and Cowell (1992); their headline result was that 'contrary to the slogan of the previous [Franco] régime "Spain is *not* different"'. But of course, in general, 'country' does not equal 'culture', nor should it be assumed that a distinctive culture would make one country dramatically different from others in terms of distributional judgments. Within our sample (see table B.1) there are several cases illustrating these points: for example, is the polyglot student body at the LSE 'English'? 'British'? Representative of the UK? Or is there some other aspect of British culture that is important in shaping LSE student responses? Are the differences between, say, the universities of Bonn and Karlsruhe greater than the differences between the UK (the LSE) and Germany (Bonn)? Moreover, it could also be forcefully argued that to identify 'Israel' with a specific culture is misleading since to do so would be to ignore important potential differences between religious and non-religious universities.

Nevertheless, it is evident that 'culture' – interpreted very broadly as the universe in which a person acquires his values – may have an impact upon distributional judgments at a fundamental level. For example, it might be argued that whether a person comes from a society with an 'individualistic culture' (such as the United States) or a culture that accepts as part of the order of things a benevolent interventionist state (Sweden?) may affect not only the value that the person places on inequality relative to other social issues but also on the meaning to be given to inequality rankings when comparing income distributions.

Apart from the association with country or national background there is, as we have just indicated, a second aspect of culture which should be addressed. It may be summarised in the question 'Does preknowledge of economics or economic methods matter?' This question is distinct from the issue of whether a person has preknowledge of the analysis of income distributions. This latter issue has to do with whether a person has been taught some specific technical tools, rather than with an overall approach to distributional problems and social judgments. It is the former issue that we should principally like to address, although in practice we have to accept that it may be difficult to disentangle the two.

Our questionnaires were all completed anonymously, for reasons that we set out in chapter 3, and so we have limited information on which to base a deeper study of the pattern of responses. Although we can, and do, check internal evidence of answers to different questions by any one individual,[1] we do not have information about personal attributes such as the age or gender of respondents. In view of this we interpret the cross-cultural approach by focusing principally upon two issues that are raised by the pattern of our questionnaire studies:

differences between academic disciplines, and differences between countries and institutions. Let us consider how this information may be effectively deployed.

8.2 A statistical approach

Systematic comparisons of different subgroups of the combined sample can provide practical insights on cultural differences. It may be possible to reduce the question of cultural perspective to a series of narrowly defined statistical hypotheses. For example, it would be interesting to know if there were a significant difference between the pattern of responses of subgroup X and that of subgroup Y on certain specific issues in the questionnaire experiments.

The appropriate formal method of checking whether or not there are significant differences of this sort between subgroups is to use a chi-squared test to compare distributions of responses to the numerical questions. Suppose the results of a particular study are available for groups of respondents $i = 1, 2, \ldots, r$ and the responses can be classified into categories $j = 1, 2, \ldots, c$ where a typical element a_{ij} gives the number of observations from subgroup i in response category j. We can then construct a table with r rows (one for each subgroup) and c columns (one for each response category): for example, in the case of pairwise (X, Y) comparisons of subgroups' responses on issues with the three possible responses 'Agree', 'Disagree' and 'Strongly Disagree', we would have a 2×3 table. We can address the question of whether the pattern of responses in each of the r rows is essentially the same by computing the statistic

$$\sum_{i=1}^{r} \sum_{j=1}^{c} \frac{(a_{ij} - e_{ij})^2}{e_{ij}} \tag{8.1}$$

where e_{ij} is the expected number of observations in cell (i, j) of the table if all the subgroup response patterns were to be the same, and applying a standard test.[2]

Given the range of coverage of our student respondents in terms of countries, institutions and subject specialisations there are obviously a great many pairwise (X, Y) comparisons possible. Many of these could appear somewhat recondite to the non-specialist reader – it might not be terribly exciting to know that, let us say, the students at Tel Aviv think primarily in terms of scale independence, while those in Alabama give replies in line with translation independence. Nevertheless, it would be interesting to concentrate upon the big questions that have emerged in the preceding chapters and to see whether there are important differences between groups in terms of their attitudes towards those questions.

We do not expect there to be wide agreement about what are the 'big questions'. However, we suggest that the following programme of action would be a reasonable way of addressing the questions of cross-cultural perspective:

*   Firstly, we will focus on the main principles of distributional judgments and consider the intergroup differences of support for those principles.

- Secondly, we will examine whether the pattern of responses differs significantly as between the direct and indirect approaches to the analysis of inequality.
- Finally, we will look at the extent to which thinking about economics may influence thinking about inequality.

8.3 Principles of distributional judgments

Which principles? A brief glance through the technical material in appendix A is enough to show that there is a depressingly long list of principles (axioms) in the main fields of inequality, social welfare and poverty; in principle we might run statistical tests to compare various subgroups' responses on any of the principles in the list. Should we single out just a few of these for special treatment perhaps? The logical purist will claim – rightly – that in a true axiomatic approach no one axiom is more 'basic' than any other. The horny-handed pragmatist might well reply 'Yes, but there some axioms which appear to embody the main idea of a subject and we should concentrate on those.' On reviewing the discussion of the three interrelated fields of distributional analysis we might reasonably claim that the most important general issues are:

- the transfer principle
- monotonicity
- the use of a relative rather than an absolute poverty line.

Let us then examine the evidence of cross-cultural diversity that may lie underneath the overall results reported earlier in chapters 4, 5 and 7.

The transfer principle

As we have seen, many would consider the transfer principle to be the defining concept of inequality analysis. Remember that the principle requires that *any* pairwise poorer-to-richer income transfer will increase income inequality, irrespective of the rest of the income distribution.

Table 8.1 extends the discussion of page 40. It gives a breakdown of the responses to the first inequality questionnaire (A1) by subsample of student respondents just on the issue of the transfer principle. We report what happened both when we presented the key numerical example (which was illustrated by figures 1.1–1.3) and when we posed the issue verbally. As we can see from the left-hand side of table 8.1 we have students from five countries and eight university institutions; there is also a group of 'non-economists' at the Hebrew University of Jerusalem who were students whose principal subjects were philosophy and education.

One apparent cultural difference emerges strikingly from the verbal responses (right-hand half of the table): the economics students at the Hebrew University of Jerusalem appear to be well out of line with other groups in that their verbal

Table 8.1. *Breakdown of views on the transfer principle: direct approach (percentages)*

	N	Numerical			Verbal		
		Agree	Strongly disagree	Disagree	Agree	Strongly disagree	Disagree
North Texas	37	22	51	27	41	38	19
Southern Methodist	108	32	51	14	44	29	29
LSE	106	45	39	16	66	23	11
Bonn	356	31	45	24	54	28	15
Karlsruhe	53	45	34	19	57	30	13
Koblenz	50	46	46	8	62	26	12
Ruppin	174	33	38	29	62	24	14
Hebrew Univ. (Econ)	170	42	38	19	83	7	6
Hebrew Univ. (Non-econ.)	54	24	43	33	50	28	20
All	1,108	35	42	22	60	24	14

Notes:
Results are based on responses to questions 4 (numerical) and 13 (verbal) of questionnaire A1. For interpretation of 'Agree' and 'Disagree', see text and note 3 of chapter 4. For full names of academic institutions, see table B.1.

responses are consistent with the conventional view that distributional orderings should respect the transfer principle: we shall have more to say on this point in a moment. What of other possible aspects of diversity amongst the numerical responses?

In order to investigate the possibility of divergent views we addressed the question 'What is the probability that group X's and group Y's patterns of responses come from the same distribution?' The results of this chi-square test are reported in table 8.2. We have highlighted in bold the cases which satisfy the standard criterion for rejecting the hypothesis that the two patterns are identical (i.e. the probability is less than 5%).

On this basis it is clear that we cannot reject the hypothesis that the views of the US and Europe subsamples are the same; the same conclusion applies to comparisons of the USA and individual European countries. By contrast, we can reject the hypothesis that the pattern of responses is identical in the USA and Israel; but this may be because of the special nature of the economics students at the Hebrew University, Jerusalem. Furthermore, it is apparent that, with the exception of Koblenz and Bonn, we cannot reject the hypothesis that the pattern of responses is identical in pairs of individual institutions within one country.

Finally, and perhaps surprisingly, the hypothesis that the distributions of numerical responses and verbal responses amongst the 1,108 students who participated in the A1 questionnaire study are the same was rejected.

Table 8.2. *Do X and Y have the same pattern of responses on the transfer principle? Direct approach*

	Probability (%)
North Texas & Southern Methodist	15.2
Karlsruhe & Bonn	9.4
Koblenz & Bonn	**1.8**
Karlsruhe & Koblenz	20.6
Hebrew Univ. (Econ.) & Ruppin	6.7
USA & Europe	14.7
USA & Germany	22.8
USA & UK	6.4
USA & Israel	**2.0**
Germany & UK	9.5
Germany & Israel	28.7
Israel & UK	16.7
Non-econ. & econ. (Hebrew Univ.)	**2.4**
Numerical & verbal	**0.0**

Notes: Implied probabilities based on detailed breakdown of responses to numerical questions in table 8.1. Figures in bold indicate cases where the probability that the two responses are identical is less than 5%. For full names of academic institutions, see table B.1.

Monotonicity

Because monotonicity is closely related to the idea of the Pareto principle it is often regarded as basic to the welfare-economic comparison of income distributions. Recall its meaning: if a list of incomes B can be derived from A just by increasing one or more of the incomes in A then B is considered to have a higher level of social welfare than A.

As we noted in chapter 5 (n. 14, p. 68) the results of questionnaire B1 seem to suggest a considerable divergence of view on monotonicity, in contrast with the views expressed on other welfare principles (the divergence of view was less pronounced in the control study B2). Does the same divergence of view between sub-samples emerge clearly when we apply the same statistical approach as we have just applied in the case of responses on the transfer principle? From tables 8.3 and 8.4 we can see, for example, that the hypothesis that Israeli respondents and European respondents have the same views is clearly rejected: whether or not there is substantial heterogeneity of view within each country subsample, it is clear that the pattern of responses to numerical questions does differ significantly between the country groups.

Furthermore, as we can see from the summary distributions by universities in tables 8.3 and 8.4, there appears to be a close correspondence between the pattern of verbal and numerical responses. Detailed cross-checking of the responses by

Table 8.3. *Agreement with monotonicity: does B exhibit higher social welfare than A? (Percentage expressing areement)*

	N	(q. 4) A: (5, 5, 5, 5) B: (5, 5, 5, 10)	(q. 6) A: (4, 8, 9) B: (4, 8, 20)	(q. 5) A: (5, 5, 5, 5) B: (5, 5, 5, 30)
LSE	*29*	97	86	76
Stockholm	*51*	84	81	77
Bonn	*211*	67	59	57
Koblenz	*84*	79	73	62
Tel Aviv (Economics)	*133*	59	59	53
Tel Aviv (Sociology)	*112*	36	30	26
All	*620*	*64*	*59*	*54*

Notes:
Results are based on responses to questions 4, 5 and 6 of questionnaire B1. For full names of academic institutions, see table B.1.

the same individuals to different questions confirms this observation. So the unconventional responses which consistently appear in certain of the subsamples do not appear to be the outcome of a fluke reaction to one particular type of question. As we noted in chapter 5 it is reasonable to conclude that the monotonicity axiom is indeed in dispute as a general principle of welfare analysis, at least by some important subgroups within our sample.

The poverty line

Cultural differences over the approach to poverty could take many forms. For example, they could just be focused on those differences that emerge on questions which are well known from the inequality and social welfare fields such as the transfer principle, monotonicity and subgroup decomposability. As we reported in chapter 7 these issues can be addressed using a poverty questionnaire experiment (P1) in which respondents are asked about distributional comparisons using a given poverty line. The numerical examples in these experiments are carefully arranged so that none of the comparisons involves individuals crossing the poverty line. As we discussed on page 112 on these distributional principles, the results from the poverty question generally reflect the conclusions drawn from the earlier chapters on inequality and social welfare. The principal heterogeneity within the P1 responses is that students in the two subgroups from Bar-Ilan University generally have more markedly 'conventional' views than the overall sample on the issues of anonymity, decomposability, the population principle and the transfer principle.[3]

However, this no-line-crossing approach to poverty questionnaire experiments may miss the main point. It is arguable that the crucial question in this area of

Table 8.4. *Breakdown of verbal responses on the monotonicity principle (percentage responses)*

	N	Agree	Disagree
LSE	*29*	93	7
Bonn	*211*	68	28
Koblenz	*84*	87	13
Tel Aviv (Economics)	*133*	37	42
Tel Aviv (Sociology)	*112*	30	62
All	*569*	*55*	*37*

Notes:
Results are based on responses to question 14 of questionnaire B1. For interpretation of 'Agree' and 'Disagree', see text and note 3 of chapter 4. For full names of academic institutions, see table B.1.

distributional analysis is whether the poverty line should be considered as exogenous to the distributional problem in question, or as essentially endogenous, one that is to be inferred from the data themselves. For that type of question one has to have a reference point to give meaning to an exogenous poverty line and an agreed system of values for evaluating how the poverty line and poverty comparisons change as economic circumstances change. This was the purpose behind the P2 questionnaire study, which has the potential of revealing whether there are cultural differences on the meaning of a poverty line.

As we saw in chapter 7 (p. 112) the context of the questions concerning poverty line changes or comparisons appears to have an important effect upon responses on this topic, and the key point emerges in the final verbal question, for which the results are reported in table 7.13. Table 8.5, which gives the breakdown of these results by samples, shows that the general conclusion – support for the absolute rather than the relative poverty line approach – applies to all the subgroups in the P2 poverty sample.

But are there differences in viewpoint across countries? Applying the standard test criteria (table 8.6) we find that the hypothesis that the USA and Europe have the same views on the poverty line question cannot be rejected. However, we can reject the corresponding hypothesis in the case of the Europe/Israel and the USA/Israel comparisons.

Drawing together the results in these three subsections we may conclude that, on some key issues, there does appear to be a 'cultural difference' between subgroups. This is most marked in the case of the issue of monotonicity. However, this leaves open the question of whether it is attributable to something in the national outlook or is principally an aspect of the way in which students accept and apply conventional economic wisdom; we return to this in section 8.5.

Table 8.5. *Breakdown of views on the poverty line: verbal question (percentage responses)*

	N	Basic needs	Relative	Neither
Alabama	*80*	85	9	2
Southern Methodist	*19*	63	5	5
LSE	*34*	71	18	12
Koblenz	*31*	87	3	10
Warsaw	*34*	79	6	15
Tel Aviv (Sociology)	*43*	56	26	12
Ruppin	*64*	61	13	13
ANU	*35*	71	6	20
All	*340*	*72*	*11*	*10*

Notes:
Results are based on responses to question 7 of questionnaire P2. For interpretations of 'basic needs' and 'relative' poverty lines, see chapter 7 (p. 106). For full names of academic institutions, see table B.1.

Table 8.6. *Do X and Y have the same pattern of verbal responses on the poverty line question?*

	Probability (%)
USA & Europe	20.9
Europe & Israel	**0.0**
USA & Israel	**0.0**

Note: Implied probabilities based on detailed breakdown of responses to verbal questions in table 8.5. Figures in bold indicate cases where the probability that the two responses are identical is less than 5%.

8.4 Direct and indirect approaches to inequality

Does it matter how you approach the subject of inequality? We started the book by dealing with inequality in a 'free-standing' fashion, as an entity to be considered in its own right. But, as we have seen in chapter 5, one can come to inequality via the indirect route of social welfare analysis, and this raises the question of whether it matters if a 'front-door' or a 'back-door' route is used. We tackled this in part on pages 60ff. when we examined some of the standard inequality axioms that are commonly applied to the specification of social welfare criteria. There are two aspects of interest here: first, whether the overall pattern of responses on each of the principles differs betweeen the direct and indirect approaches to inequality; second, whether cross-cultural issues show up in the indirect approach to inequality analysis as in section 8.3 above.

The first of these two aspects can be dealt with quite swiftly. Consider the basic principles summarised in table 5.10: are the differences in the percentages of agreement with each principle important? The hypothesis to be considered for any one of the axioms can be stated thus: 'the proportion of responses conforming to the axiom is the same for the direct and the indirect approach'. Applying the same type of test as before to the responses from the A1 and B1 questionnaires we find that for anonymity and the population principle this hypothesis is rejected both for numerical questions and for verbal questions; but the hypothesis cannot be rejected in the case of the decomposability principle. Applying the test to the verbal responses on the transfer principle from the A4 and B1 questionnaires we again find that the hypothesis cannot be rejected. This result has a bearing on the cross-cultural issue because characteristics such as educational background may affect whether people think about these inequality issues primarily via the front-door or back-door route.

Now consider the second aspect of the indirect approach. Do differences between countries show up in inequality questions that are dressed up in social welfare clothes? The detail of the B1 questionnaire enables us to deal with this point using the same technique as earlier.

Remarkably we find the same general picture as for the detail of the responses on the transfer principle using the direct approach; see table 8.2. From table 8.8 we again find that the cross-country differences[4] in the pattern of responses on the transfer principle are insignificant but that the differences between economists and non-economists and between the patterns of verbal and non-verbal responses are significant.

8.5 Does economics matter?

The concept of culture is commonly interpreted in terms of where people live and the kind of political and social norms that they may have absorbed through their home background and education. This is essentially the way that we have treated the topic up to this point in the discussion, by focusing upon the differences in the patterns of responses between subgroups defined by country or educational institution. However, these differences form only part of the story. It is possible that the subject matter of a person's educational background may exert a powerful impact upon his attitudes and behaviour. In particular it is possible that the study of economics has this sort of effect: we might then speak about 'the culture of economics'. So one of the most important aspects of the question 'Is thinking

Table 8.7. *Breakdown of views on the transfer principle: indirect approach (percentages)*

	N	Agree	Strongly disagree	Disagree
LSE	29	52	41	7
Bonn	211	46	29	24
Koblenz	84	50	19	31
Stockholm	51	47	22	28
Tel Aviv (Economics)	133	58	14	26
Tel Aviv (Sociology)	112	33	10	54
All	620	47	21	30

Notes:
Results are based on responses to question 1 of questionnaire B1. For interpretation of 'Agree' and 'Disagree', see text and note 3 of chapter 4. For full names of academic institutions, see table B.1.

Table 8.8. *Do X and Y have the same pattern of responses on the transfer principle? Indirect approach*

	Probability (%)
Israel & Europe	11.0
Economics & Sociology (Tel Aviv)	**0.0**
Numerical & verbal	**0.0**

Notes:
Implied probabilities based on detailed breakdown of responses to numerical questions in table 8.7. Figures in bold indicate cases where the probability that the two responses are identical is less than 5%.

about inequality affected by such things as cultural background?' can be roughly translated 'Is thinking about inequality affected by whether you have been taught economics?'

The supposition that the culture of economics does make a difference is not original to this book. This is hardly surprising in view of the fact that the study of economics focuses upon an important slice of human activity. Because the subject does not just deal with theoretical abstraction but can provide practical everyday rules and recommendations, it is reasonable to expect some of this to rub off on those who specialise in the subject. So when one compares those who have and have not studied economics, one might expect to find differences in behaviour that may be informed by individuals' awareness of certain principles and methods in guiding their own choices and actions in everyday life. If the

Table 8.9. *Do X and Y have the same*
pattern of responses on monotonicity?

	Probability (%)
Israel & Europe	**0.00**
Economics & Sociology (Tel Aviv)	**0.04**

Notes:
Implied probabilities based on detailed breakdown
of responses to numerical questions in table 8.4.
Figures in bold indicate cases where the probability
that the two responses are identical is less than 5%.

study of economics 'matters' in this sense we would expect this to show up not only in economists' management of their personal finances and expenditures but also in their behaviour as social creatures, their approach to the provision of public goods, for example; there is indeed evidence that economists do behave differently from others in this respect.[5] We should, of course, admit that it is difficult, and perhaps dangerous, to make more than a vague conjecture as to causation here: although it is possible that exposure to economic reasoning may corrupt the innocent, converting good citizens into self-centred maximisers, it may also be that those with certain characteristics – certain social attitudes, for example – select themselves by choosing to study economics rather than some other subject.

It is clear from the discussion of the material in sections 8.3 and 8.4 that there is a substantial difference in the response pattern of the economics and non-economics subgroups within a particular institution. This comes out very clearly in the cross-tabulations and formal tests on the pattern of responses to the transfer principle: non-economists believe in it even less than do economists; see tables 8.1, 8.2, 8.7 and 8.8. The same picture also emerges in respect of the fundamental principle of monotonicity: table 8.9 gives the test result for the cross-tabulations that we saw earlier in table 8.4.[6] It is clear that once again the sociologists really do believe in the monotonicity principle less than their economist colleagues.

Is all this evidence of a kind of 'programming' – not to say brainwashing – of economics students that induces a characteristic approach to distributional questions? If so, how does it occur, and does it matter? A possible explanation for this phenomenon is the extent to which students study welfare economics, including such things as the Pareto principle, as part of their standard intellectual diet. The conventional approach to welfare economics, by focusing upon individuals in isolation, may create a climate of acceptance of principles – such as the transfer principle, monotonicity and decomposability – that fit most easily within this individualistic framework. This 'programming' of views matters in so far as alternative approaches to distributional comparisons deserve to be considered on their own merits rather than being casually dismissed by a general uncritical acceptance of the conventional economic wisdom.

8.6 An appraisal

Culture interpreted as 'country' matters perhaps rather less than one might have supposed: there are instances where, for example, the US students' responses differ from the Israelis' on the transfer principle, but this sort of thing is not very common. Culture interpreted as 'subject' seems to be rather important: it appears that on key issues the approach of the economists is different from others in its bias towards the conventional. Here lies a danger: uncritical acceptance of the culture of economics may serve to impede the process of thinking about inequality.

Notes

1 See, for example, our discussion on page 44 of the use of individual responses to several questions to check agreement with Lorenz ordering.
2 The statistic in (8.1) is distributed as a χ^2 variable with $(r-1)(c-1)$ degrees of freedom. See also Harrison and Seidl (1994a, 1994b) for an application of this approach.
3 However, in the P2 questionnaire, the students from the other subgroup of Israelis (the Ruppin Institute) did not respond in this way.
4 In this case we have just the comparison of respondents from Israel and from Europe (Germany, the UK and Sweden).
5 See, for example, Marwell and Ames (1981), and Frank et al. (1993, 1996).
6 For the corresponding numerical questions (4, 5 and 6) one may safely reject the hypothesis that the pattern of responses of the economists and non-economists is identical; in every case the probability is less than 0.005%.

9 Thinking again about inequality

9.1 Second thoughts about second thoughts

Why is thinking about inequality so necessary? Why is thinking about economic inequality so necessary? The short answer is that analysing wealth and income distributions in terms of inequality, social welfare or poverty is essentially different from the idea of inequality in other contexts and other subjects. As Dalton (1920, p. 348) remarked:

An American writer has expressed the view that 'the statistical problem before the economist in determining upon a measure of the inequality in the distribution of wealth is identical with that of the biologist in determining upon a measure of the inequality in the distribution of any physical characteristic' [Persons 1908]. But this is clearly wrong. For the economist is primarily interested, not in the distribution of income as such, but in the effects of the distribution of income upon the distribution and total amount of economic welfare, which may be derived from that income.

Thinking about inequality is essential because the main ideas of inequality require detailed assumptions if they are to be made workable. Even if the idea of economic equality were to be based upon an agreed set of ethical principles or some widely accepted mathematical axioms about the meaning of distributional comparisons, there would remain a problem. As in other fields of study there is, of course, a question of where the agreed set of principles or the accepted axioms come from. This whole book is predicated on the advisability of rethinking the standard approach to inequality analysis and the related topics of social welfare and poverty. Rethinking in this way opens up the possibility of new avenues of theoretical and empirical research on the economic analysis of income distribution and related topics. In this final chapter we wish both to take stock of the empirical evidence on people's thinking about inequality and to suggest some ways in which this type of investigation may be taken forward.

9.2 Applying inequality judgments

The standard approach to the treatment of inequality in the economics literature can be caricatured as the Lorenz curve method. Almost all the battery of inequality statistics that have become standard equipment for empirical researchers and policy analysts can be seen as new twists or simplifications of the basic Lorenz insight, and take as given the assumptions underlying the formal theory that has become accepted as standard in the profession. However, powerful though the Lorenz insight is, it is not the only, nor necessarily the best, way forward to the analysis of income distribution.

Right from the elementary puzzle depicted in chapter 1 we have seen that there are problems with this approach to distributional comparisons. The basis of inequality comparison that is almost universally adopted in the theoretical and applied literature seems to be at variance with the way untrained people interpret inequality comparisons. One might just respond to that with a dismissive shrug: the theory is what it is. But do heretical views matter? Should they? Well, of course they should matter if economists want to address the same kind of questions as are commonly addressed in other fields of study such as the analysis of preference rankings in consumer theory.

Following the analogy with the modelling of individual preferences in consumer theory we might enquire whether the responses to income-distribution questionnaires can be used to chart a coherent picture of views about income distribution. As a basis for consumer theory it is commonly assumed that the 'maps' that people make of alternative baskets of goods are well-defined: the maps are complete (people know their own mind and never find two baskets of goods that they cannot compare), transitive (a basic consistency property) and continuous (there are no sudden jumps in preference). So are the views about income distribution similarly well defined? Do they exhibit the basic properties of an ordering, in the sense explained on page 10? The picture revealed by our series of questionnaire studies is encouraging.

- *Completeness.* We have indirect evidence that the completeness assumption is reasonable. We never found a case where the respondents said they were unable to compare distributions, although we did not ask our respondents directly about this issue.
- *Transitivity.* However, we do have direct evidence from the very first questionnaire study that people's inequality orderings of distributions are transitive; see pages 44 and 58 and Amiel and Cowell (1992).
- *Continuity.* The experiments that focused upon a number of similar comparisons in income space (for example, those dealing with the iso-inequality curves and with income growth reported in chapter 6) suggest that individual orderings are continuous, except possibly in the neighbourhood of perfect equality.

Table 9.1. *Standard axioms in three related fields*

	Inequality	Social welfare	Poverty
Anonymity	✓	✓	✓
Monotonicity		✓	✓
Transfer	✓	✓	✓
Population	✓	✓	✓
Decomposability	✓	✓	✓
Scale independence	✓	*	✓
Translation independence	✓	*	✓

Note: * In the case of social welfare neither form of the independence axiom makes much sense, but scale- or translation-invariance may be relevant.

If we take as granted the basic criteria for an ordering, what are the commonly accepted standard assumptions about orderings in distributional analysis? These are summarised in table 9.1 under the three main headings that correspond to the discussions of chapters 4, 5 and 7. Notice that the standard criteria for social welfare comparisons do not include all of those commonly applied to inequality analysis, nor vice versa. The analysis of poverty inherits some elements from the approach to inequality and some elements from that to social welfare comparisons. As we have seen, some of the axioms that would normally be considered as basic in one or more of these three fields are those which are called into question by the results of our questionnaire studies.

Can something be learned from this that would be applicable to the more general problem of comparing distributions of economic entities other than income, perhaps in areas that have little or nothing to do with economics? There are, broadly speaking, two views on this. The first is that the problem of inequality measurement is just one part of a general problem of the approach to measuring dispersion in the social sciences or in the physical sciences. The second view can be introduced by continuing the passage from Dalton's seminal article, quoted above:

A partial analogy would be found in the problem of measuring the inequality of rainfall in the various districts of a large agricultural area. From the point of view of the cultivator, what is important is not rainfall as such, but the effects of rainfall upon the crop which may be raised on the land. Between rainfall and crop there will be a certain relation, the discovery of which will be a matter of practical importance. The objection to great inequality of rainfall is the resulting loss of potential crop. The objection to great inequality of incomes is the resulting loss of potential economic welfare. (Dalton 1920, pp. 348–9)

It is clear that, for Dalton, the difference in underlying approach between the two types of distribution problem lies in some kind of valuation process (of rainfall or of personal income): without clear principles on which to judge the loss of economic welfare it would be impossible, from his standpoint, to have a soundly based approach to inequality measurement. Not all economists – and few from other disciplines – would be automatically persuaded that welfare loss is the right way to tackle the subject. However, the general point implicit in Dalton's remarks seems to have some force: rules for appraising income distributions should be grounded in principles that in some sense incorporate the generally accepted evaluation of individual income or of income differences.

We should then be cautious about drawing parallels between responses to questions set in the context of income distribution – inequality, social welfare and poverty – and responses to distributional questions in other contexts. Nevertheless, these considerations may have a bearing upon the direction in which this type of analysis may fruitfully be taken.

9.3 Where next?

Picking over fundamental principles like the transfer principle and monotonicity might seem a little like thinking the unthinkable. But why stop there? Once we have set out on the heretical trail of inquiry, we might try following it back to its source.

One of the most important intellectual sources of modern inequality analysis is the literature on ranking probability distributions. Some of the seminal pieces in inequality analysis – Atkinson (1970) foremost amongst them – started from the insight that the problem of ordering income distributions in terms of inequality is essentially similar to the problem of ordering distributions in other contexts. Also, as we discussed in chapter 3, some economists and philosophers have suggested a formal basis for social attitudes to inequality using individual attitudes to uncertainty.[1] So we do not only find a possible similarity of approach between the analysis of income distribution and the analysis of risk (as there is between income distribution and, say, the distribution of firms by size or the geographical dispersion of rainfall), but we must also address the argument that the analysis of probability distributions may be a basis for the analysis of income distributions.

In view of this it may be appropriate to wonder whether useful insights can be obtained by reversing the chain of thought. We have made the case for thinking about inequality in a way that leaves open the question of whether the 'basic' axioms are to be adopted or not. What would emerge if one were to adopt the same kind of approach to an examination of the problem of comparing risky prospects?

In principle the questionnaire approach could be easily adapted from either the inequality questionnaires (the A series) or the social welfare questionnaires (the B series). The two routes lead to different concepts in the analysis of individual preference orderings in the face of uncertainty. On the one hand the inequality questions can be made to correspond to the concept of risk; on the other hand, questions on social welfare rankings can be shown to be parallel to the questions

Table 9.2. *Standard axioms in the analysis of income and probability distributions*

	Inequality	Risk	Social welfare	Preferences over prospects
Anonymity	✓	✓	✓	✓
Monotonicity		✓	✓	✓
Transfer	✓	✓	✓	✓
Population	✓	✓	✓	✓
Decomposability	✓	✓	✓	✓
Scale independence	✓	✓	*	*
Translation independence	✓	✓	*	*

Note: * In the case of social welfare and preferences over prospects neither form of the independence axiom makes much sense, but scale- or translation-invariance may be relevant.

on individual preference rankings of prospects;[2] see table 9.2 for a summary comparison. Some of the more recondite points in the two subject areas can also be related: for example, the issue of violations of the independence axiom in the analysis of risk,[3] and the issue of externalities in the assessment of income distributions.

There is, of course, a substantial literature on the experimental approach to people's behaviour in situations of choice under risk and some well-known counterparts to the unconventional results that we have found from our own questionnaire experiments.[4] However, to carry through an effective comparison of perceptions in the two fields it is more useful to mimic the approach to income distribution by constructing a questionnaire experiment in the field of perceptions of risk and uncertainty of the same format.

Questionnaire R3 (appendix B, pp. 171–2) is almost identical to questionnaire A3 on inequality perceptions which was discussed in chapter 6: when drafting it on the word processor we simply replaced all occurrences of 'inequality' by 'risk' and made a very few other changes for the sake of euphony. The experiment was run on a sample of students similar to the one used for the A3 experiment. The results are reported in tables 9.3 and 9.4 which have been set out in the same format as those containing the results of the corresponding inequality questionnaire experiment (A3).

We may note the apparent similarity between the results reported in tables 9.3 and 9.4 and what we established in chapter 6 about people's views on inequality at different income levels (see tables 6.1 and 6.2). In particular, the evidence – from both the numerical and the verbal questions – about what happens when you add a fixed absolute amount to incomes at various income levels is particularly striking: here the pattern of responses is almost identical. It is also clear that the same sort of phenomenon emerges as one increases the reference level of income: at low income levels a proportionate income addition will reduce risk or

Table 9.3. *What happens to risk when you increase people's incomes? (Percentage responses)*

	'Risk decreases'	'Risk increases'	'Risk stays same'
Adding a fixed absolute sum			
(q. 1) (200, 400) → (400, 600)	77	9	14
(q. 4) (600, 900) → (900, 1200)	65	11	24
(q. 7) (1200, 1800) → (1800, 2400)	53	17	29
Adding a compromise* sum			
(q. 2) (200, 400) → (400, 700)	77	17	5
(q. 5) (600, 900) → (900, 1300)	61	29	9
(q. 8) (1200, 1800) → (1800, 2550)	53	34	12
Adding a fixed proportionate sum			
(q. 3) (200, 400) → (400, 800)	70	18	12
(q. 6) (600, 900) → (900, 1350)	55	32	12
(q. 9) (1200, 1800) → (1800, 2700)	43	38	18

Notes:
* 'Compromise' means 'between absolute and proportionate'.
Results are based on numerical responses to questionnaire R3 ($N = 346$).

Table 9.4. *What income change will leave risk unchanged? (Percentage responses)*

The same proportionate amount added to all incomes	19
A fixed sum added to all incomes	13
Depends on the income level	45
None of the above	14

Notes:
Results are based on resonses to questionnaire R3
($N = 235$). Results from the University of Osnabrück were
unavailable for this question.

inequality, whereas at moderate or high income levels a proportionate income addition will increase inequality (the dependence hypothesis again). However, there are important differences. In particular, the 'natural' assumption of scale independence which appears to have common currency in the inequality literature appears to be less well supported when individuals are asked the corresponding questions about risk: for example, in the verbal question on inequality, 32% supported the scale-independence principle (table 6.1) but, as table 9.4 shows, the corresponding proportion in the context of risk is only 19%.

This has some interesting implications for the direction of future research. Firstly, the finding that risk attitudes conform less closely to the pattern of scale independence than do inequality attitudes is in line with the approach commonly adopted in the related literature on risk: in the case of risk analysis the 'natural' assumption appears to be that of translation independence, as is evident in the widespread use of the mean-variance approach in the analysis of risk.[5] Secondly, it suggests that it would be worth enquiring whether some of the other inequality axioms discussed in chapters 2 and 4 are appropriate in the context of risk attitudes: one could run through the first two columns of table 9.2, while a similar exercise could be done with the last two columns of the same table to see whether the results on social welfare reported in chapter 5 were matched by similar results on preferences over uncertain prospects.

Moreover, the results raise certain more basic questions for both theoretical and applied experimental work in the field:

- Should research methodologies pursue experimentation that allows one to investigate attitudes in both fields – risk and inequality – jointly (Davidovitz 1998)?
- Do perceptions of distributional orderings of risk and distributional orderings of inequality have the same basic structure? Preliminary research results suggest that they do not (Amiel and Cowell 1998b). If so, then it may be inappropriate to base the theory of inequality comparisons exclusively on the analysis of risk.
- But if inequality comparisons are not to be based on risk analysis, then on what? Should they be based on individual perceptions of levels of income and differences? (Broome 1988; Temkin 1986)

These issues, which go beyond the scope of the present book, are the subject of current research.

9.4 A final word

As we admitted at the beginning, income inequality is a subject that has been vulnerable to the whim of fashion within the domain of economic thought. Our idea has not been to set a new fashion but to see why a fresh look at the intellectual basis for distributional analysis could reveal some curious anomalies and arbitrary assumptions in the accepted wisdom.

Should experimentation continue? Of course, we have a vested interest in the answer to this question. But the reason we feel that this approach should be pursued is not that of further experiments for experiments' sake. Some of the lessons to be drawn from the preceding chapters suggest that understanding of the meaning of inequality comparisons and the like can be considerably enhanced by trying to see how other people see these comparisons.

A brief list of the key points of this enhanced understanding might include the following.

The plurality of theory. The standard approach to inequality appears to present an ever-narrower focus on the 'right' way to compare one distribution with another. But this is not a subject where statements of mathematical truth of the '2 + 2 = 4' variety should predominate. Intellectual judgment is required and it would be undesirable for a monopoly on thinking about inequality to be established. Put bluntly it probably does not matter if we 'lose' some key axioms. Alternative approaches are conceivable and alternative axioms can provide a coherent basis for the comparison of income distributions.

The building blocks of inequality. The 'new axioms for old' idea suggests that it may be worth reconsidering the elements from which the theory is to be constructed. One of the most crucial issues is whether one should work with individual incomes or with income differences. The distinction is important because it will affect not only the specification of formal abstract principles but also the choice of practical tools which one brings to bear on empirical studies: we need to consider seriously measures defined in terms of income differences or gaps. If we follow the income-difference approach then some familiar tools such as the Lorenz curve may no longer be appropriate in all circumstances. However, Gini-type indices survive because they are defined in terms of income differences.

The nature of distributional judgments. Inequality judgments can have a 'life of their own', distinct from welfare judgments. Of course, social welfare remains as one basis for developing an approach to inequality, but it is one of several. The connection between inequality and social welfare remains one of personal value judgment. Likewise with poverty comparisons: they, too, may or may not have a formal root in inequality analysis or social welfare theory. What is more, it may make good sense to work simultaneously with more than one approach to distributional comparison: the word 'poverty' or the idea of poverty comparisons can simultaneously mean quite different things to different people. The same sort of idea could apply to 'inequality' or 'social welfare'.

Some of these avenues have been opened up by the research reported here. It would have been intriguing to have gone further within this book. But if it stimulates new thinking about inequality then our purpose will have been accomplished.

Notes

1 See the discussion of the Harsanyi and Rawls approach on pages 25ff.
2 On risk and inequality, see Nermuth (1993) and Rothschild and Stiglitz (1970, 1971, 1973). On distributional rankings and first- and second-order concepts of dominance see, for example, Atkinson and Bourguignon (1982), Kolm (1969), Marshall and Olkin (1979), Saposnik (1981, 1983) and Shorrocks (1983). For higher-order concepts of dominance, see Davies and Hoy (1995), Fishburn and Willig (1984), Kolm (1974, 1976b) and Shorrocks and Foster (1987).

3 This is manifested in the phenomenon of 'regrets' in choice under uncertainty.
4 Perhaps one of the best known of these is the 'Allais paradox' (Allais 1953; Allais and Hagen 1979; Drèze 1974; Raiffa 1968).
5 See, for example, Hicks (1935), Hirshleifer (1970, ch. 10; 1989, pp. 78–82), Markowitz (1959) and Tobin (1958).

Appendix A
Inequality analysis: a summary of concepts and results

This appendix covers some of the principal concepts and results in the formal literature on inequality measurement and related topics in the analysis of income distribution. For surveys of this field, see, for example, Champernowne (1974), Cowell (1995, 1999), Foster (1985), Jenkins (1991), Lambert (1993), Sen (1973) and Sen and Foster (1997).

A.1 The axiomatic approach

Assuming that the concepts 'income' and 'income receiver' have been defined, we index the members of the population by $i = 1, 2, \ldots, n$, and assume that person i's income is a non-negative scalar x_i. The symbol $\mathbf{x}$ denotes a vector of such incomes $(x_1, x_2, \ldots, x_n)$, and $\mathbf{1}$ denotes a vector of ones. For convenience we write $n(\mathbf{x})$ and $\mu(\mathbf{x})$ respectively for the number of components and the arithmetic mean of the components of vector $\mathbf{x}$. Also we let $\mathbf{x}[m] := (\mathbf{x}, \mathbf{x}, \ldots, \mathbf{x})$, a mn-vector that represents a concatenation of m identical n-vectors $\mathbf{x}$.

Write N for the set of integers $\{1, 2, \ldots, n\}$ and X for the set of all possible income vectors, which we will take to be the set of all finite-dimensioned non-negative vectors excluding the zero vector. Also write X' for the subset of X that excludes all vectors of the form $a\mathbf{1}$, $a > 0$. By an inequality comparison we mean a binary relation on the members of X. Since our questionnaire is phrased in terms of inequality, the statement '$\mathbf{x} \geqslant \mathbf{x}''$' is to be read as '$\mathbf{x}$ represents an income distribution that is at least as unequal as distribution $\mathbf{x}''$'. It is possible, of course, that this does not represent a complete ordering on X. We define the strict inequality comparison $>$ and inequality equivalence $\sim$ in the usual way.

To give economic meaning to the relation $\geqslant$ a number of assumptions are conventionally imposed. The principal assumptions which are commonly used as building blocks in an axiomatic approach to inequality measurement can be expressed in the following way:

- *Anonymity.* For all $\mathbf{x} \in X$ and any permutation matrix $\mathbf{P}$, $\mathbf{x} \sim \mathbf{Px}$.
- *Scale invariance.* For all $\mathbf{x}, \mathbf{y} \in X$ and positive scalars a, $\mathbf{x} \geqslant \mathbf{y}$ implies $a\mathbf{x} \geqslant a\mathbf{y}$.
- *Translation invariance.* For all $\mathbf{x}, \mathbf{y} \in X$ and any scalar b (such that $\mathbf{x} + b\mathbf{1} \in X$ and $\mathbf{y} + b\mathbf{1} \in X$) $\mathbf{x} \geqslant \mathbf{y}$ implies $\mathbf{x} + b\mathbf{1} \geqslant \mathbf{y} + b\mathbf{1}$.
- *Scale independence.* For any $\mathbf{x} \in X$ and positive scalars a, $a\mathbf{x} \sim \mathbf{x}$.
- *Translation independence.* For all $\mathbf{x} \in X$ and any scalar b such that $\mathbf{x} + b\mathbf{1} \in X$, $\mathbf{x} + b\mathbf{1} \sim \mathbf{x}$.
- *Population principle.* For all $\mathbf{x} \in X$ and positive integers m, $\mathbf{x}[m] \sim \mathbf{x}$.
- *Transfer principle.* For all $\mathbf{x} \in X'$, for any $i, j \in N$, and for any scalar $d > 0$ such that $x_i > x_j$ and $x_i - d > x_j + d$, $\mathbf{x} > (x_1, x_2, \ldots, x_i - d, \ldots, x_j + d, \ldots, x_n)$.
- *Decomposability.* Let $\mathbf{x}_g \in X$ and $\mathbf{x}'_g \in X$, $g = 1, 2, \ldots, G$ be income vectors such that $n(\mathbf{x}_g) = n(\mathbf{x}'_g)$, $\mu(\mathbf{x}_g) = \mu(\mathbf{x}'_g)$ and $\mathbf{x}_g \geqslant \mathbf{x}'_g$ for all g, then $(\mathbf{x}_1, \mathbf{x}_2, \ldots, \mathbf{x}_G) \geqslant (\mathbf{x}'_1, \mathbf{x}'_2, \ldots, \mathbf{x}'_G)$.

The anonymity axiom says that if people are identical in all relevant characteristics other than income then inequality comparisons treat them equally. This axiom is of fundamental importance in related fields as well as in inequality analysis, and – as long as incomes and income receivers have been appropriately defined – some form of the anonymity axiom may be taken as essential to a rational discussion of the meaning of inequality comparisons.[1] The rest of the assumptions are presented in an order that is convenient for comparison with the format of our first questionnaire (A1) rather than that suggested by a logical sequence.

Except in trivial cases scale independence and translation independence must be treated as mutually exclusive alternatives: a simple mathematical argument is provided by Aczél (1987) and Amiel (1981), and the choice between the two principles was discussed by Dalton (1920) and Kolm (1969, 1976a). However, other, similar assumptions may also be reasonable. It has been argued,[2] for example, that some compromise position between scale independence and translation independence may be appropriate; thus one might require that inequality should remain unchanged under some transformation such as $a\mathbf{x} + b\mathbf{1}$ where a and b are specific constants with $a > 0$. Notice that scale (translation) independence implies scale (translation) invariance but not vice versa, and that there is no problem with an index possessing the properties of scale invariance and translation invariance simultaneously.

The population principle has an important implication for inequality indices that one might construct on the basis of one's axiom system. Given this assumption, such indices would be invariant under replications of the population. Note that this is considerably stronger than the requirement that inequality comparisons be invariant under replication: i.e. $\mathbf{x}'[m] \geqslant \mathbf{x}[m]$ if and only if $\mathbf{x}' \geqslant \mathbf{x}$.

The transfer principle states simply that if a small income transfer is made between two persons of unequal income, inequality rises (falls) according as the recipient is richer (poorer) than the donor. Observe that this property is required to hold independently of the incomes possessed by any other members of the community.

The decomposability assumption can be viewed as a type of 'independence of irrelevant alternatives' axiom. In this book we have investigated a weaker form of this property where $G=2$ and $\mathbf{x}_2 = \mathbf{x}_2'$. The transfer principle and the decomposability principle have tremendous consequences for the selection of appropriate tools with which to carry out inequality analysis. There is a simple proposition which connects the transfer principle with the ordering of distributions using the Lorenz curves.[3] If $\mathbf{x}$ and $\mathbf{y}$ have the same mean then the following statements are equivalent:

- $\mathbf{x} > \mathbf{y}$ for all inequality rankings satisfying the principle of transfers;
- the Lorenz curve of $\mathbf{x}$ lies somewhere below and nowhere above the Lorenz curve of $\mathbf{y}$;
- $\mathbf{x}$ can be reached from $\mathbf{y}$ by a sequence of poorer-to-richer pairwise income transfers.

The greater part of the received wisdom on the positive and normative approaches to economic inequality is founded upon this principle and its corollaries.

Furthermore, the acceptance of population decomposability significantly affects the structure of the class of indices that are admissible as inequality measures: for example, it rules out popular indices such as the Gini coefficient, the relative mean deviation and the logarithmic variance.[4] Scale invariance, the transfer principle and population decomposability require that the measure is of a form that is ordinally equivalent to the generalised entropy index

$$I_{\mathrm{GE}}(\mathbf{x}) = \frac{1}{\alpha^2 - \alpha}\left[\frac{1}{n(\mathbf{x})}\sum_{i=1}^{n(\mathbf{x})}\left[\frac{x_i}{\mu(\mathbf{x})}\right]^{\alpha} - 1\right] \tag{A.1}$$

where α is a sensitivity parameter that may be assigned any real value.[5] An important related family of indices is the Atkinson class of inequality measures

$$I_{\mathrm{Atkinson}}(\mathbf{x}) = 1 - \left[\frac{1}{n(\mathbf{x})}\sum_{i=1}^{n(\mathbf{x})}\left[\frac{x_i}{\mu(\mathbf{x})}\right]^{1-\epsilon}\right]^{\frac{1}{1-\epsilon}} \tag{A.2}$$

where $\epsilon \geq 0$ is an 'inequality aversion' parameter: An index (A.2) will rank income distributions in the same order as an index (A.1) if $\epsilon = 1 - \alpha$ for $-\infty < \alpha < 1$.

However, if one were to consider relaxing the core principles mentioned above, would one have sensible inequality tools available? Relaxing decomposability is not too serious: if one were to insist only on non-overlapping decomposability but not full decomposability, then the Gini coefficient[6]

$$I_{\mathrm{Gini}}(\mathbf{x}) = \frac{1}{2n(\mathbf{x})^2\mu(\mathbf{x})}\sum_{i=1}^{n(\mathbf{x})}\sum_{j=1}^{n(\mathbf{x})}|x_i - x_j| \tag{A.3}$$

would be an admissible inequality index; if one were to relax even this weaker requirement, then the relative mean deviation

$$I_{\text{RMD}}(\mathbf{x}) = \frac{1}{n(\mathbf{x})} \sum_{i=1}^{n(\mathbf{x})} \left| \frac{x_i}{\mu(\mathbf{x})} - 1 \right| \qquad (A.4)$$

would be admissible. What if the transfer principle were to be relaxed? One might then consider using the logarithmic variance

$$I_{\text{logvar}}(\mathbf{x}) = \frac{1}{n(\mathbf{x})} \sum_{i=1}^{n(\mathbf{x})} \left[\log \frac{x_i}{\mu(\mathbf{x})} \right]^2 \qquad (A.5)$$

or the variance of logarithms.[7] However, the region in which these indices violate the transfer principle is quite different from the situations that we have been considering: the logarithmic variance has the property that the principle of transfers is violated for any pair of incomes if they exceed 2.7183 times the mean; see Cowell (1995). Our questionnaires have not involved transfers between the very rich and the super-rich. An alternative index has been suggested by Gastwirth (1974) and discussed by Nygård and Sandström (1981, p. 264):

$$I(\mathbf{x}) = \frac{1}{n(\mathbf{x})^2} \sum_{i=1}^{n(\mathbf{x})} \sum_{j=1}^{n(\mathbf{x})} \left| \frac{x_i - x_j}{x_i + x_j} \right| \qquad (A.6)$$

Notice that the index looks superficially similar to the Gini coefficient (A.3) but that each pairwise difference is normalised by the average of that particular pair of incomes rather than by mean income $\mu(\mathbf{x})$. The index (A.6) satisfies anonymity, scale independence and the principle of population but not the transfer principle.

A.2 Inequality and welfare rankings

Let W denote the social welfare function: this is assumed to be a continuous function from X to $\mathfrak{R}$. Many of the properties of the inequality ordering can be immediately restated in terms of the welfare function W: this applies to the properties of anonymity, scale invariance and translation invariance, to the population principle and to decomposability. For example, one would write the first of these as:

- *Anonymity.* For all $\mathbf{x} \in X$ and any permutation matrix $\mathbf{P}$, $W(\mathbf{x}) = W(\mathbf{Px})$.

   One principle requires a minor restatement:

- *Transfer principle.* For any $\mathbf{x} \in X'$, for any $i, j \in N$, and for any scalar $d > 0$ such that $x_i > x_j$ and $x_i - d > x_j + d$, $W(\mathbf{x}) < W(x_1, x_2, \ldots, x_i - d, \ldots, x_j + d, \ldots, x_n)$.

   In addition we may state

- *Monotonicity.* For any $\mathbf{x} \in X'$, for any $i \in N$, and for any scalar $d > 0$, $W(\mathbf{x}) < W(x_1, x_2, \ldots, x_i + d, \ldots, x_n)$.

In many cases it is convenient to restrict the class of admissible functions to those that are in additive form:

$$W(\mathbf{x}) = \sum_{i=1}^{n(\mathbf{x})} \varphi(x_i) \tag{A.7}$$

A number of standard results linking distributional comparisons and welfare and inequality propositions are available. For simplicity of expression let us suppose that we are comparing two distributions $\mathbf{x}, \mathbf{y} \in X$ with the same population ($n(\mathbf{x}) = n(\mathbf{y})$), although the results are valid more generally; also assume that $x_1 \leq x_2 \leq x_3 \ldots$ and $y_1 \leq y_2 \leq y_3 \ldots$ (given the anonymity assumption it is always valid to relabel the population so that these ordering properties are true). Then the following two statements are equivalent (Saposnik 1981, 1983):

- '$x_i \geq y_i$, $i = 1, 2, 3 \ldots$' (first-order dominance);
- '$W(\mathbf{x}) \geq W(\mathbf{y})$ for all welfare functions of the form (A.7) that satisfy monotonicity.'

Furthermore, the following two statements are also equivalent (Kolm 1969; Marshall and Olkin 1979; Shorrocks 1983):

- '$\sum_{j=1}^{i} x_j \geq \sum_{j=1}^{i} y_j$, $i = 1, 2, 3 \ldots$' (second-order dominance);
- '$W(\mathbf{x}) \geq W(\mathbf{y})$ for all welfare functions of the form (A.7) that satisfy monotonicity and the transfer principle.'

From this second result other important consequences flow. For example, if also we have $\mu(\mathbf{x}) = \mu(\mathbf{y})$ then these two equivalent conditions are also equivalent to the Lorenz curve of $\mathbf{x}$ lying everywhere on or above the Lorenz curve of $\mathbf{y}$ (Atkinson 1970).

A.3 Poverty comparisons

As in the discussion of inequality and social welfare, individuals are assumed to be identical in every respect other than their incomes. We suppose that there is also a given poverty line, an exogenously given number z; individual i is said to be poor, or in poverty, if $x_i < z$. The assumption that people are alike other than in their incomes simplifies the analysis (otherwise we would have to consider multiple poverty lines depending on persons' characteristics) but is not essential for stating the main principles of poverty measurement. For any $\mathbf{x} \in X$ we will write the set of poor persons as

$$\Pi(\mathbf{x}, z) := \{i : i \in N(\mathbf{x}), x_i < z\}.$$

The axioms of anonymity, the population principle and decomposability are essentially the same as in the discussion of inequality orderings; the principle of transfers and monotonicity are almost the same as in the discussion above. In the following descriptions of the first five axioms it is to be understood that $\mathbf{x} \in X$,

$\mathbf{x}' \in X$ and $n(\mathbf{x})=n(\mathbf{x}')$. A *poverty index* is a function $P:X\rightarrow\Re$ which is given meaning by a number of axioms:

- *Weak monotonicity.* If $z>x_i>x_i'$ and $x_j=x_j', j\neq i$, then $P(\mathbf{x})<P(\mathbf{x}')$.
- *Strong monotonicity.* If $x_i>x_i'$ and $x_j=x_j', j\neq i$, for $i\in\Pi(\mathbf{x}, z)$, then $P(\mathbf{x})<P(\mathbf{x}')$.
- *Weak principle of transfers.* If $x_i'=x_i-d<x_j+d=x_j'<z$ for some $d>0$, and $x_k=x_k', k\neq i, j$, then $P(\mathbf{x})<P(\mathbf{x}')$.
- *Strong principle of transfers.* If $x_i'=x_i-d<x_j+d=x_j'$ for some $d>0$, for $j\in\Pi(\mathbf{x}, z)$ and $\mathbf{x}_k=\mathbf{x}_k', k\neq i, j$, then $P(\mathbf{x})<P(\mathbf{x}')$.
- *Focus.* If $x_j=x_j'$ for all $x_j<z$, then $P(\mathbf{x})=P(\mathbf{x}')$.

In addition there are two axioms which are sometimes invoked concerning cases where $n(\mathbf{x})$ and $n(\mathbf{x}')$ are different. Suppose $\mathbf{x}'=(\mathbf{x}, \tilde{x})$: in other words the vector $\mathbf{x}'$ is formed by concatenating $\mathbf{x}$ with one extra component $\tilde{x}$.

- *Growth of the poor.* If $\tilde{x}<z$, then $P(\mathbf{x})<P(\mathbf{x}')$.
- *Growth of the non-poor.* If $\tilde{x}\geq z$ then, $P(\mathbf{x})>P(\mathbf{x}')$.

Notice that the difference between the 'weak' and 'strong' versions of monotonicity and the transfer principle lies in whether or not we consider the possibility that one individual crosses the poverty line. This is different from the distinction between 'weak' and 'strong' as used in the social welfare and inequality literature.

Monotonicity and the focus axiom might at first glance seem to be self-evident properties of a sensible poverty index. However, caution is required. One commonly used poverty index – the head-count ratio – does not satisfy the requirement of monotonicity, and the focus axiom would be called into question if, for example, it was considered appropriate that the poverty line be some function of overall mean income, $\mu(\mathbf{x})$, or the median (a complication that we have excluded). Finally, although it seems clear that 'growth of the poor' is reasonable and defensible, it is not clear *a priori* that 'growth of the non-poor' is an appropriate assumption: it could be argued that the numbers of the non-poor are irrelevant (in which case the axiom would have read 'if $\tilde{x}<z$, then $P(\mathbf{x})=P(\mathbf{x}')$'); our version of the property follows Seidl (1988).

Notes

1 Nygård and Sandström (1981) comment that 'a rejection of SYM [the anonymity axiom] would deprive us of all means of judging inequality'. If there are subgroups in the population between which income comparisons are not possible – for example, groups where income receivers have different personal characteristics such as family size – then the anonymity axiom cannot apply universally; see Cowell (1980).
2 See, for example, Bossert and Pfingsten (1990) and Kolm (1976b).
3 See Atkinson (1970) and Dasgupta *et al.* (1973).
4 See Cowell (1988) and Shorrocks (1984). For an axiomatic approach to the Gini coefficient, see Pyatt (1985) and Thon (1982).

5 As α increases the index becomes more sensitive to the top of the income distribution; as α decreases (towards $-\infty$) the index becomes more sensitive to the bottom of the income distribution. For the cases $\alpha = 1$ and $\alpha = 0$, respectively, this expression reduces to Theil's first and second indices (Theil 1967). See Cowell (1995, 1999) for further details.

6 If the index (A.3) is multiplied by mean income, one obtains the so-called absolute Gini, or Gini's mean difference.

7 This is found by replacing the arithmetic mean in (A.5) by the geometric mean.

Appendix B
The questionnaires

The first questionnaires (A1) were administered in 1989, and studies continued over the following seven years. The procedure for conducting the questionnaires was the same in each country and educational institution. The lecturer or teacher ran the questionnaire during class time and the completed questionnaires were returned to the Ruppin Institute for collation and coding. The overall sample characteristics for the nine questionnaire experiments reported in this book are given in table B.1.

The English text of the questionnaires is provided on the following pages. Notice that the rubric at the head of each questionnaire sheet was essentially the same, and that in every case the numerical question appeared on the first page of the questionnaire sheet, and the rubric for the verbal questionnaire was at the top of the second page.

In practice, questionnaire B2 was rather different from the others since it was designed to check whether the ordering of numerical problems and questions would seriously affect the responses. The basic text of questionnaire B2 (pp. 161–3) was derived from B1 (pp. 157–60) and then four variants prepared as follows:

- *B2a:* The basic version of the questionnaire.
- *B2b:* Reverse the order of numerical questions and of verbal questions from B2a (i.e. top to bottom).
- *B2c:* Order of questions as for B2a but wherever there is 'A' and 'B', transpose them (i.e. left to right).
- *B2d:* Both switches as in B2b and B2c.

All four subtypes were used simultaneously in each experiment on each group of student respondents. Although the questionnaires were labelled differently, students were not informed that they were tackling slightly different questionnaires.

Finally, note that there were no questionnaires R1 and R2. The risk questionnaire R3 was given this label because of its close similarity to the inequality questionnaire A3.

Table B.1. *Breakdown of the combined sample*

Country	Institution	Discipline	Sample size
A1			
USA	North Texas University	Economics	37
USA	Southern Methodist University	Economics	108
UK	London School of Economics	Economics	106
Germany	University of Bonn	Economics	356
Germany	University of Karlsruhe	Economics	53
Germany	HU,* Koblenz	Economics	50
Israel	Ruppin Institute	Econ. & Management	174
Israel	Hebrew University, Jerusalem	Economics	170
Israel	Hebrew University, Jerusalem	Phil. & Education	54
Subtotal			*1,108*
A2			
Israel	Ruppin Institute	Econ. & Management	21
Israel	Tel Aviv University	Economics	89
Israel	Hebrew Univeristy, Jerusalem	Sociology	71
Subtotal			*181*
A3			
Israel	Hebrew University, Jerusalem	Psychology	49
Israel	Ruppin Institute	Econ. & Management	18
Israel	Tel Aviv University	Economics	62
Israel	Tel Aviv University	Economics	19
Israel	Hebrew Univeristy, Jerusalem	Sociology	38
Subtotal			*186*
A4			
Israel	Ruppin Institute	Econ. & Management	106
Israel	Tel Aviv University	Economics	46
Israel	Bar-Ilan University	Economics	48
UK	London School of Economics	Economics	158
Subtotal			*358*
B1			
Germany	University of Bonn	Economics	211
Germany	HU,* Koblenz	Economics	84
Sweden	Stockholm School of Economics	Economics	51
UK	London School of Economics	Economics	29
Israel	Tel Aviv University	Economics	133
Israel	Tel Aviv University	Sociology	112
Subtotal			*620*

Table B.1. (*cont.*)

Country	Institution	Discipline	Sample size
B2			
UK	London School of Economics	Economics	213
Israel	Bar-Ilan University	Economics	105
Israel	Ruppin Institute	Economics	83
Subtotal			*401*
P1			
Israel	Bar-Ilan University	Economics	17
Israel	Bar-Ilan University	MBA	42
Israel	Ruppin Institute	Econ. & Management	67
USA	University of Alabama	Economics	83
USA	Southern Methodist Univeristy	Economics	23
Australia	University of Melbourne	Economics	234
Australia	Australian National University	Economics	20
Subtotal			*486*
P2			
USA	University of Alabama	Economics	80
UK	London School of Economics	Economics	34
Germany	HU,* Koblenz	Economics	31
Poland	Warsaw University	Economics	34
USA	Southern Methodist Univeristy	Economics	19
Israel	Tel Aviv University	Sociology	43
Israel	Ruppin Institute	Econ. & Management	64
Australia	Australian National University	Economics	35
Subtotal			*340*
R3			
Germany	University of Osnabrük	Economics	93
NZ	Massey University	Economics	27
UK	London School of Economics	Economics	103
Israel	Ruppin Institute	Econ. & Management	123
Subtotal			*346*
Total			**4,026**

Note: * Hochschule für Unternehmungsführung.

A1

INCOME INEQUALITY QUESTIONNAIRE

*This questionnaire concerns people's attitudes to income inequality. We would be interested in **your** views, based on some hypothetical situations. Because it is about **attitudes** there are no "right" answers. Some of the suggested answers correspond to assumptions commonly made by economists: but these assumptions may not be good ones. Your responses will help to shed some light on this, and we would like to thank you for your participation. The questionnaire is anonymous: please do not write your name on it.*

In each of the first nine questions you are asked to compare two distributions of income. Please state which of them you consider to be the **more unequally** distributed by circling A or B. If you consider that both of the distributions have the same inequality then circle both A and B.

1)   A = (5, 8, 10)   B = (10, 16, 20)

2)   A = (5, 8, 10)   B = (10, 13, 15)

3)   A = (5, 8, 10)   B = (5, 5, 8, 8, 10, 10)

4)   A = (1, 4, 7, 10, 13)   B = (1, 5, 6, 10, 13)

5)   A = (4, 8, 9)   B = (5, 6, 10)

6)   A = (4, 7, 7, 8, 9)   B = (5, 6, 7, 7, 10)

7)   A = (5, 5, 5, 10)   B = (5, 5, 10, 10)

8)   A = (5, 5, 10, 10)   B = (5, 10, 10, 10)

9)   A = (5, 5, 5, 10)   B = (5, 10, 10, 10)

In each of questions 10 to 14 you are presented with a hypothetical change and three possible views about that change, labelled a, b, c. Please circle the letter alongside the view that corresponds most closely to your own. Feel free to add any comments which explain the reason for your choice.

10) Suppose we double the "real income" of each person in a society, when not all the initial incomes are equal.

a) *Each person's share remains unchanged, so inequality remains unchanged.*

b) *Those who had more also get more, so inequality has increased.*

c) *After doubling incomes more people have enough money for basic needs, so inequality has fallen.*

In the light of the above, would you want to change your answer to question 1? If so, please write your new response - "A" or "B" or "A and B" (if you now consider the two distributions to have the same inequality):

11) Suppose we add the same fixed amount to the incomes of each person in a society, when not all the initial incomes are equal.

a) *Inequality has fallen because the share of those who had more has fallen*

b) *Inequality remains the same.*

c) *Inequality has increased.*

Suppose instead of adding we deduct a fixed amount from each person's income. Then inequality...

a) *is the same*

b) *increases*

c) *decreases*

In the light of both of the above, would you want to change your answer to question 2?   If so, please write your new response ("A" or "B" or "A and B") here:

12) Suppose we replicate a three-person society by merging it with an exact copy of itself (so that we now have a society of six people consisting of three sets of identical twins).

  a) *The income inequality of the six-person community is the same as that of the three-person community because the relative income shares remain unchanged.*

  b) *The income inequality of the six-person community is less than that of the three-person community because in the six-person community there are some people who have the same income.*

  c) *The income inequality of the six-person community is greater than that of the three-person community.*

In the light of the above, would you want to change your answer to question 3?   If so, please write your new response ("A" or "B" or "A and B") here:

13) Suppose we transfer income from a person who has more income to a person who has less, without changing anyone else's income. After the transfer the person who formerly had more still has more.

  a) *Income inequality in this society has fallen.*

  b) *The relative position of others has also changed as a consequence of this transfer. Therefore we cannot say, a priori, how inequality has changed.*

  c) *Neither of the above.*

In the light of the above, would you want to change your answer to question 4?   If so, please write your new response ("A" or "B" or "A and B") here:

14) Suppose there are two societies A, B with the same number of people and with the same total income, but with different distributions of income. Society A is now merged with C, and society B is merged with C' where C and C' are identical.

a) *The society which had the more unequal income distribution before the merger still has the more unequal distribution after the merger.*

b) *We can't say which society has the more unequal income distribution unless we know the exact distributions.*

c) *Neither of the above.*

In the light of the above (and your answer to question 5) would you want to change your answer to question 6?   If so, please write your new response ("A" or "B" or "A and B") here:

15)   Suppose there is a society consisting of n people. There is one rich person and n-1 identical poor people. One by one, some of those who were poor acquire the same income as the rich person, so that eventually there are n-1 (identical) rich people and just one poor person. Please circle the appropriate response:

a) *Inequality increases continuously.*

b) *Inequality decreases continuously.*

c) *Inequality at first increases and then decreases.*

d) *Inequality at first decreases and then increases.*

e) *Inequality remains the same throughout.*

f) *None of the above*

In the light of the above would you want to change your answer to questions 7,8 and 9? If so please note your new responses here...
    7:
    8:
    9:

Please write your special subject here:

Thanks once again for your help!

INCOME INEQUALITY QUESTIONNAIRE

*This questionnaire concerns people's attitude to income inequality. We would be interested in **your** views, based on some hypothetical situations.   Because it is about **attitudes** there are no "right" answers. Some of the suggested answers correspond to assumptions commonly made by economists: but these assumptions may not be good ones. Your responses will help to shed some light on this, and we would like to thank you for your participation. The questionnaire is anonymous. Please do not write your name on it.*

In each of the first seven questions you are asked to compare two distributions of income. Please state which of them you consider to be **more unequally** distributed by circling A or B.   If you consider that both of the distributions have the same inequality then circle both A and B.

1)   A = (5, 5, 5, 5)   B = (5, 5, 5, 10)

2)   A = (5, 5, 5, 10)   B = (5, 5, 10, 10)

3)   A = (5, 5, 10, 10)   B = (5, 10, 10, 10)

4)   A = (5, 10, 10, 10)   B = (10, 10, 10, 10)

5)   A = (5, 5, 5, 5)   B = (10, 10, 10, 10)

6)   A = (5, 5, 5, 10)   B = (5, 10, 10, 10)

7)   A = (7, 5, 10, 9)   B = (9, 5, 7, 10)

continued/...

In each of questions 8 to 10 you are presented with possible views about inequality comparisons labelled *a,b,...,* . Please circle the letter alongside the view that corresponds most closely to your own.

8)   Suppose income inequality in Alfaland is higher than income inequality in Betaland and income inequality in Betaland is higher than income inequality in Gamaland. Then

   a) *Inequality in Alfaland is higher than inequality in Gamaland.*

   b) *It is not clear that inequality in Alfaland is higher than inequality in Gamaland.*

In the light of the above would you want to change your answer to questions 1, 2, 3, 4, 5 and 6?   If so, please note your new responses here:

1:                              4:
2:                              5:
3:                              6:

9)   Suppose there is a society consisting of *n* persons. All of them are identical poor people. One by one each person receives in turn an identical large bonus and thus becomes a rich person: so eventually there are *n* identical rich people. Please circle the appropriate response:

   a)   *Inequality increases continuously*

   b)   *Inequality decreases continuously*

   c)   *Inequality at first increase and then decrease*

   d)   *Inequality at first decrease and then increase*

   e)   *Inequality remains the same throughout*

   f)   *None of the above*

In the light of the above would you want to change your answer to questions 1, 2, 3, 4, 5 and 6?   If so please note your new responses here:

1:                              4:
2:                              5:
3:                              6:

10)   Suppose we permute the incomes of people who are identical

in every respect other than income. (So person *i* gets the income that *j* had previously, *j* gets the income that person *k* had previously, etc.). Then:

a) Inequality remains the same

b) Inequality may change

In the light of the above, would you want to change your answer to question 7? If so, please write your new response ("A", "B" or "A and B", if you now consider the two distributions to have the same inequality) here:

A3

INCOME INEQUALITY QUESTIONNAIRE

*This questionnaire concerns people's attitude to income inequality. We would be interested in **your** view, based on hypothetical situations. Because it is about attitudes there are no "right" answers. Some of the possible answers correspond to assumptions consciously made by economists: but these assumptions may not be good ones. Your responses will help to shed some light on this, and we would like to thank you for your participation. The questionnaire is anonymous. Please do not write your name on it.*

In Alfaland there are some areas with different levels of income. All areas have the same number of people which are identical except in their incomes. In each area half of the people have one level of income and the other half have another level of income. The average income in Alfaland by local currency is 1000 Alfa-dollars and the income which ensures a supply of basic needs is 400 Alfa-dollars.

In each of the following questions you are asked to compare two distributions of income - one per each area. Please state which of them you consider to be the more unequally distributed by circling A or B. If you consider that both of the distributions have the same inequality then circle both A and B.

1)   A = (200, 400)   B = (400, 600)

2)   A = (200, 400)   B = (400, 700)

3)   A = (200, 400)   B = (400, 800)

4)   A = (600, 900)   B = (900, 1200)

5)   A = (600, 900)   B = (900, 1300)

6)   A = (600, 900)   B = (900, 1350)

7)   A = (1200, 1800)   B = (1800, 2400)

8)   A = (1200, 1800)   B = (1800, 2550)

9)   A = (1200, 1800)   B = (1800, 2700)

continued/...

In the next question you are presented with possible views about inequality comparisons labelled *a,b,c,d*. Please circle the letter alongside the view that corresponds most closely to your own. Feel free to add any comments which explain the reason for your choice.

10) Suppose we change the real income of each person in a society, when not all the initial incomes are equal.

  a) If we add (or deduct) an amount to the income of each person that is proportional to his initial income then inequality remains unaltered.

  b) If we add (or deduct) the same fixed amount to the incomes of each person inequality remains unaltered.

  c) Inequality may remain unaltered: whether it does so depends not only on the change but also on initial and final levels of real income.

  d) None of the above.

In the light of the above would you want to change your answers to questions 1-9? If so, please note your new responses here:

1)   6)

2)   7)

3)   8)

4)   9)

5)

A4

INCOME INEQUALITY QUESTIONNAIRE

*This questionnaire concerns people's attitude to income inequality. We would be interested in **your** view, based on hypothetical situations. Because it is about attitudes there are no "right" answers. Some of the possible answers correspond to assumptions consciously made by economists: but these assumptions may not be good ones.   Your responses will help to shed some light on this, and we would like to thank you for your participation. The questionnaire is anonymous.*

Alfaland consists of five persons who are identical in every respect other than their income. Two economic policy proposals A and B are being considered for implementation in Alfaland next year. It is known that - apart from their impact on personal incomes - the two policies would have the same effect on the population. The impact upon incomes would depend upon the particular state of the Alfaland economy at the time the policy (A or B) is to be introduced.

In each of the questions (1) to (5) two alternative lists of incomes A and B (in Alfaland local currency) are given. Each of these pairs represents the outcomes of the A-policy and the B-policy in each of five different situations in which Alfaland might find itself. In each case please state which policy you consider would result in higher **inequality** in Alfaland by circling A or B. If you consider that the two policies will result in the same inequality than circle both A and B.

1)   A = (2, 5, 9, 20, 30)   B = (2, 6, 8, 20, 30)

2)   A = (2, 5, 9, 20, 30)   B = (3, 5, 9, 20, 29)

3)   A = (2, 5, 9, 20, 30)   B = (2, 6, 9, 20, 29)

4)   A = (2, 5, 9, 20, 30)   B = (2, 10, 9, 15, 30)

5)   A = (10, 10, 10, 10, 30)   B = 10, 10, 10, 20, 20)

\...Continued

In question 6 you are presented with a hypothetical income change and some possible views about that change. The views are labelled *a),...e)*. Please circle the letter alongside the view that corresponds most closely to your own. You can check more than one answer, provided that you consider they do not contradict each other. Feel free to add any comment which explains the reason for your choice.

6)   Suppose we transfer income from a person who has more income to a person who has less, without changing anyone else's income. After the transfer the person who originally had more income still has more.

   a) Income inequality in this society has fallen if the ranking of the income of all the people remains the same. If there is any change in the rank of all the incomes then it is possible that income inequality increases or remains the same.

   b) If the transfer was from the richest to the poorest, and after the transfer the richest remains the richest and the poorest remains the poorest, than income inequality has fallen. In other cases we cannot say a priori how inequality has changed.

   c) The relative position of others has also been changed by the transfer. So we cannot say a priori how inequality has changed.

   d) Inequality in this society has fallen, even if there is a change in the ranking of the income of people as a result of this transfer, and even if the transfer is not from the richest in the society to the poorest.

   e) None of the above

In the light of your answer to question 6, would you want to change your answer to question 1-5? If so, please state your new response here.

1)

2)

3)

4)

5)

B1

INCOME DISTRIBUTION QUESTIONNAIRE

*This questionnaire concerns peoples attitude to income distribution. We would be interested in **your** views, based on some hypothetical situations. Because it is about attitudes there are no "right" answers. Some of the suggested answers correspond to assumptions commonly made by economists; but these assumptions may not be good ones. Your responses will help to shed some light on this, and we would like to thank you for your participation. The questionnaire is anonymous.*

In Alfaland two economic programmes are proposed. It is known that both programmes will have the same effect on the population except on their incomes and all the people are identical in every respect other than income.

In each of the first ten questions there are given two alternative lists of incomes A and B (in Alfaland local currency) which result from these two programmes respectively. Please state which programme you consider would make the community of Alfaland better off by circling A or B. If you consider that each of the programmes is just as good as the other then circle both A and B.

1)   A = (1, 4, 7, 10, 13)   B = (1, 5, 6, 10, 13)

2)   A = (4, 8, 9)   B = (5, 6, 10)

3)   A = (4, 7, 7, 8, 9)   B = (5, 6, 7, 7, 10)

4)   A = (5, 5, 5, 5)   B = (5, 5, 5, 10)

5)   A = (5, 5, 5, 5)   B = (5, 5, 5, 30)

6)   A = (4, 8, 9)   B = (4, 8, 20)

7)   A = (5, 10, 15, 20)   B = (6, 8, 16, 20)

8)   A = (6, 8, 16, 20)   B = (6, 9, 14, 21)

9)   A = (6, 9, 14, 21)   B = (5, 10, 15, 20)

10)   A = (7, 5, 10, 9)   B = (9, 5, 7, 10)

Continued/...

Now there are two other islands, Betaland and Gammaland. In Betaland there are three people and in Gammaland there are six people. All the people (on both islands) are identical in every respect other than income. Both islands have the same currency and prices.

Question 11 gives the list of income in Betaland (labelled B) and in Gammaland (labelled C). Please state which community you consider better off by circling B or C. If you think that the two communities are equally well off then circle both B and C.

11)   B = (5, 8, 10)   C = (5, 5, 8, 8, 10, 10)

In each of questions 12 to 17 you are presented with hypothetical change and some possible views about that change, labelled *a*, *b*, *c*,... Please write the letter alongside the view that corresponds most closely to your own. Feel free to add any comments which explain the reason for your choice.

12) Suppose there are two economic programmes A and B which have only the following difference: The income of person *i* in programme A is *x* units higher than his income in programme B while the income of person *j* in programme A is *x* units lower than his income in programme B. In both programmes the income of person *i* is higher than the income of person *j*. The incomes of all other people are unaffected by the choice of programme A or programme B.

   a) *Programme A would make the community better off.*

   b) *Programme B would make the community better off.*

   c) *The relative position of other people is also different by A and B. Therefore we cannot say which programme would make the community better off.*

   d) *None of the above.*

In the light of the above, would you want to change your answer to question 1? If so please write your new response ("A" or "B" or "A and B") here:

13) Suppose there are two islands A,B with the same number of
     people and with the same total income, but with different
     distributions of income. Island A is now merged with island
     C, and island B is merged with island C', where C and C'
     are identical.

     a) *The community of the island which was better off
        before the merger is still better off after the
        merger.*

     b) *We can't say which community is better off unless
        we know the exact distributions.*

     c) *Neither of the above.*

In the light of the above, (and your answer to question 2) would
you want to change your answer to question 3? If so please write
your new response ("A" or "B" or "A and B") here:

14) Suppose there are two economic programmes A and B which
     have only one difference: there is one person whose income
     under programme B is higher than under programme A. For
     every other person his income under programme B equals his
     income under programme A.

     a) *Programme B would make the community better off
        because no one is worse off and someone is better
        off.*

     b) *The relative positions of others is also different
        as between A and B; therefore we cannot say, a
        priori, which programme is better off.*

     c) *Neither of the above.*

In the light of the above would you want to change your answers
to questions 4, 5 and 6?   If so please write your new response
("A" or "B" or "A and B") here:

4:
5:
6:

15)   Suppose the community is better off under programme A than under programme B; suppose also that it is better under programme B than under programme C.

   a) *The community is better off under programme A than under programme C.*

   b) *It is not clear that the community is better off under programme A than under programme C.*

In the light of the above would you want to change your answer to questions 7, 8 and 9? If so please write your new responses here:

7:
8:
9:

16)   Suppose we permute the incomes of people who are identical in every respect other than income. (So person i gets the income that j had previously, j gets the income that person k had previously, etc.)

   a) *The community is equally well off in the two situations.*

   b) *It is not clear that the community is equally well off in the two situations.*

In the light of the above would you want to change your answer to question 10? If so please note your new response here:

17)   Suppose two identical islands with the same income distribution are amalgamated into one state without any other change.

   a) *The position of the amalgamated state is as good as each island separately because the relative incomes shares remain unchanged.*

   b) *The position of the amalgamated state is better than either island separately because there are more people who have the same income.*

   c) *The position of the amalgamated state is worse than that of either island separately.*

In the light of the above would you want to change your answer to question 11?   If so please note your new response ("A" or "B" or "A and B") here:

B2

INCOME DISTRIBUTION QUESTIONNAIRE

*This questionnaire concerns people's attitude to income distribution. We would be interested in **your** views, based on some hypothetical situations. Because it is about attitudes there are no "right" answers. Some of the suggested answers correspond to assumptions commonly made by economists; but these assumptions may not be good ones. Your responses will help to shed some light on this, and we would like to thank you for your participation. The questionnaire is anonymous.*

Alfaland is a small country for which two economic programmes have been proposed. It is known that the programmes will have an identical effect on the population - except in so far as incomes are concerned (all the people in Alfaland are identical in every respect other than income). In questions 1 to 7 you are asked about two alternative lists of incomes A and B (in Alfaland local currency) which result from each of these programmes. Please state which programme you consider would make the community of Alfaland better off by circling A or B. If you consider that each of the programmes is just as good as the other then circle both A and B.

1)   A = (4, 8, 9)   B = (4, 8, 20)

2)   A = (5, 5, 5,5)   B = (5, 5, 5, 30)

3)   A = (5, 5, 5, 5)   B = (5, 5, 5, 10)

4)   A = (4, 7, 7, 8, 9)   B = (5, 6, 7, 7, 10)

5)   A = (4, 8, 9)   B = (5, 6, 10)

6)   A = (1, 4, 7, 10, 13)   B = (1, 4, 8, 9, 13)

7)   A = (1, 4, 7, 10, 13)   B = (1, 5, 6, 10, 13)

Continued/..

Now suppose that there are two other islands, Betaland and Gammaland. In Betaland there are three people and in Gammaland there are six people. All the people (on both islands) are identical in every respect other than income. Both islands have the same currency and prices.

Question 8 gives the list of income in Betaland (labelled B) and in Gammaland (labelled C). Please state which community you consider better off by circling B or C. If you think that the two communities are equally well off then circle both B and C.

8)   B = (5, 8, 10)   C = (5, 5, 8, 8, 10, 10)

In each of questions 9 to 12 you are presented with hypothetical change and some possible views about that change, labelled *a, b, c,...*   Please write the letter alongside the view that corresponds most closely to your own.   Feel free to add any comments which explain the reason for your choice.

9)   Suppose two economic programmes A and B differ only in their effect on the incomes of Irene and Janet. Irene (who is richer than Janet) gets $1 more under programme A than she would get under B; Janet would get $1 less under A than she would under B. (For everyone else income under B is the same as it would be under A.)

   a)   *Programme A would make the community better off.*

   b)   *Programme B would make the community better off.*

   c)   *The relative positions of other people will be changed in different ways by programme A and programme B; so we can't say which is better.*

   d)   *None of the above.*

In the light of the above, would you want to change your answer to questions 1 and 2?   If so please write your new response ("A" or "B" or "A and B") here:

   question 1:
   question 2:

10)   Suppose there are two islands A and B with the same number of people and with the same total income, but with different distributions of income. Island A is now merged with island C, and island B is merged with island Ç where C and Ç are identical.

   a)   *If the population of A was better off than the population of B (before the merger) then the population of A+C must be better off than the population of B+C' (after the merger).*

   b)   *We can't say which community is better off unless we know the exact distributions.*

   c)   *Neither of the above.*

B2a

In the light of the above, (and of your answer to question 3) would you want to change your answer to question 4? If so please write your new response ("A" or "B" or "A and B") here:

question 4:

11)   Suppose two economic programmes A and B differ in only one respect: there is one person who would get a higher income under programme B than he would under A. (For everyone else income under B is the same as it would be under A.)

   a)   *Programme B would make the community better off because no one is worse off and someone is better off.*

   b)   *The relative positions of other people will be changed in different ways by programme A and programme B; so we can't say which is better.*

   c)   *Neither of the above.*

In the light of the above would you want to change your answers to questions 5, 6 and 7? If so please write your new response ("A" or "B" or "A and B") here:

question 5:
question 6:
question 7:

12)   Suppose there are two islands that are identical in every respect, including their population structure, total income and income distribution. Now suppose the two islands are amalgamated into one state without any other economic or social change.

   a)   *The position of the amalgamated state is as good as each island separately because the relative income shares remain unchanged.*

   b)   *The position of the amalgamated state is better than either island separately because there are more people who have the same income.*

   c)   *The position of the amalgamated state is worse than that of either island separately.*

   d)   *None of the above.*

In the light of the above would you want to change your answer to question 8? If so please note your new response ("A" or "B" or "A and B") here:

question 8:

B2a

Poverty Questionnaire

*This questionnaire concerns people's attitude to poverty.   We would
be interested in **your** views, based on some hypothetical   situations.
Because it is about attitudes there are no "right answers".   Some of
the suggested answers correspond to assumptions   commonly made by
economists, but these assumptions may not be good ones.   Your
responses will help to shed some light on this, and we would like to
thank you for your participation.*

The questionnaire is anonymous.

In Alfaland there are two regions which have different
levels   of income.   All the people of Alfaland are
identical in every respect other than their incomes. The
level of income which ensures a supply of basic needs
anywhere in Alfaland is 15 Alfadollars.

In each of the ten following questions you are asked to
compare two distributions of income – one for each region.
Please indicate the region in which you consider poverty to
be greater by circling A or B. If you consider that poverty
is the same in the two regions then circle both A and B.

1)   A = (4,8,12,30,40,50,66)   B = (4,9,12,30,40,50,66)

2)   A = (4,8,12,30,40,50,66)   B = (4,9,11,30,40,50,66)

3)   A = (4,8,12,30,66,50,40)   B = (12,8,4,30,40,50,66)

4)   A = (4,8,12,30,40,50,66)   B = (4,4,8,8,12,12,30,30,
                                           40,40,50,50,66,66)

5)   A = (4,8,12,30,40,50,66)   B = (5,6,13,30,40,50,66)

6)   A = (4,7,8,12,30,40,50,53,66)   B = (5,6,7,13,30,40,50,53,66)

7)   A = (4,8,12,30,40,50,66)   B = (4,8,12,30,140,150,166)

8)   A = (4,8,12,30,40,50,66)   B = (4,8,12,20,30,40,50,66)

9)   A = (4,8,12,30,40,50,66)   B = (4,8,12,30,40,50,66,100)

10)   A = (4,8,12,30,40,50,66)   B = (4,8,12,14,30,40,50,66)

\...Continued

In each of the following questions you are presented with a hypothetical change and several possible views about that change, labelled *a*, *b*, *c*,... Please circle the letter alongside the view that corresponds most closely to your own. Feel free to add any comments which may explain the reason for your choice.

In question 11 and 12 we consider two regions A and B that have "almost identical" income distributions. By this we mean that A and B have the same numbers of inhabitants and - with just a few exceptions - we can find matching pairs of one A-resident and one B-resident who have identical incomes.

11)   Suppose there are two regions A and B which have almost identical income distribution;the only exception is that a particular person *i* in region B has a higher income than the corresponding person *i* in region A. In both regions the income of person *i* is less than the level that ensures a supply of basic needs.

    a)   *Poverty in region A is higher.*

    b)   *The relative position of other people is also different in A and B; therefore we cannot say, a priori, in which region poverty is greater.*

    c)   *Neither of the above*

In the light of the above would you want to change your answer to question 1? If so, please note your new response ("A" or "B" or "A and B") here:

12)   Suppose there are two regions A and B which have almost identical income distributions. The only exceptions are that the income of one particular poor person *i* in region A is *x* units higher than the income of the corresponding poor person *i* in region B, and that the income of another, very poor person *j* in region A is *x* units lower than the income of the corresponding very poor person in region B.

    a)   *Poverty in region A is greater than in region B.*

    b)   *Poverty in region B is greater than in region A.*

    c)   *The relative position of other people is also different in A and B. Therefore we cannot say in which region poverty is greater.*

    d)   *None of the above.*

In the light of the above, would you want to change your answer to question 2? If so, please write your new response ("A", or "B" or "A and B") here:

2

13) Suppose people are identical in every respect other than income, and that one income distribution is a permutation of another income distribution.

a)   *Poverty is the same in the two situations*

b)   *It is not clear that poverty is the same in the two situations.*

In the light of the above would you want to change your answer to question 3? If so, please note your new response ("A" or "B" or "A and B") here:

14) Suppose two identical regions with identical income distribution and the same "basic-needs" income level were to be amalgamated into one region without any other change.

a)   *Poverty in the amalgamated region would be the same as in each region separately.*

b)   *Poverty in the amalgamated region would be higher than in each region separately.*

c)   *Poverty in the amalgamated region would be less than in each region separately.*

In the light of the above would you want to change your answer to question 4? If so, please note your new response ("A" or "B" or "A and B") here:

15) Suppose there are two regions A, B with the same number of inhabitants and with the same total income and the same basic-needs income level. Region A is now merged with region C, and region B is merged with region C', where C and C' have identical income distribution and have the same basic-needs level as in regions A and B.

a)   *If poverty in A was higher (lower) than in B before the merger, then it is also higher (lower) than B after the merger.*

b)   *We cannot say in which region poverty is higher unless we know the exact distributions.*

c)   *Neither of the above.*

In the light of the above, (and your answer to question 5) would you want to change your answer to question 6? If so, please write your new response ("A" or "B" or "A and B") here:

16)   Suppose we increase the income of some of the people whose
       incomes are higher than the basic-needs income level.

    a)   *Poverty will increase because the poor compare their own
          incomes to those of other people.*

    b)   *Poverty will remain unaltered because poverty has nothing
          to do with the incomes of those who are not poor.*

    c)   *Poverty will decrease because in order to alleviate
          poverty we shall need to transfer to the poor a smaller
          share of the total income.*

    d)   *None of the above.*

In the light of the above would you want to change your answer to
question 7? if so, please note your new response ("A" or "B" or "A
and B") here:

17)   Suppose a person whose income is above the basic-needs
       level is allowed to immigrate to a region and that there is
       no change in the incomes of all others and that the
       basic-needs level in this region remains unchanged.

    a)   *Poverty goes up.*

    b)   *Poverty goes down.*

    c)   *Poverty remains the same.*

    d)   *We cannot say whether poverty goes up, goes down or remains
          the same unless we know the exact income distributions.*

    e)   *None of the above.*

In the light of the above, would you want to change your answers to
question 8 and 9? If so, please write your new responses ("A"   or
"B" or "A and B") here:

18)   Suppose a person whose income is lower than the basic-needs
         level is allowed move into a region. (The region's basic-
       needs income level and the incomes of all other persons in
       the region remain unchanged.)

    a)   *Poverty goes up because there is one more poor person.*

    b)   *We cannot say whether poverty goes up, goes down or remains
          the same unless we know the exact distributions.*

    c)   *Neither of the above.*

In the light of the above, would you want to change your answer to
question 10? If so, please note your new response ("A" or "B" or "A"
and "B") here:

Poverty Questionnaire

*This questionnaire concerns people's attitude to poverty. We would be interested in **your** views, based on some hypothetical situations. Because it is about attitudes there are no "right answers". Some of the suggested answers correspond to assumptions commonly made by economists, but these assumptions may not be good ones. Your responses will help to shed some light on this, and we would like to thank you for your participation. The questionnaire is anonymous.*

In Alfaland there are two regions A and B. All the people of Alfaland are identical in every respect other than their incomes. The people of region A consider that the level of income which ensures a supply of basic needs in their region is 10 Alfa-dollars, and the people of region B consider that the basic-needs income level in their region is 20 Alfa-dollars. Prices in A and in B are the same.

In each of the three following questions you are asked to compare two distributions of income - one for each region. Please indicate the region in which you consider poverty to be greater by circling A or B. If you consider that poverty is the same in the two regions then circle both A and B.

1)   A = (4,8,12,20,24,32,40)   B = (4,8,12,20,24,32,40)

2)   A = (4,8,12,20,24,32,40)   B = (8,16,24,40,48,64,80)

3)   A = (4,8,12,20,24,32,40)   B = (14,18,22,30,34,42,50)

\...Continued

In each of the following questions you are presented with a hypothetical change and several possible views about that change, labelled *a*, *b*, *c*,... Please circle the letter alongside the view that corresponds most closely to your own. Feel free to add any comments which explain the reason for your choice.

4) Suppose two regions A and B have the same income distribution. Suppose the level of income which ensures a supply of basic needs is higher in region B.

   a)   *It is clear that poverty in B is greater than in A.*

   b)   *The basic-needs income level does not effect the level of poverty. So poverty is the same in A and B.*

   c)   *Neither of the above.*

In the light of the above would you want to change your answer to question 1? If so, please note your new response ("A" or "B" or "A and B") here:

5) Suppose the real income of each person and the basic needs income level are doubled

   a)   *Poverty increases*

   b)   *Poverty decreases*

   c)   *Poverty remains the same*

   d)   *The direction of change of poverty depends on initial and final levels of real income.*

In the light of the above, would you want to change your answer to question 2? If so, please write your new response ("A", or "B" or "A and B") here:

6)   Imagine a region in which some persons' incomes are less than the basic-needs level. Suppose the real income of each person in the region is increased by the same fixed amount and that the basic-needs income level is also increased by the same fixed amount.

    a)   *Poverty increases.*

    b)   *Poverty decreases.*

    c)   *Poverty remains the same.*

    d)   *The direction of change of poverty depends on initial and final levels of real income.*

Suppose instead that the real income of each person in the same region is decreased by the same fixed amount and that the basic needs income level is also decreased by the same fix amount.

    a)   *Poverty increases*

    b)   *Poverty decreases*
    c)   *Poverty remains the same*
    d)   *The direction of change of poverty depends on initial and final levels of real income.*

In the light of the above would you want to change your response to question 3? If so, please note your new response ("A" or "B" or "A and B") here:

7)   Poverty is a situation in which incomes are:

    a)   *Not enough for a supply of basic needs.*

    b)   *Below a level which is relative to the income distribution (for example 50% of the median income).*

    c)   *Neither of the above.*

R3

INCOME RISK QUESTIONNAIRE

This questionnaire concerns people's attitude to risk. We would be interested in **your** *view, based on hypothetical situations. Because it is about attitudes there are no "right" answers. Some of the possible answers correspond to assumptions commonly made by economists: but these assumptions may not be good ones. Your responses will help to shed some light on this, and we would like to thank you for your participation. The questionnaire is anonymous. Please do not write your name on it.*

In Alfaland there are areas with different levels of income. All areas have the same number of people who are identical in every respect except their incomes: in each area half of the people have a relatively low income and the other half have a relatively high income. The income of a migrant into any area would effectively be determined by a lottery: the person would get the higher or the lower income of that area with probability 50%. The average income in Alfaland in terms of local currency is 1000 Alfa-dollars and the income that ensures a supply of basic needs is 400 Alfa-dollars.

In each of the following questions you are asked to compare two distributions of income, one per area. Please state which of the two you consider to be more risky to a potential migrant by circling A or B. If you consider that the distributions exhibit the **same** risk then circle **both** A and B.

1)   A = (200, 400)   B = (400, 600)

2)   A = (200, 400)   B = (400, 700)

3)   A = (200, 400)   B = (400, 800)

4)   A = (600, 900)   B = (900, 1200)

5)   A = (600, 900)   B = (900, 1300)

6)   A = (600, 900)   B = (900, 1350)

7)   A = (1200, 1800)   B = (1800, 2400)

8)   A = (1200, 1800)   B = (1800, 2550)

9)   A = (1200, 1800)   B = (1800, 2700)

continued/...

In the next question you are presented with possible views about risk-comparisons labelled *a,b,c,d*. Please circle the letter alongside the view that corresponds most closely to your own. Feel free to add any comments to explain the reason for your choice.

10) Suppose we change all the payoffs in a lottery simultaneously:

a)   *If we add to (or deduct from) each payoff an amount that is proportional to the original payoff then the riskiness of the lottery remains unchanged.*

b)   *If we add to (or deduct from) each original payoff the same fixed amount then the riskiness of the lottery remains unchanged.*

c)   *Whether the riskiness of the lottery remains unaltered depends not only on the changes but also on initial and final levels of the payoffs*

d)   *None of the above.*

In the light of the above would you want to change your answers to questions 1-9? If so, please note your new responses here:

1)   6)

2)   7)

3)   8)

4)   9)

5)

References

Aczél, J. (1987). *A Short Course on Functional Equations: Based upon Recent Applications to the Social and Behavioural Sciences*. Dordrecht: D. Reidel.

Allais, M. (1953). Le comportement de l'homme rationnel devant le risque: critique des postulats et axiomes de l'école américaine. *Econometrica* 21: 503–46.

Allais, M. and O. Hagen (1979). *The Expected Utility Hypothesis and the Allais Paradox*. Dordrecht: D. Reidel.

Amiel, Y. (1981). Some remarks on income inequality, the Gini index and Paretian social welfare functions. Technical Report 17–81, Foerder Institute for Economic Research, Tel Aviv University.

Amiel, Y. and F. A. Cowell (1992). Measurement of income inequality: experimental test by questionnaire. *Journal of Public Economics* 47: 3–26.

(1994a). Income inequality and social welfare. In J. Creedy (ed.), *Taxation, Poverty and Income Distribution*. Aldershot: Edward Elgar, pp. 193–219.

(1994b). Inequality changes and income growth. In W. Eichhorn (ed.), *Models and Measurement of Welfare and Inequality*. Berlin: Springer-Verlag, pp. 3–26.

(1994c). Monotonicity, dominance and the Pareto principle. *Economics Letters* 45: 447–50.

(1995). The measurement of poverty: an experimental questionnaire investigation. Distributional Analysis Discussion Paper 5, STICERD, London School of Economics.

(1996). Distributional orderings and the transfer principle: a re-examination. Distributional Analysis Discussion Paper 14, STICERD, London School of Economics.

(1997a). The measurement of poverty: an experimental questionnaire investigation. *Empirical Economics* 22: 571–88.

(1997b). Poverty perceptions and the poverty line. In *Distribution of Welfare and Household Production: An International Perspective*. Cambridge: Cambridge University Press, pp. 179–93.

(1998a). Distributional orderings and the transfer principle: a re-examination. Research on *Economic Inequality* 8: 195–215.

(1998b). Risk perceptions and distributional judgments. Conference draft, London School of Economics.

(1999). Income transformations and income inequality. In D. Slottje (ed.), *Festschrift for Camilo Dagum*. Heidelberg: Springer-Verlag.

Amiel, Y., J. Creedy and D. Hurn (1999). Attitudes towards inequality. *Scandinavian Journal of Economics* 101: 83–96.

Arrow, K. J. (1981). Optimal and voluntary income distribution. In S. Rosefielde (ed.), *Economic Welfare and the Economics of Soviet Socialism: Essays in Honor of Abram Bergson.* Cambridge: Cambridge University Press.

Atkinson, A. B. (1970). On the measurement of inequality. *Journal of Economic Theory* 2: 244–63.

(1987). On the measurement of poverty. *Econometrica* 55: 749–64.

(1995). Capabilities, exclusion and the supply of goods. In *Choice, Welfare and Development: A Festschrift in honor of Amartya K. Sen.* Oxford: Clarendon Press.

Atkinson, A. B. and F. Bourguignon (1982). The comparison of multi-dimensional distributions of economic status. *Review of Economic Studies* 49: 183–201.

Ballano, C. and J. Ruiz-Castillo (1992). Searching by questionnaire for the meaning of income inequality. Technical Report 43, Departmento de Economia, Universidad Carlos III de Madrid.

Beckman, S., D. Cheng, J. P. Formby and W. J. Smith (1994). Preferences for income distributions and redistributions: evidence from experiments with real income at stake. Technical Report, University of Colorado at Denver and University of Alabama.

Boskin, M. J. and E. Sheshinski (1978). Optimal income redistribution when the individual welfare depends on relative income. *Quarterly Journal of Economics* 92: 589–602.

Bossert, W. and A. Pfingsten (1990). Intermediate inequality: concepts, indices and welfare implications. *Mathematical Social Science* 19: 117–34.

Brennan, G. (1973). Pareto-optimal redistribution: the case of malice and envy. *Journal of Public Economics* 2: 173–83.

Brittan, S. E. (1973). *Is There an Economic Consensus?* London: Macmillan.

Broome, J. (1988). What's the good of equality? In J. Hey (ed.), *Current Issues in Microeconomics.* Basingstoke: Macmillan.

Callan, T. and B. Nolan (1991). Concepts of poverty and the poverty line. *Journal of Economic Surveys* 5: 243–61.

Castagnoli, E. and P. Muliere (1990). A note on inequality measures and the Pigou–Dalton principle of transfer. In C. Dagum and M. Zenga (eds.), *Income and Wealth Distribution, Inequality and Poverty.* Berlin: Springer-Verlag, pp. 171–82.

Champernowne, D. G. (1974). A comparison of measures of income distribution. *Economic Journal* 84: 787–816.

Cowell, F. A. (1980). On the structure of additive inequality measures. *Review of Economic Studies* 47: 521–31.

(1985). 'A fair suck of the sauce bottle' – or what do you mean by inequality? *Economic Record* 6: 567–79.

(1988). Inequality decomposition – three bad measures. *Bulletin of Economic Research* 40: 309–12.

(1990). *Cheating the Government.* Cambridge, Mass.: MIT Press.

(1995). *Measuring Inequality* (2nd edn.). Hemel Hempstead: Harvester Wheatsheaf.

(1999). Measurement of inequality. In A. B. Atkinson and F. Bourguignon (eds.), *Handbook of Income Distribution.* Amsterdam: North-Holland, ch. 2.

Dagum, C. (1990). On the relationship between income inequality measures and social welfare functions. *Journal of Econometrics* 43: 91–102.

Dahlby, B. G. (1987). Interpreting inequality measures in a Harsanyi framework. *Theory and Decision* 22: 187–202.

Dalton, H. (1920). Measurement of the inequality of incomes. *Economic Journal* 30: 348–61.

Dasgupta, P. S., A. K. Sen and D. A. Starrett (1973). Notes on the measurement of inequality. *Journal of Economic Theory* 6: 180–7.

Davidovitz, L. (1998). Risk aversion and inequality aversion. Conference draft, Ruppin Institute, Emek Hefer, Israel.

Davies, J. B. and M. Hoy (1995). Making inequality comparisons when Lorenz curves intersect. *American Economic Review* 85: 980–6.

Drèze, J. H. (1974). Axiomatic theories of choice, cardinal utility and subjective probability: a review. In J. H. Drèze (ed.), *Allocation Under Uncertainty: Equilibrium and Optimality*. New York: Macmillan, pp. 3–23.

Duesenberry, J. S. (1949). *Income, Saving and the Theory of Consumer Behavior*. Cambridge, Mass.: Harvard University Press.

Ferber, R. and W. Z. Hirsch (1982). *Social Experimentation and Economic Policy*. Cambridge: Cambridge University Press.

Fields, G. S. (1987). Measuring inequality change in an economy with income growth. *Journal of Development Economics* 26: 357–74.

Fishburn, P. C. and R. D. Willig (1984). Transfer principles in income redistribution. *Journal of Public Economics* 25: 323–8.

Foster, J. E. (1985). Inequality measurement. In H. P. Young (ed.), *Fair Allocation*. Providence, R.I.: American Mathematical Society, pp. 38–61.

Frank, R. H., T. D. Gilovich and D. T. Regan (1993). Does studying economics inhibit cooperation? *Journal of Economic Perspectives* 7(2): 159–71.

(1996). Do economists make bad citizens? *Journal of Economic Perspectives* 10(1): 187–92.

Galbraith, J. K. (1971). *Economics, Peace and Laughter: A Contemporary Guide*. London: André Deutsch.

Gastwirth, J. L. (1974). A new index of income inequality. *International Statistical Institute Bulletin* 45(1): 437–41.

Hagenaars, A. J. M. (1986). *The Perception of Poverty*. Amsterdam: North-Holland.

Harrison, E. and C. Seidl (1994a). Acceptance of distributional axioms: experimental findings. In W. Eichhorn (ed.), *Models and Measurement of Welfare and Inequality*. Berlin: Springer-Verlag, pp. 67–99.

(1994b). Perceptional inequality and preferential judgements: an empirical examination of distributional judgements. *Public Choice* 19: 61–81.

Harsanyi, J. C. (1955). Cardinal welfare, individualistic ethics and interpersonal comparisons of utility. *Journal of Political Economy* 63: 309–21.

Hey, J. (1991). *Experiments in Economics*. Oxford: Basil Blackwell.

Hicks, J. R. (1935). A suggestion for simplifying the theory of money. *Economica* 2: 1–9.

Hirschman, A. and M. Rothschild (1973). The changing tolerance for income inequality in the course of economic development. *Quarterly Journal of Economics* 87: 544–66.

Hirshleifer, J. (1970). *Investment, Interest and Capital*. Englewood Cliffs: Prentice Hall.

(1989). *Time, Uncertainty, and Information*. Oxford: Basil Blackwell.

Hochman, H. and J. D. Rodgers (1969). Pareto-optimal redistribution. *American Economic Review* 59: 542–57.

Jenkins, S. P. (1991). The measurement of economic inequality. In L. Osberg (ed.), *Readings on Economic Inequality*. Armonk, N.Y.: M. E. Sharpe.

Kahneman, D., P. Slovic and A. Tversky (1982). *Judgment under Uncertainty: Heuristics and Biases*. Cambridge: Cambridge University Press.

Kapteyn, A. and F. G. van Herwaarden (1980). Interdependent welfare functions and optimal income distribution. *Journal of Public Economics* 14: 375–97.

Kolm, S.-C. (1969). The optimal production of social justice. In J. Margolis and H. Guitton (eds.), *Public Economics*. London: Macmillan, pp. 145–200.

(1974). Rectifiances et dominances intégrales de tous dégrés. Technical Report, CEPREMAP, Paris.

(1976a). Unequal inequalities I. *Journal of Economic Theory* 12: 416–42.

(1976b). Unequal inequalities II. *Journal of Economic Theory* 13: 82–111.

Kundu, A. and T. R. Smith (1983). An impossibility theorem on poverty indices. *International Economic Review* 24: 423–34.

Lambert, P. J. (1993). *The Distribution and Redistribution of Income* (2nd edn.). Manchester: Manchester University Press.

Layard, P. R. G. (1980). Human satisfactions and public policy. *Economic Journal* 90: 737–50.

Levy, H. (1994). Absolute and relative risk aversion: an experimental study. *Journal of Risk and Uncertainty* 8: 289–307.

Markowitz, H. M. (1959). *Portfolio Selection*. New York: Wiley.

Marshall, A. W. and I. Olkin (1979). *Inequalities: Theory and Majorization*. New York: Academic Press.

Marwell, G. and R. E. Ames (1981). Economists free ride, does anyone else? Experiments on the provision of public goods. *Journal of Public Economics* 15: 295–310.

McClelland, G. and J. Rohrbaugh (1978). Who accepts the Pareto axiom? The role of utility and equity in arbitration decisions. *Behavioural Science* 23: 446–56.

Morawetz, D. (1977). Income distribution and self-rated happiness: some empirical evidence. *Economic Journal* 87: 511–22.

Nermuth, M. (1993). Different economic theories with the same formal structures: risk, income inequality, information structures, etc. In W. E. Diewert, K. Spremann and F. Stehling (eds.), *Mathematical Modelling in Economics – Essays in Honour of Wolfgang Eichhorn*. Heidelberg: Springer-Verlag, pp. 271–7.

Nygård, F. and A. Sandström (1981). *Measuring Income Inequality*. Stockholm: Almqvist and Wiksell.

Oswald, A. (1983). Altruism, jealousy and the theory of optimal nonlinear taxation. *Journal of Public Economics* 20: 77–87.

Panel on Poverty and Public Assistance (1995). *Measuring Poverty: A New Approach*. Washington, D.C.: National Academy Press.

Persons, W. M. (1908). The variability in the distribution of wealth and income. *Quarterly Journal of Economics* 23: 416–49.

Pigou, A. C. (1912). *Wealth and Welfare*. London: Macmillan.

Plous, S. (1993). *The Psychology of Judgments and Decisions*. New York: McGraw-Hill.

Pyatt, G. (1985). An axiomatic approach to the Gini coefficient and the measurement of welfare. In R. L. Basmann and G. G. Rhodes (eds.), *Advances in Econometrics*, vol. IV. Stamford, Conn.: JAI Press.

Raiffa, H. (1968). *Decision Analysis: Introductory Lectures on Choice Under Uncertainty*. Reading, Mass.: Addison-Wesley.

Ravallion, M. (1994). *Poverty Comparisons: A Guide to Concepts and Methods*. Chur, Switzerland: Harwood Academic Publishers.

Rawls, J. (1972). *A Theory of Justice*. Oxford: Oxford University Press.

Rothschild, M. and J. E. Stiglitz (1970). Increasing risk: I. A definition. *Journal of Economic Theory* 2: 225–43.

(1971). Increasing risk: II. Its economic consequences. *Journal of Economic Theory* 3: 66–84.

(1973). Some further results on the measurement of inequality. *Journal of Economic Theory* 6: 188–203.

Saposnik, R. (1981). Rank dominance in income distribution. *Public Choice* 36: 147–51.

(1983). On evaluating income distributions: rank dominance. *Public Choice* 40: 329–36.

Schokkaert, E. and B. Capeau (1991). Interindividual differences in opinions about distributive justice. *Kyklos* 44: 325–45.

Schokkaert, E. and K. Devooght (1995). The empirical acceptance of compensation axioms. Working Paper 45, Centrum Voor Economische Studien, Leuven, Belgium.

Schokkaert, E. and L. Lagrou (1983). An empirical approach to distributive justice. *Journal of Public Economics* 21: 33–52.

Schokkaert, E. and B. Overlaet (1989). Moral intuitions and economic models of distributive justice. *Social Choice and Welfare* 6: 19–31.

Schuman, H. and S. Pressler (1981). *Questions and Answers in Attitude Surveys*. New York: Academic Press.

Seidl, C. (1988). Poverty measurement: a survey. In D. Bös, M. Rose and C. Seidl (eds.), *Welfare and Efficiency in Public Economics*. Berlin: Springer-Verlag, pp. 71–147.

Sen, A. K. (1970). *Collective Choice and Social Welfare*. Edinburgh: Oliver and Boyd.

(1973). *On Economic Inequality*. Oxford: Clarendon Press.

(1976). Poverty: an ordinal approach to measurement. *Econometrica* 44: 219–31.

(1983). Poor, relatively speaking. *Oxford Economic Papers* 35: 153–69.

Sen, A. K. and J. E. Foster (1997). *On Economic Inequality* (2nd edn.). Oxford: Clarendon Press.

Shorrocks, A. F. (1984). Inequality decomposition by population subgroups. *Econometrica* 52: 1369–85.

Shorrocks, A. F. and J. E. Foster (1987). Transfer-sensitive inequality measures. *Review of Economic Studies* 5: 485–98.

Summers, R. and A. Heston (1988). A new set of international comparisons of real product and price levels: estimates for 130 countries, 1950–1985. *Review of Income and Wealth* 34: 1–25.

(1991). The Penn world table (mark 5): an expanded set of international comparisons 1950–1988. *Quarterly Journal of Economics* 106: 327–68.

Temkin, L. S. (1986). Inequality. *Philosophy and Public Affairs* 15: 99–121.

(1993). *Inequality*. Oxford: Oxford University Press.

Theil, H. (1967). *Economics and Information Theory*. Amsterdam: North-Holland.

Thon, D. (1982). An axiomatization of the Gini coefficient. *Mathematical Social Science* 2: 131–43.

Tobin, J. (1958). Liquidity preferences as behavior towards risk. *Review of Economic Studies* 25: 65–86.

Tversky, A. and D. Kahneman (1981). The framing of decision and the psychology of choice. *Science* 211: 453–8.

World Bank (1990). *World Development Report*. Washington, D.C.

Yaari, M. and M. Bar-Hillel (1984). On dividing justly. *Social Choice and Welfare* 1: 1–24.

Index